Pick, A.   (2nd. ed)   769.

Catalogue of   559
European Paper   Pic
Money since 1900

4/12

SECOND EDITION

Catalogue of

EUROPEAN

PAPER MONEY

since 1900

By ALBERT PICK

 STERLING
PUBLISHING CO., INC.   NEW YORK

 Oak Tree Press Co., Ltd.
London & Sydney

COIN AND STAMP BOOKS

Revised Edition
Copyright © 1974, 1971 by PRESIDENT COIN CORP.
4 Warwick Place, Port Washington, N.Y. 11050
Translated from "Papiergeld Katalog Europa seit 1900"
© 1970 by Ernst Battenberg Verlag, Munich, Germany
British edition published by Oak Tree Press Co., Ltd., Nassau, Bahamas
Distributed in Australia and New Zealand by Oak Tree Press Co., Ltd.,
P.O. Box J34, Brickfield Hill, Sydney 2000, N.S.W.
Distributed in the United Kingdom and elsewhere in the British Commonwealth
by Ward Lock Ltd., 116 Baker Street, London W 1
Manufactured in the United States of America
All rights reserved
Library of Congress Catalog Card No.: 76–151707
Sterling ISBN 0–8069–6030 2 Trade   Oak Tree 7061–2497–9
6031 0 Library

CONTENTS

FOREWORD

During the past few years, interest in collecting paper money has greatly increased. The number of collectors specializing in paper currency is still small compared to those whose main interest is stamps or coins but more and more numismatists and philatelists are bringing printed notes into their field of interest.

North American and European notes of the 20th century have been the most popular among collectors. Aside from a few plentiful issues such as the French assignats, notes issued before 1900 are seldom seen and those that do still exist are treasured by their owners and seldom offered for sale. A complete collection of just the 20th century notes would be nearly impossible to put together. Completeness alone should not, therefore, be a collector's goal.

The literature previously available has consisted mainly of mimeographed catalogues and price lists, mostly full of errors, which unfortunately have not always guided the collector properly. This is not surprising, of course, in a hobby so relatively new and with so few serious studies available. The following books, however, are excellent sources of information and are highly recommended: Dr. Arnold Keller "Das Papiergeld des ersten Weltkrieges" and "Das Papiergeld des zweiten Weltkrieges"; A. Platbarzdis "Coins and Notes of Estonia, Latvia and Lithuania" and "Sveriges Sedlar 1661–1961"; Maurice Muszynski "Catalogue des Billets de la Banque de France."

This catalogue deals only with paper money issued by governments and banks plus those regional and military notes that were widely circulated. Germany has contributed perhaps the greatest number of local notes, so of the bank issues only those after 1900 are taken up and the local and private issues of Notgeld (emergency money) have been excluded altogether. The catalogue numbers of regional notes are preceded by an R, the military notes by an M.

Arranging the notes of all the countries according to a uniform scheme was not practical but, so far as possible, the listings are in order by date of issue. The dates are given in the European manner as they appear on the notes with the first numeral indicating the day, the second numeral the month, and the third numeral the year of issue. Dates of issue which do not actually appear on the notes are given within parentheses. The dates following the listings are examples taken from notes actually observed. The listings further indicate the principal devices and vignettes that appear on the obverses of the notes and the main colors of each. Further description is given only where it was necessary to distinguish a note from other issues. Signature and serial variety numbers are noted and watermarked paper is pointed out.

Catalogue evaluations have previously, for the most part, been geared to types only with all notes of the same design shown at one price rather than with a separate value for each of the various issues which can be differentiated by date, series, etc. Consequently, it has been very difficult for a collector to determine the right price at which to buy, sell or trade. In this catalogue, only one price is given for each note, this for notes in average used condition as they are generally available. Very fine condition or uncirculated notes are naturally higher priced, poorly preserved notes are worth less.

A base price of 15¢ was established for the commonest notes and actual dollar prices were quoted only up to $50. An R signifies a price range of $50 to $100, RR indicates a price upwards from $100, and RRR denotes an issue that would realize well in excess of $100. Current notes are not given any valuation at all since they are usually available from foreign exchange dealers for their face value plus perhaps a small service charge. Some notes that now seem to be scarce may be lying unknown and unappreciated in some dealer's stock or in someone's bureau drawer. Government emission offices may sell off retired or cancelled notes or whole issues that were never officially released. Searching through archives and printers' records may turn up some previously unreported issues. Any of these factors can make further price adjustments necessary.

In general, specimen notes are rarer than regular issues. Collectors nevertheless usually favor the actual notes. For certain issues with high face value such as the German 500 and 1,000 rentenmark notes of 1923, it has been practical to quote a value only for specimens. The price given in such a case is understandably for these specimen notes. Only under Czechoslovakia were separate values given for specimen notes, since most of the issues up to 1953 were given out in large quantity to collectors and dealers.

The notes illustrated are through the courtesy of the Bayerischen Hypotheken und Wechsel Bank of Munich and Coin & Currency Institute, Inc. of New York.

Munich 1970

FOREWORD TO SECOND EDITION

The steadily growing interest in collecting paper money has resulted in some substantial increases in the values of notes. The scarcer German and French issues especially now command substantially higher prices than just a few years ago. In the first edition, actual dollar prices were quoted only up to $50. In this revised edition, actual dollar prices have been used up to $850 where enough information is available to justify them. An R now signifies a price range of $100 to $250, RR indicates a price upwards from $250, and RRR denotes an issue that might be worth several times $250. In a few instances where large quantities of hitherto rare notes have come to light, price reductions were made. Some examples are Czechoslovakia #44, Greece #158–161, and Hungary #137, 145 and 146.

Many collectors and dealers reported new information and I would especially like to thank the following:

Joseph Boling, Seattle; Urs Graf, Nyon; Karl Jaksch, Wien; Maurice Muszynski, Clermont-Ferrand; Dr. Alexander Persijn, Kaiserslautern; Beate Rauch, Los Angeles; Rudolf Richter, Wals; Dr. Jens-Uwe Rixen, Tubingen; Karl Scheuch, Biebertal; Carl Siemsen, Fredensborg; Georges Thomas, Paris.

In order to avoid changing the number sequences to take account of additions and insertions in the listings, the number of the preceding note was used with the addition of a small letter—a, b, c, etc. The notes of Great Britain had to be completely rearranged with separate listings for the various signature varieties. To avoid shifting numbers again in the future, each division of the country has been given its own number sequence with distinctive identifying numbers.

Munich 1974   Albert Pick

NOTE

The values in this catalogue are quoted in U.S. dollars, a unit familiar in all parts of the world and one which readers everywhere can readily convert into their own currencies.

ALBANIA (Shqipni)

From the Middle Ages until 1912 when it became a principality, Albania was a province of Turkey. During World War I, both Italy and Austria occupied the country. A republic was proclaimed in 1925 under President Achmed Zogu who assumed the title of king in 1928. Albania was occupied by Italy from 1939 to 1943 and thereafter by Germany until the end of World War II. The country was declared a communist People's Republic on January 12, 1946.

1 Frank Ar (gold franc) = *5 Lek* = *100 Quindtar Ar* (gold cent)

Banka Kombetare e Shqipnis, Banca Nazionale d'Albania (National Bank of Albania)

1.	(1925)	5 Lek — 1 Frank Ar, brown with green, grey and rose background. Printed by Richter & Co., Naples	$45.00
2.	(1926)	5 Franka Ari, green. Boy's head at right (two signature varieties)	10.00
3.	(1926)	20 Franka Ari, blue. Youth's head at left	15.00

190 × 104

4.	(1926)	100 Franka Ari, lilac. President Achmed Zogu at right	100.00
5.	(1939)	100 Franka Ari. Same as #4 but head of Zogu overprinted with black double-headed eagle	175.00
6.	(1939)	5 Franga, green and blue. Watermarked with head of King Victor Emmanuel III	6.50
7.	(1939)	20 Franga, green. Seated figure of Roma with she-wolf at right	8.50
8.	(1944)	100 Franga, lilac brown. Peasant woman with sickle and sheaves at right	18.50
9.	(1944)	2 Lek, violet on brown. Man's head at right	2.25
10.	(1944)	5 Lek, blue on yellow. Female profile on reverse	2.50
11.	(1944)	10 Lek, red on brown. Female profile on reverse	3.00

#7
185 × 105

Banka e Shtetit Shqiptar

12.	(1945)	20 Franka Ari. Same as #3 but with impressed double-headed eagle and new bank name	250.00
13.	(1945)	20 Franga. Same as #7 but impression as #12	175.00
14.	(1945)	100 Franga. Same as #8 but impression as #12	250.00
15.	1.5.1945	1 Franga	100.00
16.		5 Franga, green, blue and brown. Helmeted man's head at left	125.00
17.		20 Franga	RR
18.		100 Franga	RR
19.	1947	10 Leke, green on brown. Soldier with weapon at right	25.00
20.		50 Leke, brown on green. Type of #19	35.00
21.		100 Leke, violet. Type of #19	65.00
22.		500 Leke, brown on violet. Type of #19	85.00

178 × 90

23.		1,000 Leke, brown, blue and yellow. Type of #19	RR
24.	1949	10 Leke, red, blue and green. Double-headed eagle	12.50
25.		50 Leke, violet on green. Bearded man's head at right	16.50
26.		100 Leke, green. Soldier at left	25.00
27.		500 Leke, brown violet. Peasant woman with sheaf at left	65.00
28.	1957	10 Leke. Type of #24	3.50
29.		50 Leke. Type of #25	6.50

30.		100 Leke. Type of #26	8.50
31.		500 Leke. Type of #27	12.50
32.		1,000 Leke, brown, lilac and green. Bearded man's head at left	15.00
33.	1964	1 Lek, green and blue. Peasant man and woman	—
34.		3 Leke, brown and lilac. Woman with basket of grapes	—

125 × 65

35.		5 Leke, lilac and blue. Truck and train	—
36.		10 Leke, dark green. Woman at loom	—
37.		25 Leke, dark blue. Peasant woman with sheaf	—
38.		50 Leke, red brown. Marching soldiers	—
39.		100 Leke, brown lilac. Worker and youth on dike	—

Berat, Bashkia e Beratit

R1.	19. Dhetuer (Dec) 1925	50 Quindtar	65.00

Koritza (Korce), a republic founded by the French in 1917

R2.	1. 3.1917	½ Franc. Double-headed eagle with inscription "Shqiperie Vetqeveritare, Korce." Serial letter "A"	45.00
R3.		1 Franc. Type of #R2	45.00
R4.	25. 3.1917	½ Franc. Type of #R2 but serial letter "B"	20.00
R5.		1 Franc. Type of #R4	20.00
R6.	10.10.1917	½ Franc. Type of #R2 but inscription "Republika Shqipetare, Korce." Serial letter "C"	25.00

108 × 71

R7.		1 Franc. Type of #R6	20.00
R8.	Feb. 1918	½ Franc	45.00
R9.		1 Franc	45.00
R10.	1.11.1918	50 Centimes. Serial letter "A." City view on reverse	45.00
R11.		1 Franc. Type of #R10	45.00

R12.	1.12.1918	50 Centimes. Type of #R10 but serial letter "B"	45.00
R13.		1 Franc. Type of #R12	45.00
R14.	10.12.1918	50 Centimes. Type of #R10 but serial letter "C"	45.00
R15.		1 Franc. Type of #R14	45.00
R16.	March 1920	50 Centimes. Type of #R2 with "Territoire de Koritza"	45.00
R17.		1 Franc. Type of #R16	45.00
R18.	1. 4.1920	1 Franc, multicolored	65.00
R19.		2 Franc, multicolored	65.00
R20.	1. 8.1920	1 Franc	45.00
R21.	1. 8.1921	1 Skender. With "Katundari e Korces" in red, bust of Skanderbeg at left	65.00
R22.	9.11.1921	25 Qindtar. With "Katudnari e Korces," peasant plowing. Skanderbeg on horseback on reverse	65.00
R23.		50 Qindtar	65.00
R24.		1 Skender	65.00

Skutari (Shkodre)

R25.	30. 1.1920	5 Qindtar. Text reads "Sigurim arke i perlimt ares se Shkodres permbi"	25.00
R26.		10 Qindtar. Type of #R25	25.00
R27.		20 Qindtar. Type of #R25	25.00
R28.		50 Qindtar. Type of #R25	25.00

Vlora, Bashkia e Vlores

R29.	1. 5.1924	10 Qindtar	35.00
R30.		25 Qindtar	35.00
R31.		1 Frank	35.00
R32.		2 Frank	35.00

ANDORRA

Tracing its history back for more than 1,000 years, Andorra is an independent free state on the Franco-Spanish border high in the Pyrenees mountains. The republic is under the joint protection of the President of France and the Spanish Bishop of Urgel. During the Spanish civil war of 1936–39, necessity money was issued with text printed in the Catalonian dialect.

1 Peseta = 100 Centimes

1.	19.12.1936	1 Peseta, blue with colored stamp	$35.00
2.		2 Pesetas. Type of #1	35.00
3.		5 Pesetas. Type of #1	45.00
4.		10 Pesetas. Type of #1	52.50
5.		50 Centimes, brown with impressed stamp	25.00
6.		1 Peseta. Type of #5	20.00

100 × 75

7.	2 Pesetas. Type of #5	20.00
8.	5 Pesetas. Type of #5	20.00
9.	10 Pesetas. Type of #5	35.00

AUSTRIA (Osterreich)

In 1869, Austria was linked with Hungary in a dual monarchy under Emperor Francis Joseph (1848–1916). The old monarchy was broken up after World War I with parts going to make up the present-day republics of Austria, Hungary, Czechoslovakia and Yugoslavia. Other pieces went to Italy and to Rumania. The Austrian Republic was called "Ostmark" while under German control from 1938 until 1945. Occupied by Allied troops after World War II, Austria was restored to independence and guaranteed neutrality under a 1955 treaty.

1 Gulden = 100 Kreuzer (until 1892)
1 Krone = 100 Heller (until 1924)
1 Schilling = 100 Groschen (1924–38 and 1945-   )

Osterreichisch-Ungarische Bank, Osztrak-Magyar Bank (Austro-Hungarian Bank)

1.	1. 5.1880	10 Gulden, blue. Woman's head at left and right	$30.00

154 × 108

2.		100 Gulden, blue. Boy with sickle and sheaf at left, boy with book at right	85.00
3.		1,000 Gulden, blue. Child's head at left and right	RR
4.	31. 3.1900	10 Kronen, lilac. Putti (cupids) at left and right	18.50
5.		20 Kronen, red and green. Woman's head with putti	25.00
6.	2. 1.1902	50 Kronen, blue. Seated woman at left and right	15.00
7.		100 Kronen, green. Seated woman and child at left, blacksmith at right	150.00
8.		1,000 Kronen, blue. Woman's head at right	3.50
9.	2. 1.1904	10 Kronen, blue violet on red and green. Girl's head (Princess Rohan) at right	8.50
10.	2. 1.1907	20 Kronen, blue on red brown and green. Woman's head at right	10.00
11.	2. 1.1910	100 Kronen, blue. Woman with flowers at right	85.00

12.	2. 1.1912	100	Kronen, green on red and blue. Woman's head at right	1.50
13.	2. 1.1913	20	Kronen, blue on green and red. Woman's head at left	1.25
14.		20	Kronen. Type of #13 but with "*II Auflage* (2nd issue)"	1.25
15.	2. 1.1914	50	Kronen, blue and green. Woman's head	1.75
16.	5. 8.1914	1	Krone. Woman's head. Trial printing	RRR
17.		2	Kronen, blue. Girl's head	
			a. Thin paper with serial letter "A" or "B" (two control number varieties)	6.50
			b. Hard paper with serial letter "C"	1.50
18.		5	Kronen. Woman's head. Trial printing	RRR
19.	2. 1.1915	10	Kronen, blue and green. Boy's head at right	1.00
20.	1.12.1916	1	Krone, red. Woman's head at left and right. Serial numbers 1,000–1,700	.40
			For serial numbers over 7,000 see Hungary # 10.	
21.	1. 3.1917	2	Kronen, red. Woman's head at left and right. Serial numbers 1,000–1,600 and A1,000–1,100 (two control number varieties)	.40
			For serial numbers over 7,000 see Hungary # 11.	
22.	1.10.1918	5	Kronen. Woman's head at left and right. Trial printing	RRR
23.	27.10.1918	25	Kronen, blue on grey brown. Girl's head at left. Serial numbers to 2,000	8.50
			For serial numbers over 3,000 see Hungary #12 and #13.	
24.		200	Kronen, green on rose. Girl's head at left. Serial letter "B"	15.00
			For serial letter "A," see Hungary #14 and #16.	
25.	2.11.1918	10,000	Kronen, violet. Woman's head at right	5.00

Kriegsdarlehenskasse (War Loan Office Notes)

26.	26. 9.1919	250	Kronen, red and green. Three allegorical figures at right	45.00
27.		2,000	Kronen, green and brown. Type of #26	45.00
28.		10,000	Kronen, lilac and blue. Type of #26	45.00
			Also see Hungary #1–3.	

Osterreichisch-Ungarische Bank (Austro-Hungarian Bank, Treasury Notes)

29.	3.10.1918	100,000	Kronen, violet and brown. Printed reverse	RR
30.	25.10.1918	5,000	Kronen	RRR
31.	26.10.1918	1,000	Kronen. Printed reverse	RR
32.	28.10.1918	1,000	Kronen, green. Blank reverse	RR
33.	30.10.1918	1,000	Kronen, green. Type of #32 except date	RR
34.	4.11.1918	10,000	Kronen. Printed reverse	RR
35.	18.11.1918	1 Million	Kronen, red brown. Blank reverse	RR
36.	5. 2.1919	5,000	Kronen. Printed reverse	RR
37.	23.12.1921	1,000	Kronen, green	150.00
38.		5,000	Kronen, olive	250.00
39.	23.12.1921	10,000	Kronen, blue	250.00

217 × 128

40.   100,000 Kronen, violet   RR

For Treasury Notes of the Hungarian branches of the Bank, see Hungary #4–9.

Osterreichisch-Ungarische Bank (Austro-Hungarian Bank), overprinted *"Ausgegeben nach dem 4. Okt. 1920"*

41.	1.12.1916	1 Krone. Same as #20 but overprinted in green	4.50
42.	1. 3.1917	2 Kronen. Same as #21 but overprinted in green	5.00
43.	2. 1.1915	10 Kronen. Same as #19 but overprinted in red	6.50
44.	2. 1.1913	20 Kronen. Same as #13 but overprinted in red	12.50
45.		20 Kronen. Same as #14 but overprinted in red	6.50
46.	2. 1.1914	50 Kronen. Same as #15 but overprinted in red	6.50
47.	2. 1.1912	100 Kronen. Same as #12 but overprinted in red	6.50
48.	2. 1.1902	1,000 Kronen. Same as #8 but overprinted in red	8.50

Osterreichisch-Ungarische Bank (Austro-Hungarian Bank), overprinted *"Deutschoster-reich 1919"* or *"1920"*

49.	1.12.1916	1 Krone. Same as #20 but overprinted in green	.40
50.	1. 3.1917	2 Kronen. Same as #21 but overprinted in green	.40
51.	2. 1.1915	10 Kronen. Same as #19 but overprinted in red	.40
52.	2. 1.1913	20 Kronen. Same as #13 but overprinted in red	.40
53.		20 Kronen. Same as #14 but overprinted in red	.40
		a. With additional stamp *"Note echt, Stempel falsch* (note genuine, stamp false)"	20.00
54.	2. 1.1914	50 Kronen. Same as #15 but overprinted in red	.40
		a. With additional stamp as #53a	20.00
55.	2. 1.1912	100 Kronen. Same as #12 but overprinted in red. Hungarian reverse	.40
		a. With additional stamp as #53a	20.00
		b. With additional stamp *"Note echt, Stempel nicht konstantierbar* (note genuine, stamp not verified)"	35.00
56.		100 Kronen. Same as #55 but German reverse	.40
57.	2. 1.1902	1,000 Kronen. Same as #8 but overprinted in red. Hungarian reverse	2.50
		a. With additional stamp as #53a	20.00

128 × 192

58.		1,000 Kronen. Same as #57 with additional black overprint *"Echt, Osterr.-ungar. Bank, Hauptanstalt Wien* (Genuine, Austro-Hungarian Bank, Head Office, Vienna)"*	25.00
59.		1,000 Kronen. Same as #57 but German reverse	.40
60.		1,000 Kronen. Obverse same as #57 but reverse has ornaments and woman's head at left and right	.40
61.		1,000 Kronen. Same as #60 but additional red overprint *"II Auflage* (2nd issue)"*	.40
62.	2.11.1918	10,000 Kronen. Same as #25 but overprinted in red. Hungarian reverse	65.00
		a. With additional stamp as #53a	35.00
63.		10,000 Kronen. Same as #62 with additional overprint as #58	57.50
64.		10,000 Kronen. Obverse same as #62 but German reverse	4.50
65.		10,000 Kronen. Obverse same as #64 but reverse has ornaments and woman's head at left and right	2.50
66.		10,000 Kronen. Same as #65 but additional overprint *"II Auflage"*	3.50

Donaustaadt Noten (Danube Area Notes)

Only half printed, these unissued notes were used as lottery tickets. All have numerals but no indication of denomination. The first column is the value for the note only while the second column is the price for a specimen with the lottery overprint.

67.	No date	10 Green and red brown. Girl's head at right	25.00	2.25
68.		20 Green and violet. Girl's head at right	25.00	1.75
69.		50 Blue and lilac. Woman's head at right	25.00	2.50
70.		100 Blue and brown. Woman's head at right	25.00	1.75

71.		1,000	Green and blue. Girl's head at right	35.00	3.00
72.		10,000	Red brown and olive. Rev. Heads of 11 children	45.00	3.50

Osterreichisch-Ungarische Bank, Osterreichische Geschaftsfuhrung (Austro-Hungarian Bank, Austrian Management)

73.	2. 1.1922	1	Krone, red		.40
74.		2	Kronen, red. Woman's head at right		.40
75.		10	Kronen, blue violet. Child's head at right		.40
76.		20	Kronen, lilac. Bearded man's head at right		.40
			a. Error: Without colored background		100.00
77.		100	Kronen, green. Girl's head (Princess Rohan) at right		.40
78.		1,000	Kronen, blue. Woman's head at right		.40
79.		5,000	Kronen, green and red brown. Woman's head in picture frame at right		3.50
80.		50,000	Kronen, red brown and green. Woman's head in picture frame at right		15.00

195 × 131

81.		100,000	Kronen, blue and green. Woman's head in picture frame at right	18.50
82.	11. 9.1922	1,000,000	Kronen, blue green	RRR
83.		5,000,000	Kronen, blue green	RRR
84.	20. 9.1922	500,000	Kronen, brown lilac. Woman and three children at right	57.00

Osterreichische Nationalbank (Austrian National Bank)

Currency Reform, 1924: *10,000 Kronen = 1 Schilling*

85.	2. 1.1924	10,000	Kronen, violet and green. Girls head at right	2.50
86.		1	Schilling. Same as #85 but overprinted with new denomination	3.50
87.	1. 7.1924	1,000,000	Kronen	RRR

88.	2. 1.1925	5 Schilling, green. Youth's head (E. Zwiauer, painter) at right	18.50
89.		10 Schilling, brown violet. Man's head at right	25.00
90.		20 Schilling, green. Woman's head at right	35.00
91.		100 Schilling, blue on multicolored. Woman's head at right	65.00

204 × 97

92.		1,000 Schilling, blue on green and red brown. Woman's head at right	250.00
93.	3. 1.1927	10 Schilling, blue on green and red. Mercury	25.00
94.		100 Schilling, violet on green. Woman's head (personification of Knowledge) at right	95.00
95.	1. 7.1927	5 Schilling, blue on green. Young man with pair of dividers at left	12.50
96.	2. 1.1928	20 Schilling, green. Girl's head at left, peasant at right	25.00
97.	2. 1.1929	50 Schilling, blue on brown olive. Woman's head at left, man's head at right	45.00
98.	2. 1.1930	1,000 Schilling, blue violet on green. Woman with a statuette of Athena	150.00
99.	2. 1.1933	10 Schilling, blue. Young woman in native costume	
		a. Corner numerals on diagonal lines	12.50
		b. Numerals on cross hatched lines	12.50
100.	2. 1.1935	50 Schilling, blue violet on green. Boy's head at right (Hubert Sterrer)	35.00
101.	2. 1.1936	100 Schilling, dark green on multicolored. Young woman with edelweiss (not officially issued)	85.00

From 1938 through 1945, the following German bank notes were in circulation: #171, #173, #174, #179–190.

Alliierte Militarbehorde (Allied Military Authority)

102.	1944	50 Groschen, red brown	
		a. Watermarked with "Military Authority" (not visible on most notes, occasionally part of a word shows)	8.50
		b. Watermarked with wavy lines	1.25

103.		1 Schilling, blue on green	
		a. Watermarked as #102a	6.50
		b. Watermarked as #102b	1.00
104.		2 Schilling, blue	
		a. Watermarked as #102a	6.50
		b. Watermarked as #102b	1.25
105.		5 Schilling, lilac	1.75
106.		10 Schilling, green	2.25
107.		20 Schilling, blue on blue violet	2.40

138 × 78

108.	25 Schilling, brown on lilac	35.00
109.	50 Schilling, brown on yellow brown	4.50
110.	100 Schilling, green	6.50
111.	1,000 Schilling, blue on green and multicolored	50.00

Republik Osterreich (Austrian Republic), issues of the Russian border garrison

112.	(20.12.1945)	50 Reichspfennig, brown on orange (not issued, pattern notes only)	150.00
113.		1 Reichsmark, green	10.00

Osterreichische Nationalbank (Austrian National Bank)

114.	29. 5.1945	10 Schilling, blue. Type of #99 — color varies from blue to violet (two control number varieties)	1.75
115.		10 Schilling, blue. Type of #114 but "Zweite Ausgabe" below design (two control number varieties)	15.00
116.		20 Schilling, blue green. Type of #96 but many color shades (two control number varieties)	1.75
117.		50 Schilling, dark green. Type of #100 but many color shades	12.50
118.		100 Schilling, blue violet to violet. Type of #94 but many color shades	2.00
119.		100 Schilling, blue violet. Type of #118 but design and "Zweite Ausgabe" at right	65.00
120.		1,000 Schilling, green. Type of #98	85.00
121.	4. 9.1945	5 Schilling, blue or violet on grey green. Type of #95 but many color shades (Also see #131)	3.75

| 122. | 2. 2.1946 | 10 Schilling, multicolored. Woman's head at right | 6.50 |

145 × 76

| 123. | | 20 Schilling, multicolored. Woman's head in middle | 8.50 |
| 124. | 2. 1.1947 | 100 Schilling, dark green. Young woman in native costume at right | 25.00 |

184 × 92

125.	1. 9.1947	1,000 Schilling, dark brown on grey green. Type of #120 but design and "Zweite Ausgabe" at left	125.00
126.	3. 1.1949	100 Schilling, dark green. Cupids at left, woman's head at right	16.50
127.		100 Schilling, dark green. Same as #126 but overprinted "2 Auflage" at bottom left	12.50
128.	2. 1.1950	10 Schilling, violet. Prince Eugen on horseback	4.50
129.		10 Schilling, violet. Same as #128 but overprinted "2 Auflage" on upper reverse	4.50
130.		20 Schilling, brown on multicolored. Joseph Haydn at right	6.50
		Error: "OESTERREICHISC*Æ*E" in background printing on obverse	50.00
131.	1951	5 Schilling, violet on grey green. Same as #121 but overprinted "Ausgabe 1951" at left	4.50
132.	2. 1.1951	50 Schilling, lilac and violet. Jakob Prandtauer at right	8.50
133.	2. 1.1953	500 Schilling, dark brown on blue and red. Wagner v. Jauregg at right	50.00

134.	2. 1.1954	100 Schilling, green. Franz Grillparzer at right	12.50
135.		1,000 Schilling, blue. Anton Bruckner at right	85.00
136.	2. 7.1956	20 Schilling, brown on red brown and olive. Auer von Welsbach at right	4.50
137.	1. 7.1960	100 Schilling, green, violet and multicolored. Johann Strauss at right	8.50
138.	2. 1.1961	1,000 Schilling, dark blue and multicolored. Viktor Kaplan at right (size 148 × 75 mm)	150.00
139.		1,000 Schilling, dark blue and multicolored. Type of #138 but blue lined background to edge (size 158 × 85 mm)	85.00
140.	2. 7.1962	50 Schilling, violet. Richard Wettstein at right	5.00
141.	1. 7.1965	500 Schilling, red brown. Josef Ressel at right	—
142.	1. 7.1966	1,000 Schilling, dark blue and violet. Bertha von Suttner at right	—
143.	2. 7.1967	20 Schilling, brown. Carl Ritter von Ghega at right	—
144.	2. 1.1969	100 Schilling, dark green. Angelika Kauffmann at right	—
145.	2. 1.1970	50 Schilling, violet. Ferdinand Raimund at right	—

AUSTRIA (continued)

Notes of the Austrian Provinces 1918-1921

Karnten (Carinthia)

R1.	11.11.1918	10 Kronen, black. One-sided trial printing (not issued)	$4.50
R2.		10 Kronen, orange. Type of R1	4.50

124 × 72

R3.		20 Kronen, blue. Both sides printed with control numbers (not issued)	12.50
R4.		100 Kronen, black. One-sided trial printing (not issued)	5.00
R5.		100 Kronen, orange. Type of R4	5.00
R6.	1. 3.1920	10 Heller, black and lilac on light brown	.40
R7.		20 Heller, black and blue on light brown	.40
R8.		50 Heller, black and green on light brown	.40

Niederosterreich (Lower Austria)

R9.	May 1920	10 Heller, dark green. Mountains with railroad bridge	.40
R10.		20 Heller, blue grey. Steamboat on the Danube	.40
R11.		50 Heller, brown. Peasant plowing with horses	.40
R12.	July 1920	10 Heller, green to dark green. Peasant woman with cows, "II Auflage"	.40
		Error: Picture on both sides	12.50
		Trial printing: One-sided on orange or lilac colored paper	12.50
R13.		20 Heller, blue to dark blue. Landscapes with horse and wagon, "II Auflage"	.40
		Trial printing: One-sided on white or lilac colored paper	16.50
R14.		50 Heller, brown. Castle, "II Auflage"	.40
		Error: Picture on both sides	12.50
		Trial printing: Light blue ink	20.00
		Trial printing: One-sided on lilac colored paper	12.50

Oberosterreich (Upper Austria)

R15.	1. 3.1920	20 Heller	
		a. Green blue, white paper	.40
		b. Green blue, bluish paper	.40
		c. Blue, grey paper	3.50
		d. Violet	1.75
		e. Green	12.50
		f. Brown	16.50
R16.		50 Heller	
		a. Dark brown	.40
		b. Red	.60
R17.	1. 6.1920	10 Heller	
		a. Rose paper	.40
		b. Grey violet paper	.40

78 × 53

R18.	21. 6.1920	80 Heller, red and grey	.60
R19.	1921	10 Heller	
		a. Red	.40
		b. Green	.40
		c. Orange	.75
		d. Brown	.40
		e. Blue	.40
R20.		20 Heller	
		a. Brown	.40
		b. Violet	.40
		c. Black	.40
		d. Green	.40
		Error: Wrong reverse picture (Steyr with fountains) in nine different colors, each	25.00
R21.	1. 2.1921	50 Heller, orange	.60

Osterreich ob der Enns (Austria on the Enns)

R22.	30.11.1918	5 Kronen, brown on green	3.50
R23.		10 Kronen, green on blue grey	4.50
R24.		20 Kronen, blue on grey brown	8.50
R25.		50 Kronen, brown on light brown	20.00

Salzburg

R26.	1.10.1919	10 Heller, blue on green	.40
		Error: No background color	4.50
R27.		20 Heller, black on yellow	.40
R28.		50 Heller, blue on rose	.40
		Error: No background color	4.50

R29.	May 1920	10 Heller, black and red. View of Salzburg about 1500	.45
		Error: Obverse or reverse without red plate	4.50
R30.		20 Heller, black and red. View of Salzburg about 1600	.45

78 × 61

R31.		50 Heller, black and red. View of Salzburg about 1700	.45
		Error: Obverse or reverse without red plate	4.50
R32.	1921	5 Kronen. Mirabelle Castle on reverse (not issued)	
		a. Obverse brown on red-brown background, reverse brown. Name of printing firm in middle (with and without control numbers)	4.50
		b. Type of R32a but name of printing firm at right, design at left	4.50
		c. Type of R32a but reverse lilac. Without name of printing firm	6.50
		d. Type of R32a but obverse brown on green	20.00
R33.		10 Kronen. Summer riding school in Salzburg on reverse (not issued)	
		a. Type of R32a	4.50
		b. Type of R32b	4.50
		c. Type of R32c	6.50
		d. Type of R32d	20.00
R34.		20 Kronen. Residenz Castle in Salzburg on reverse (not issued)	
		a. Type of R32a	4.50
		b. Type of R32b	4.50
		c. Type of R32c	6.50
		d. Type of R32d	20.00

Steiermark (Styria)

R35.	17.10.1919	10 Heller, blue	.40
R36.		20 Heller, green	.40
R37.		50 Heller, red brown on grey green	.40
R38.		50 Heller, red brown, "II Auflage"	
		a. Blue background	.45
		b. Green background	.45
		c. Yellow-brown background	.45
		d. Rose background	.45

Tirol (Tyrol)

R39.	1. 9.1919	10 Heller, orange	.60
R40.		20 Heller, grey	.60
R41.		50 Heller, green	.60
R42.	1.10.1920	10 Heller, green	.60
R43.		20 Heller, brown	.60
R44.		50 Heller, blue	.60

Vorarlberg

R45.	1.10.1919	10 Heller, green	.60
R46.		20 Heller, light brown	.60
R47.		50 Heller, blue	.60
R48.	1. 5.1921	50 Heller	
		a. Brown	.75
		b. Violet	.75
		Error: Reverse inverted	6.50

AZORES (Acores)

A group of islands in the Atlantic Ocean, the Azores is now a self-supporting province of Portugal.

1 Milreis = 1,000 Reis (Insulanos)
1 Escudo = 100 Centavos

Various notes of the Bank of Portugal are known with black imprints "Moeda Insulana" and "Acores" or a red imprint "Acores." Each new type of note has a different plate number ("Ch" for chapa = plate).

 124 × 82

1.	2,500	Reis. Alf. de Albuquerque, "Ch.1"	$35.00
2.	5,000	Reis. Tejo u. Douro, "Ch.3"	65.00
3.	10,000	Reis. Don Henrique, "Ch.3"	85.00
4.	10,000	Reis. Symbolic figures, "Ch.4"	85.00
5.	20,000	Reis. Symbolic figures of Mechanics and History, "Ch.3"	100.00
6.	50,000	Reis. Pero de Alenquer and Diogo Cao, "Ch.2"	150.00
7.	20	Escudos. Marques de Pombal, "Ch.4"	RR
8.	50	Escudos. Christovao da Gama, "Ch.3"	RR
9.	100	Escudos	RRR
10.	500	Escudos	RRR
11.	1,000	Escudos	RRR

Since 1931, regular Portuguese notes without imprints have circulated.

BELGIUM (Belgique - Belgie)

After Napoleon's defeat in 1815, Belgium became a part of the Netherlands but in 1830 it proclaimed its independence and chose Prince Leopold of Saxe-Coburg as King. The same ruling family has continued ever since. The country was occupied by Germany during both World Wars. King Leopold III (1937–51) was held a prisoner by the Germans during World War II and, in 1945, a regency was set up under Prince Charles (brother of Leopold III) until Prince Baudouin came of age in 1951.

1 Franc (Frank) = 100 Centimes (Centiemen)
1 Belga = 5 Francs

Most of the Belgian notes carry the date of printing, so many types exist with several different date varieties. The official designations of the note types are thus usually the name of the designer or engraver. Because of the two official languages, French and Flemish, Belgian notes carry inscriptions in both languages.

Banque Nationale de Belgique—Nationale Bank van Belgie (National Bank of Belgium)

Notes issued before World War I with printings continuing to 1922

1.	1.7.1914	5 Francs, brown and orange. (Hendrickx-Doms type) Allegorical figures	$25.00
		a. 25.1.1919 date (two signature varieties)	35.00
2.	1.7.1914	5 Francs, green and brown. Similar to #1 (Hendrickx-Doms type)	12.50
		a. 29.12.1918 date	8.50
		b. 30.12.1919 date	8.50
		c. 3.1.1921 date (two signature varieties)	8.50
3.	Various dates	20 Francs, wine red and green. Minerva with lion at left (Titz-Biet type, four signature varieties)	20.00
4.		50 Francs, blue and black. Woman's head in medallion and children (1887 type, three signature varieties)	150.00

#5

159 × 97

5.	50 Francs, green. Man with scythe at left, two women with book at right (Montald type, four signature varieties)	65.00
6.	100 Francs, blue and black. Man seated at left, woman with scepter at right (Hendrickx-Doms-Ligny type)	175.00
7.	100 Francs, blue, red and black. Type of #6 but denomination in red	175.00
8.	100 Francs, green. Quadriga with lions at left and right, lion in middle (Montald type)	150.00
9.	100 Francs, brown and black. Type of #8 but watermarked with medallion, white border below and arabesque imprinted at right (dated to 1914, two signature varieties)	25.00
10.	100 Francs, brown and black. Type of #9 but no arabesque (dated after 1914, two signature varieties)	20.00
11.	500 Francs, blue, red and black. Women and cupids (Hendrickx-Doms type). Bank name and value in red (three signature varieties)	RR
12.	500 Francs, blue and green. Type of #11 but bank name and denomination (Francs only) in green (three signature varieties)	175.00
13.	1,000 Francs, black and blue. Neptune with trident at left, woman with scepter at right (Hendrickx-Pannemaker-Doms type)	RR

220 × 134

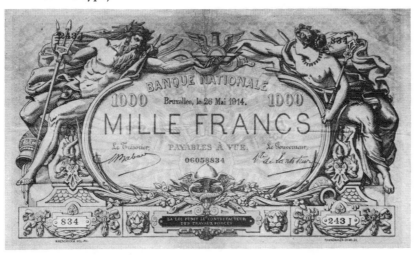

14.	1,000 Francs, green and brown. Type of #13 (three signature varieties)	250.00
15.	1,000 Francs, green and brown. Type of #14 but no edge printing (provisional)	RR

Banque Nationale de Belgique—Nationale Bank van Belgie (National Bank of Belgium)

Comptes Courants (War Issues)

16.	27.8.1914	1 Franc, blue on grey	4.50

17.	2 Francs, brown on grey	8.50
18.	20 Francs, grey and brown. Leopold I	45.00
19.	100 Francs, grey, blue and red. Leopold I	125.00
20.	1,000 Francs, brown and red. Leopold I	RR

Societe Generale de Belgique

The notes issued by this bank during the German occupation and after the war show various printing dates between 1915 and 1920.

21.	1 Franc, violet. Queen Louise-Marie	1.50
22.	2 Francs, brown. Queen Louise-Marie	2.50
23.	5 Francs, green. Queen Louise-Marie	12.50

137 × 88

24.	20 Francs, blue. Peter Paul Rubens	45.00
25.	100 Francs, brown. Queen Louise-Marie	175.00
26.	1,000 Francs, green. Peter Paul Rubens	RRR

Bank Nationale de Belgique—Nationale Bank van Belgie (National Bank of Belgium)

Post war types, denominations in francs only, various dates from 1920

27.	1 Franc, blue. King Albert and Queen Elizabeth (Nationale type)	1.25
28.	5 Francs, blue. Type of #27 (two signature varieties)	2.50
	See #46 and 47 for notes overprinted "Tresorerie."	
29.	20 Francs, brown. Type of #27 (two signature varieties)	25.00
	See #48 and 49 for notes overprinted "Tresorerie."	

182 × 105

| 30. | 100 Francs, lilac brown. Type of #27 (three signature varieties) | 10.00 |
| 31. | 1,000 Francs, blue. Type of #27 (three signature varieties) | 45.00 |

Denominations in both francs and belgas, various dates from 1927

32.	50 Francs = 10 Belgas, green. Type of #5 (Montald)	100.00
33.	50 Francs = 10 Belgas, blue. Peasant woman with sheaves and two horses (Anto-Carte type)	65.00
34.	50 Francs = 10 Belgas, green. Type of #33 but dated after 1928 See #50 for notes overprinted "Tresorerie."	12.50
35.	100 Francs = 20 Belgas, blue. King Albert and Queen Elizabeth (Nationale type)	6.50
36.	100 Francs = 20 Belgas, grey and light brown. Woman with crown and fruit in middle, Queen Elizabeth at left, King Albert at right. Serial number side in French (Vloors type, four signature varieties)	2.25

177 × 108

37.	100 Francs = 20 Belgas, grey and light brown. Type of #36 but serial number side in Flemish	6.50
38.	100 Francs = 20 Belgas, orange. Type of #36	50.00
39.	100 Francs = 20 Belgas, orange. Type of #37	50.00
40.	500 Francs = 100 Belgas, blue and green. Frame with women and cupids (Hendrickx-Doms type). Signatures on obverse only	10.00
41.	500 Francs = 100 Belgas, blue and green. Type of #40 but signatures on both sides (dated from 1938, two signature varieties)	10.00
42.	1,000 Francs = 200 Belgas, green. Type of #31 (Nationale). Signature on obverse only (three signature varieties)	6.50
43.	1,000 Francs = 200 Belgas, green. Type of #42 but signatures on both sides (two signature varieties)	6.50
44.	1,000 Francs = 200 Belgas, red. Type of #42 (issued 1944)	RRR
45.	10,000 Francs = 2,000 Belgas, blue and red. Quadrigas at left and right, lion in middle (three signature varieties)	150.00

Tresorerie-Thesaurie (State Treasury Notes)

Issues from 1926

46.	5 Francs, blue. Same as #28 (Nationale) but overprinted "Tresorerie—Thesaurie" on obverse	1.25

125 × 75

47.	5 Francs, blue. Same as #28 but overprinted "Tresorerie" on obverse, "Thesaurie" on reverse	1.75
48.	20 Francs, brown. Same as #29 but overprinted "Tresorerie—Thesaurie" on obverse (two signature varieties)	2.50
49.	20 Francs, brown. Same as #29 but overprinted "Tresorerie" on obverse, "Thesaurie" on reverse, date above middle (four signature varieties)	2.25
49a.	20 Francs, brown. Same as #49 but overprint above middle wing, date above left	2.25
50.	50 Francs = 10 Belgas, green. Same as #34 but overprinted "Tresorerie—Thesaurie" on obverse (six signature varieties)	1.50

Bank Nationale de Belgique—Nationale Bank van Belgie (National Bank of Belgium)

Printed in England, dated 1.2.1943 but issued in 1944

51.	1.2.1943	5 Francs = 1 Belga, red	.60
52.		10 Francs = 2 Belgas, green	1.00
53.		100 Francs = 20 Belgas, red and green	4.50
54.		500 Francs = 100 Belgas, violet, lilac and green	18.50
55.		1,000 Francs = 200 Belgas, brown and violet	60.00

Issues after 1944

56.	100 Francs, brown, rose and yellow. Leopold I at left, Grand Place, Brussels in middle (Dynastie type, two signature varieties)	25.00
57.	100 Francs, brown and multicolored. Leopold I at left, Frere Orban on reverse (Centenaire type, three signature varieties)	6.50
58.	100 Francs, lilac brown. Lambert Lombard at left (Lombard type)	—
59.	500 Francs, brown and yellow. Leopold II in military cap at left, view of Antwerp in middle (Dynastie type, two signature varieties)	40.00
60.	500 Francs, lilac and brown. Leopold II without cap (Centenaire type, three signature varieties)	25.00
61.	500 Francs, blue and brown. Bernard Van Orley (Van Orley Type)	—

180 × 94

62.	1,000 Francs, blue. King Albert I in steel helmet at left (Dynastie type, three signature varieties)	60.00
63.	1,000 Francs, blue and multicolored. King Albert I in civilian dress (Centenaire type, three signature varieties)	45.00
64.	1,000 Francs, brown. Gerard Kremer, known as Mercator, at left (Mercator type)	—
65.	5,000 Francs, green. Andre Vesal	—

Tresorerie—Thesaurie (State Treasury Notes)

Issues after 1945

66.	20 Francs, lilac and violet. Roland de Lassus. Dated 1.7.1950 or 3.4.1956 (two signature varieties)	2.25
67.	20 Francs, blue, green and multicolored. King Baudouin. Dated from 1964	—
68.	50 Francs, yellow, green and multicolored. Peasant woman with fruit at left, peasant man at right. Dated 1.6.1948 or 3.4.1956 (two signature varieties)	2.50
69.	50 Francs, brown. King Baudouin and Queen Fabiola. Dated from 1966	—

Armee Belge—Belgisch Leger (Belgian Army)

Notes issued for Belgian troops in Germany after World War II

M1.	1 Franc, green and blue	4.50
M2.	2 Francs, green and violet	6.50
M3.	5 Francs, green and red	6.50
M4.	10 Francs, brown and blue	15.00
M5.	20 Francs, brown and green	35.00
M6.	50 Francs, brown and red	65.00

150 × 75

M7.	100	Francs, grey blue and violet	85.00
M8.	500	Francs, grey blue and green	150.00

BOHEMIA—MORAVIA (see Czechoslovakia)

BULGARIA

Under Turkish rule from 1396, Bulgaria was declared an independent principality in 1878 under Prince Alexander Joseph. Ferdinand of Saxe-Coburg-Gotha came to the throne in 1887, declaring himself King in 1908. Bulgaria took the German side in both World Wars and was invaded by Russia in 1944. King Simeon III was deposed in 1946, the nation then becoming a communist People's Republic.

1 Lev (ЛЕВ) = *100 Stotinki* (СТОТИНКИ)
БЪЛГАРСКА НАРОДНА БАНКА = *Bulgarskata Narodna Banka* (Bulgarian National Bank)
ЦАРСТВО БЬЛГАРА = *Carstvo Bulgarija* (State Notes)
НАРОДНА РЕПЧБЛИКА БЬЛГАРИЯ = *Narodna Republika Bulgarija* (Bulgarian People's Republic)
ЛЕВ СРЕБРО = *Lev Srebro* (Silver Lev)
ЛЕВ ЗЛАТО = *Lev Zlato* (Gold Lev)

Bulgarskata Narodna Banka (Bulgarian National Bank)

Russian printing (without name of printing firm), values in "Lev Srebro." Issued from 1879 (undated) on unwatermarked paper with some signature varieties.

1.	5 Leva Srebro, blue border and red frame. Arms without script on reverse. Design in vertical format	$35.00
2.	5 Leva Srebro, green border with lilac and violet frame. Arms with "Carstvo Bulgaria" on reverse. Vertical format (issued August 1909)	16.50

91 × 142

3.	10 Leva Srebro, blue border, multicolored frame. Vertical format	12.50

4.	20 Leva Srebro, multicolored. Vertical format	35.00
5.	50 Leva Srebro, multicolored. Vertical format	45.00
6.	100 Leva Srebro, brown, blue and green. Vertical format	65.00
7.	500 Leva Srebro, grey, rose and blue. Vertical format	85.00

Russian printing (without name of printing firm), values in "Lev Zlato." Issues from 1885 (undated), on unwatermarked paper, some signature varieties.

8.	5 Leva Zlato. Same as #1 but "Srebro" crossed out and "Zlato" overprinted at left and right	15.00
9.	10 Leva Zlato. Same as #3 but "Srebro" crossed out and "Zlato" overprinted at left and right	16.50
10.	20 Leva Zlato, rose border, red and blue frame. Design in horizontal format	16.50
11.	50 Leva Zlato, rose border, blue and green frame. Horizontal format	20.00
12.	100 Leva Zlato, rose border, grey frame. Horizontal format	27.50

200 × 127

13.	500 Leva Zlato, rose border, rose and green frame. Horizontal format	35.00
13a.	20 Leva. Dated 1.8.1885	50.00

Printed at Reichsdruckerei in Berlin (without name of printing firm). Issued in 1916 but undated. Watermarked with cross and small ring pattern.

14.	1 Lev Srebro, green and blue. Horizontal format	1.25
15.	2 Leva Srebro, green and rose. Horizontal format	2.50
16.	5 Leva Srebro, yellow border, blue and grey ornamentation. Vertical format	5.00
17.	10 Leva Srebro, green-blue border, rose and lilac ornamentation. Vertical format	6.50
18.	20 Leva Zlato. Vertical format	8.50
19.	50 Leva Zlato, green-blue border, brown ornamentation. Horizontal format	20.00
20.	100 Leva Zlato, green border, blue, lilac and violet ornamentation. Horizontal format	25.00

Printed by Giesecke & Devrient, Leipzig (name imprinted on notes). Issued in August 1917 but undated. All notes are watermarked with letters.

21.	5 Leva Srebrni. Horizontal format	2.50
22.	10 Leva Zlatni. Horizontal format	3.50

158 × 100

23.	20 Leva Zlatni. Horizontal format	6.50
24.	50 Leva Zlatni. Horizontal format	7.50
25.	100 Leva Zlatni. Woman with sheaf at left. Horizontal format	16.50

Notes #8 through #25 also exist with a Serbian overprint increasing the value from 50 to 100%.

Various issues until 1928

26.	(1920)	1 Lev Srebro, green. Woman at right, buildings on the reverse. Printed by Waterlow & Sons. Watermarked with zigzag lines	1.75
27.	(1920)	2 Leva Srebro, brown. Type of #26	2.50
27a.		5 Leva. Peasant plowing on reverse. Printed by Bradbury	20.00
28.		100 Leva Zlato. Same as #20 with red overprint "БНБ" and "СЕРИЯ А"	RR
29.	(1918)	1,000 Leva Zlatni, blue green and light brown. Printed by Gebr. Parcus, Munich	65.00
30.	5.6.1924	1,000 Leva Zlatni. Same as #29 with overprint meaning "this note is good only within the kingdom"	100.00
31.	Nov. 1925	1,000 Leva Zlatni. Same as #29 with overprint meaning "This certificate has a value in the kingdom of one banknote of 1,000 Leva, Sofia, Nov. 1925"	100.00
32.		1,000 Leva Zlatni. Same as #29 but both overprints as on #30 and #31	100.00
33.	(1920)	1,000 Leva Zlatni. Same as #29 but printed by Bradbury-Wilkinson Company, London	65.00
34.	(1924)	1,000 Leva Zlatni. Same as #33 with overprint as on #30	100.00
35.	1924	5,000 Leva	RR

Carstvo Bulgarija (State Note)

36.　10.5.1916　　1,000 Leva, grey blue. Printed in Bulgaria. Water-
　　　　　　　　marked with cross and small ring pattern　　　125.00

Bulgarskata Narodna Banka (Bulgarian National Bank)

Issues after the currency reform of 1928.

37.　1922　　　　5 Leva. Printed by the American Bank Note Company　2.50
38.　　　　　　　10 Leva. Type of #37　　　　　　　　　　　　4.50
39.　　　　　　　20 Leva. Type of #37　　　　　　　　　　　　16.50
40.　　　　　　　50 Leva. Type of #37　　　　　　　　　　　　25.00

152 × 86

41.　　　　　　　100 Leva. Type of #37　　　　　　　　　　　　45.00
42.　　　　　　　500 Leva. Type of #37　　　　　　　　　　　　65.00
43.　　　　　　1,000 Leva. Type of #37　　　　　　　　　　　125.00
44.　(1928)　　　20 Leva, brown. King Boris III facing left　　　10.00
45.　1925　　　　50 Leva, brown. King Boris III at right. Printed by
　　　　　　　　Bradbury　　　　　　　　　　　　　　　　　10.00
46.　　　　　　　100 Leva, blue. Type of #45　　　　　　　　　16.50
47.　　　　　　　500 Leva, dark green. Type of #45　　　　　　50.00
48.　　　　　　1,000 Leva, brown and blue. Type of #45　　　　125.00
49.　　　　　　5,000 Leva, dark violet. Type of #45　　　　　　175.00

152 × 84

50.　1929　　　　200 Leva, green. King Boris III at right. Printed by De
　　　　　　　　La Rue & Company　　　　　　　　　　　　12.50
51.　　　　　　　250 Leva, lilac. Type of #50　　　　　　　　　25.00
52.　　　　　　　500 Leva, blue. Type of #50　　　　　　　　　65.00

53.		1,000 Leva, brown. Type of #50	100.00
54.		5,000 Leva, brown. Type of #50	200.00
55.	1938	500 Leva, lilac, brown and green. King Boris III at left. Printed by Giesecke & Devrient	25.00
56.		1,000 Leva, lilac, brown and green. Type of #55	35.00
57.		5,000 Leva, green. Type of #55	75.00
58.	1940	500 Leva, blue and green. King Boris III at right. Printed by Reichsdruckerei, Berlin	10.00
59.		1,000 Leva, red and brown. Type of #58	16.50
60.	1942	500 Leva, blue, green and brown. King Boris III at left	8.50

182 × 91

61.		1,000 Leva, red and brown. Type of #60	10.00
62.		5,000 Leva, brown. Printed by Giesecke & Devrient	45.00
63.	1943	20 Leva, blue, green and rose (date at lower right of obverse)	3.00
64.		200 Leva, brown. King Simeon III as a child at left. Printed by Reichsdruckerei, Berlin	8.50
65.		250 Leva, green. Type of #64	8.50
66.		500 Leva, blue. Type of #64	6.50
67.		1,000 Leva, dark red. King Simeon III at right. Printed by Reichsdruckerei, Berlin	8.50
68.	1944	20 Leva, brown (date at lower right of obverse)	
		a. Smooth paper, rose underprinting, brown control numbers	5.00
		b. Paper watermarked with lines, brown underprinting, brown control numbers	4.50
69.	1945	200 Leva, green and ochre. Without portrait of the Czar	16.50
70.		250 Leva, green and brown. Type of #69	16.50

155 × 81

| 71. | | 500 Leva, blue. Type of #69 | 16.50 |

| 72. | | 1,000 Leva, brown. Type of #69 | 25.00 |
| 73. | | 5,000 Leva, multicolored. Type of #69 | 40.00 |

Bulgarskata Narodna Banka (People's Republic, Bulgarian National Bank)

74.	1947	20 Leva, dark blue (date below, with name of printing firm)	6.00
75.	1948	200 Leva, brown. Arms with "9.IX.1944" at left (date below, with name of printing firm)	25.00
76.		250 Leva, green. Type of #75	35.00
77.		500 Leva, blue. Type of #75	45.00
78.		1,000 Leva. Type of #75 with soldier at right	65.00
79.	1950	20 Leva, brown	5.00
80.	1951	10 Leva, red brown. Tractor	.40
81.		25 Leva, grey blue. Track layer	.40
82.		50 Leva, brown. Peasant woman with basket and flowers	.60
83.		100 Leva, green and blue. Woman grape picker and grapes	1.25

175 × 90

84.		200 Leva, grey blue and multicolored. Tobacco harvest	2.50
85.	1962	1 Lev, brown lilac. Tower	—
86.		2 Leva, green. Woman grape picker and grapes	—
87.		5 Leva, red brown. Seashore scene	—
88.		10 Leva, blue. Factory	—
89.		20 Leva, brown lilac. Factory	—

Narodna Republika Bulgarija (Bulgarian People's Republic, State Notes)

90.	1951	1 Lev, brown	.40
91.		3 Leva, green	.40
92.		5 Leva, blue and green	.40

CROATIA (Hrvatska)

Until 1918, Croatia was part of the Kingdom of Hungary. In that year, along with Serbia and Slavonia, it became part of the Kingdom of Yugoslavia. During the 1941–44 German occupation, Croatia was declared an independent state. In 1945, Croatia was returned to Yugoslavia and is now part of the Federated Peoples Republic.

1 Kuna = 100 Banica (1941–44)

Nezavisna Drzava Hrvatska (Autonomous State of Croatia)

1.	26.5 (Svibnja).1941	50 Kuna, red brown	$2.50
2.		100 Kuna, blue grey	1.25
3.		500 Kuna, green. Three sheafs of cereal at right	3.50

168 × 90

4.		1,000 Kuna, brown. Peasant girl at left	2.25
5.	30.8 (Kolovoza).1941	10 Kuna, olive	1.75
6.	25.9 (Rujna).1942	50 Banica, blue on light brown	1.75
7.		1 Kuna, dark blue on brown	1.00
8.		2 Kuna, dark brown on red brown	1.25
9.	15.1 (Siecnja).1944	20 Kuna, brown (not issued)	16.50
10.		50 Kuna, green (not issued)	25.00

Hrvatska Drzavna Banka (Croatian State Bank)

11.	1.9 (Rujna).1943	100 Kuna, dark blue and brown	10.00
12.		1,000 Kuna, dark brown on yellow and green	4.50
13.		5,000 Kuna, red brown, blue and brown	4.50
14.	15.8 (Srpnja).1943	5,000 Kuna, brown on lilac and green. Girl in national costume at left	5.00

CZECHOSLOVAKIA (Ceskoslovenska)

When World War I brought about the collapse of the Austro-Hungarian Empire, the ancient territories of Bohemia, Moravia and Slovakia were united to form the new Republic of Czechoslovakia. In 1938, the Treaty of Munich separated the Sudetenland from the Republic and, in 1939, the independent state of Slovakia was formed. German troops occupied the rest of the country, forming the Protectorate of Bohemia-Moravia. After World War II, Czechoslovakia was re-established and, since 1948, it has been a Communist People's Republic.

1 Krone = 100 Heller

Notes of the Austro-Hungarian Bank with counterstamps or overprints added in 1919

1.	2.1.1915	10 Kronen. Austrian note #19 with "heller" over-printed in blue	$5.00
2.	2.1.1913	20 Kronen. Austrian note #13 with "heller" over-printed in red	4.50
3.	2.1.1914	50 Kronen. Austrian note #15 with "heller" over-printed in brown	4.50
4.	2.1.1912	100 Kronen. Austrian note #12 with "heller" over-printed in orange brown	4.50
5.	2.1.1902	1,000 Kronen. Austrian note #8 with "heller" over-printed in black red	10.00

> Numerous marking and overprint falsifications are known. In addition to notes #1–5 above, overprints are known on the 10 Kronen of 2.1.1904, the 20 Kronen of 2.1.1907, the 20 Kronen of 2.1.1913 (II issue) and the 100 Kronen of 2.1.1910. These are not, however, official stamps.

Most of the following notes marked "specimen" were released in large quantities for collectors. Up to 1945 the notes were perforated with holes spelling the words "Specimen" or "Neplatne." Specimen notes issued after 1945 were also perforated but with much smaller holes. The first column of prices is for regularly issued notes, the second column for specimens. The difference in value is often very large.

Bankovni urad Ministertva Financi (Authorized Bank of the Finance Ministry)

6.	15. 4 (Dubna).1919	1 Krone, blue	1.50	—
7.		5 Kronen, red. Two girls' heads	2.75	—
8.		10 Kronen, violet and yellow. Two girls' heads	10.00	—

9.		20 Kronen, red. Two men's heads	18.50	—
10.		50 Kronen, olive, green and brown. Two women's heads	57.50	—
11.		100 Kronen, violet. Two women's heads	100.00	—

175 × 119

12.		500 Kronen, red and brown. Woman's head and two eagles	RR	—
13.		1,000 Kronen, blue. Allegorical figures with globe	RR	125.00
14.		5,000 Kronen, red. Woman's head at right (like Austria #8)	RR	RR
15.	14. 1 (Ledna).1920	100 Kronen, green. Pagan priestess at right	75.00	35.00
16.	6. 7 (Cervence).1920	5,000 Kronen, brown violet. Elbe river with Rip mountain, girl in costume at right (also see #42)	85.00	10.00
17.	28. 9 (Zari).1921	5 Kronen, blue and brown. J. A. Comenius	3.50	—
18.	12. 7 (Cervence).1922	50 Kronen, blue, brown and red. Peasant with castle in background on the reverse	30.00	—
19.	6.10 (Rijna).1923	500 Kronen, brown. Head of Legionaire at right	RR	150.00

Narodna Banka Ceskoslovenska (National Bank of Czechoslovakia)

20.	1.10 (Rijna).1926	20 Kronen, blue, brown and red	2.50	1.25
21.	2. 1 (Januara).1927	10 Kronen, lilac and light brown. Type of #8	3.00	1.25
22.	2. 5 (Maja).1929	500 Kronen, red. Type of #19	20.00	2.25
23.	1.10 (Oktobra).1929	50 Kronen, red. Girl's head at left	5.00	1.75
24.	10. 1 (Ledna).1931	100 Kronen, green. Boy with falcon at left, woman's head at right	4.50	1.75
25.	8. 4 (Dubna).1932	1,000 Kronen, blue. Type of #13	35.00	4.50

198 × 105

26.   25. 5 (Kvetna).1934   1,000 Kronen, green and blue.
Woman with book and two
children at left   10.00   2.25

Protectorate of Bohemia-Moravia, 1939–1945 (Issued during German occupation).

27.   (1940)   1 Krone, blue. Girl's head at right. Unissued Czechoslovakian note with stamp
"Bohmen und Mahren"
                     a. Handstamp   6.50   —
                     b. Machine stamp   16.50   —
                     c. Without stamp   45.00   —
28.   5 Kronen, lilac and violet. Man's head at
right (J. Jungmann). Unissued Czecho-
slovakian note with stamp "Bohmen und
Mahren"
                     a. Handstamp   6.50   —
                     b. Machine stamp   20.00   —
                     c. Without stamp   50.00   —
29.   1 Krone, brown. Girl's head at right   1.75   1.00
30.   5 Kronen, green. Woman's head at right   2.25   1.00
31.   28. 8.1940 100 Kronen, blue. View of Prague with Hrad-
schin and Charles Bridges on red reverse   3.00   1.00
32.   100 Kronen, blue. Type of #31 but "II
Auflage" on blue reverse   2.25   1.00
33.   12. 9.1940   50 Kronen, dark brown and grey. Women's
head at right   5.00   2.25
34.   8. 7.1942   10 Kronen, brown. Girl's head at right (two
control number varieties)   2.25   1.25
35.   24. 1.1944   20 Kronen, green. Boy's head at right (two
control number varieties)   1.75   1.25
36.   25. 9.1944   50 Kronen, grey. Woman's head at right   3.50   1.25

Nationalbank fur Bohmen und Mahren (National Bank for Bohemia-Moravia)

37.   24. 2.1942 500 Kronen, dark brown. P. Brandl, artist, at
right   12.50   2.25

38.		500 Kronen, dark brown. Type of #37 but "II Auflage" on reverse	10.00	2.25
39.	24.10.1942	1,000 Kronen, dark green. P. Parler, sculptor, at right	20.00	8.50
40.		1,000 Kronen, dark green. Type of #39 but "II Auflage" on reverse. Ornament (guilloche) of blue and brown	16.50	2.25
41.		1,000 Kronen, dark green. Type of #39 but multicolored ornament (guilloche)	18.50	2.50
42.	6. 7.1920	5,000 Kronen, brown violet. Same as #16 with red overprint "Nationalbank fur Bohmen und Mahren." Known only as a specimen (issued 25.10.1943)	—	12.50

189 × 90

43.	24. 2.1944	5,000 Kronen, grey. St. Wencelas at right	25.00	3.00

CZECHOSLOVAK SOCIALIST REPUBLIC

State note issued by the Slovakian State Bank

44.	1945	2,000 Kronen, blue and green	125.00	6.50

State notes, Russian printing

45.	1944	1 Krone, brown	1.50	1.00
46.		5 Kronen, blue		
		a. Background of horizontal wavy lines	2.00	1.00
		b. Background of vertical wavy lines	2.00	1.00
47.		20 Kronen, dark blue on brown (two control number varieties)	2.50	1.25
48.		100 Kronen, green (two control number varieties)	3.50	1.25
49.		500 Kronen, red	12.50	1.75
50.		1,000 Kronen, dark blue on green	20.00	1.75

State notes with stamps

51.	7.10.1940	100 Kronen, blue. Slovakian note #9 with yellow stamp (issued in 1945)	8.50	2.25
52.		100 Kronen, blue. Slovakian note #10 with yellow stamp "II Emisia" on reverse	12.50	2.25

53.	12. 7.1941	500 Kronen, green. Slovakian note #13 with orange stamp (issued in 1945)	16.50	3.50
54.	25.11.1940	1,000 Kronen, brown. Slovakian note #12 with red stamp (issued in 1945)	16.50	3.75

168 × 84

55.	1944	100 Kronen, green. Same as #48 with blue stamp (issued in 1945)	5.00	1.75
56.		500 Kronen, red. Same as #49 with blue stamp	15.00	2.25
57.		1,000 Kronen, dark blue on green. Same as #50 with blue stamp	22.50	2.25

States notes issued to 1.6.1953

58.		1 Krone, blue. Type of #27c but no background	4.50	—
59.	(1945)	5 Kronen, red brown	1.75	1.25
60.		10 Kronen, green	1.75	1.25
61.		20 Kronen, blue on green. Karel Havlicek at left	3.00	1.25
62.		50 Kronen, lilac on green. General Stefanik at left	4.50	1.25
63.		100 Kronen, dark green. Tomas Masaryk at left	4.50	1.75
64.		500 Kronen, brown. J. Kollar at left	4.50	2.25
65.		1,000 Kronen, grey black. King George von Podiebrad	5.00	2.25
66.	16. 5 (Kvetna).1945	100 Kronen, grey brown. Woman's head at right	3.50	1.25
67.	3. 7.1948	50 Kronen, blue green. General Stefanik at right (three control number varieties)	5.00	1.25
68.	25. 1 (Ledna).1949	5 Kronen, red brown. Type of #59	1.75	1.25
69.	1. 5 (Kvetna).1949	20 Kronen, red brown. Girl with floral wreath at right		
		a. Bluish paper with fibers in left edge	4.50	1.25
		b. Yellowish paper without fibers	4.50	1.25

70.	4. 4.1950	10 Kronen, green. Type of #60	1.75	1.25
71.	29. 8.1950	50 Kronen, violet brown. Miner at right		
		a. Bluish paper with fibers in left edge	4.50	1.25
		b. Yellowish paper without fibers	4.50	1.25
72.	25. 2 (Unora).1953	20 Kronen, blue (not issued)	RR	—

Narodna Banka Ceskoslovenska (Czechoslovakian National Bank)

Issues to 1.6.1953

73.	16. 5 (Kvetna).1945	1,000 Kronen, grey. Girl's head at right		
		a. Thick, yellowish paper watermarked with a dark cross between light lines	7.00	2.25
		b. Transparent, bluish paper watermarked as #73a	7.00	2.25
		c. Thick, yellowish paper watermarked with a light cross and dark beams	7.00	2.25
		d. Transparent, bluish paper watermarked as #73c	7.00	2.25
74.	1.11 (Listopadu).1945	5,000 Kronen, dark brown. Smetana at right	8.50	2.25
75.	12. 3.1946	500 Kronen, brown. Type of #64	6.50	2.25

Statni Banka Ceskoslovenska (Czechoslovakian State Bank)

76.	9. 5 (Kvetna).1951	1,000 Kronen, brown. Type of #73 (not issued)	RR	—

149 × 70

77.	24.10 (Rijna).1951	100 Kronen, brown. Woman's head at right (not issued)	RR	—

States notes of the CSSR from 1.6.1953

78.	1953	1 Krone, brown	2.25	—
79.		3 Kronen, blue	4.50	—
80.		5 Kronen, green	6.50	—

| 81. | 1961 | 3 Kronen, blue | 1.25 | — |
| 82. | | 5 Kronen, green | 1.75 | — |

Statni Banka Ceskoslovenska (Czechoslovakian State Bank)

83.	1953	10 Kronen, brown	10.00	—
84.		25 Kronen, blue. Equestrian statue of J. Ziska (two control number varieties)	20.00	—
85.		50 Kronen, green. Partisan fighter and Russian soldier at left	16.50	—
86.		100 Kronen, brown. Worker and peasant at left (two control number varieties)	10.00	—
87.	1958	25 Kronen, blue. J. Ziska at left	12.50	—
88.	1960	10 Kronen, brown. Two girls with flowers	—	—
89.	1961	25 Kronen, blue. Type of #87	3.50	—
90.		100 Kronen, green. Worker and peasant girl	—	—
91.	1964	50 Kronen, red brown. Partisan fighter and Russian soldier	—	—
92.	1970	20 Kronen, light blue and multicolored. Head of J. Ziska at right	—	—

DANZIG (Gdansk)

Danzig was annexed to Prussia in 1793, declared a free city by Napoleon in 1807 and returned to Prussia in 1814. Following World War I, Danzig was made a free state again by the League of Nations. In 1939, the city was again occupied by Germany. Today, it is a part of Poland.

1 Mark = 100 Pfennig
1 Gulden = 100 Pfennig

Magistrat der Stadt (Municipal Council of the City)

Emergency issues prior to 1920

1.	10. 8.1914	50 Pfennig, violet	
		a. Watermarked with flakes	$25.00
		b. Watermarked with wavy lines	20.00
		c. Watermarked with spades	20.00
2.		1 Mark, brown	
		a. Watermarked with wavy lines	25.00
		b. Watermarked with spades	20.00
3.		2 Mark, rose	25.00
4.		3 Mark, green	
		a. Watermarked with spades	25.00
		b. Watermarked with crosses in squares	30.00
5.	9.12.1916	10 Pfennig, blue	1.75
6.		50 Pfennig, light brown	1.75
7.	12.10.1918	5 Mark, black on green	
		a. Watermarked with small drops	20.00
		b. No watermark	10.00
8.		20 Mark, black on brown	
		a. Watermarked with small drops	35.00
		b. Watermarked with spades	30.00
		c. No watermark	20.00
9.	1.11.1918	50 Pfennig, brown. Guild Hall	2.25

10.	15.11.1918	20 Mark, black on lilac brown. Sailing ship "Kogge" at left	8.50

11.	15. 4.1919	50 Pfennig, brown and violet. City view on reverse		1.00
12.		50 Pfennig, dark green and olive green. Type of #11		1.00

Senat der Stadtgemeinde (Senate of the Free City Government)

Emergency money issued after 1920 with denominations in marks

1 Milliarde = 1 Billion (American) = 1,000,000,000

13.	31.10.1922	100 Mark, green on grey. Marian church	4.50
14.		500 Mark, blue. Krantor on the reverse	4.50
15.		1,000 Mark, olive green and dark brown. Sailing ship "Kogge"	4.50
16.	15. 3.1923	1,000 Mark, dark green. Type of #15	5.00
17.	20. 3.1923	10,000 Mark, dark blue on dark brown. City view at left and right	3.00
18.		50,000 Mark, light green on yellow. Marian church	3.50
19.		50,000 Mark, dark brown and brown. Type of #18	4.50

147 × 87

20.	26. 6.1923	10,000 Mark, dark brown and blue. Painting of a Danzig merchant by Hans Holbein the Younger	3.50
21.	8. 8.1923	1,000,000 overprinted on 50,000 Mark. Note #19 with new value in red	3.50
22.		1,000,000 overprinted on 50,000 Mark. Note #19 with new value in dark blue	8.50
23.		1,000,000 Mark, lilac and green. Chodowiecki	2.25
24.		5,000,000 overprinted on 50,000 Mark. Note #19 with new value in green	2.50
25.	31. 8.1923	10,000,000 Mark, green. J. Hevelius	2.25
26.		10,000,000 Mark. Same as #25 but border imprint inverted	4.50
27.	22. 9.1923	100 Million Mark, black on orange	
		a. Watermarked with triangles	2.25
		b. Watermarked with small drops	8.50
28.	26. 9.1923	500 Million Mark, dark brown on violet. Schopenhauer. Border script light blue or light yellow	2.25
29.		500 Million Mark. Same as #28 but border script inverted	4.50

30.	11.10.1923	5 Milliarde Mark, black on blue	3.00
31.		10 Milliarde Mark, black on brown	
		a. Watermarked with entwined lines	3.00
		b. Watermarked with small drops	3.75

Danziger Zentralkasse (Danzig Central Treasury)

32.	22.10.1923	1 Pfennig	6.50
33.		2 Pfennig	8.50
34.		5 Pfennig	
		a. Paper watermarked with entwined lines	10.00
		b. Paper watermarked with octagons	20.00
35.		10 Pfennig	
		a. Paper watermarked with entwined lines	10.00
		b. Paper watermarked with sailing ship "Kogge"	12.50
36.		25 Pfennig	12.50
37.		50 Pfennig	16.50

93 × 64

38.		1 Gulden	
		a. Paper watermarked with entwined lines	25.00
		b. Paper watermarked with sailing ship "Kogge"	45.00
39.		2 Gulden	65.00
40.		5 Gulden	
		a. Paper watermarked with entwined lines	85.00
		b. Paper watermarked with sailing ship "Kogge"	100.00
41.		10 Gulden	100.00
42.		25 Gulden	175.00
43.	1.11.1923	1 Pfennig	35.00
44.		5 Pfennig	45.00
45.		10 Pfennig	65.00
46.		25 Pfennig	70.00
47.		50 Pfennig	70.00
48.		1 Gulden	85.00
49.		2 Gulden	125.00
50.		5 Gulden	175.00
51.		50 Gulden	RR
52.		100 Gulden	RR

Bank von Danzig (Bank of Danzig)

53.	10. 2.1924	10 Gulden	175.00
54.		25 Gulden	RR
55.		100 Gulden, blue	85.00
56.		500 Gulden, green	80.00

170 × 93

57.		1,000 Gulden, red orange	45.00
58.	1.10.1928	25 Gulden, dark green	65.00
59.	1. 7.1930	10 Gulden, brown	20.00
60.	2. 1.1931	25 Gulden, dark green	25.00
61.	1. 8.1931	100 Gulden, blue	35.00
62.	2. 1.1932	20 Gulden, lilac brown	16.50
63.	5. 2.1937	50 Gulden, brown	25.00
64.	1.11.1937	20 Gulden, dark green	16.50

DENMARK (Danmark)

Denmark became a constitutional monarchy in 1848 under King Frederick VII (1848–63). The present King, Frederick IX, came to the throne in 1947. The country was occupied by Germany during both World Wars.

1 Krone = 100 Ore.

Most Danish banknotes are known with many date and signature varieties

Nationalbanken i Kjobenhavn (National Bank in Copenhagen)

1.	1898–1904	5 Kroner, blue. Ornament made up of the numeral "5" and the words "Fem Kroner"	$100.00
2.	1891–1904	10 Kroner, black on brown. Arms at left. Ten one-krone coins on the reverse	175.00
3.	1883–1904	50 Kroner, brown. Crown above seated woman at left	RR
4.	1888–1904	100 Kroner, green. Woman with inscribed ribbons	RR
5.	1875–1910	500 Kroner, grey blue. Head of Hermes at left, head of Neptune at right	RR
6.	1904–11	5 Kroner, blue. Type of #1 but watermarked with wavy lines	85.00

142 × 87

7.	1904–12	10 Kroner, black on brown. Type of #2 but watermarked with wavy lines	150.00
8.	1904–10	50 Kroner, brown. Type of #3 but watermarked with wavy lines	250.00
9.	1904–10	100 Kroner, green. Type of #4 but watermarked with wavy lines	RR

Nationalbanken i Kjobenhavn (National Bank in Copenhagen)

War issue

10.	1914	1 Krone, black on reddish paper. A fish in the arms for Iceland on the reverse	20.00

120 × 76

11.		1 Krone, black on reddish paper. A falcon in the arms for Iceland on the reverse	12.50
12.	1916	1 Krone, blue on blue green	3.50
13.	1918	1 Krone, blue on blue green. Same as #12 except date	3.25
14.	1920	1 Krone, blue on blue green. Same as #12 except date	3.50
15.	1921	1 Krone, blue on blue green. Same as #12 except date	3.00

Statsbevis (State Treasury Notes)

With 5% interest, but passed as legal tender.

169 × 102

16.	1.10.1914	10 Kroner	100.00
17.		50 Kroner	175.00
18.		100 Kroner	RR
19.		500 Kroner	RRR

Nationalbanken i Kjobenhavn (National Bank in Copenhagen)

Inscription begins "Vexles med Guldmont," paper watermarked with dark numerals of the notes' denominations.

20.	1912–31	5 Kroner, blue green. Pre-historic grave	25.00
21.	1913–30	10 Kroner, brown. Head of Mercury on reverse	40.00
22.	1911–30	50 Kroner, blue green. Fisherman with boat and nets	100.00
23.	1910–30	100 Kroner, brown. Sea-god with triton horn at left and right of reverse	150.00
24.	1910–31	500 Kroner, grey blue. Farmer plowing with horse	175.00

Inscription begins "Nationalbankens Sedler," paper watermarked with light numerals of the notes' denominations.

25.	1931–36	5 Kroner, blue green. Type of #20	16.50
26.	1930–36	10 Kroner, brown. Type of #21	20.00
27.		50 Kroner, blue green. Type of #22	70.00

154 × 100

28.	1930–38	100 Kroner, brown. Type of #23	85.00
29.	1931–39	500 Kroner, grey blue. Type of #24	RR

Danmarks Nationalbank (National Bank of Denmark)

30.	1937–43	5 Kroner, blue green. Type of #20 but different bank name	1.75
31.		10 Kroner, brown. Type of #21	2.25

156 × 100

32.	1937–44	50 Kroner, blue green. Type of #22	10.00
33.	1938–44	100 Kroner, brown. Type of #23	20.00
34.	1939–44	500 Kroner, grey blue. Type of #24	85.00

For overprinted notes of above type, see Faroe Islands #1–6.

Issues after 1944

35.	1944–50	5 Kroner, blue green. New type note without illustration	6.50

131 × 80

36.	1944–45	10 Kroner, brown. Type of #35, arms on the reverse	8.50
37.	1945–50	10 Kroner, dark green. Obverse type of #31, reverse type of #36	
		a. Handmade paper, watermarked with flower design	16.50
		b. Watermarked with wavy lines (later issue)	8.50
38.	1944–55	50 Kroner, violet. Type of #32 but different design on reverse	35.00
39.	1944–45	100 Kroner, dark green. Type of #33, but only arms on reverse	85.00
40.	1946–60	100 Kroner, light green. Type of #39	45.00
41.	1944–63	500 Kroner, orange. Type of #34 but different design on reverse	125.00

Danmarks Nationalbank (National Bank of Denmark)

The modern type 5 and 10 kroner notes carry only the date of authorization, 7.4.1936. The other denominations have various dates.

42.	1952–61	5 Kroner, blue green. Thorvaldsen at left	3.50
43.	1952–53	10 Kroner, olive brown. Andersen at left, reverse printed in green	12.50
44.	1954–	10 Kroner, brown. Andersen at left, reverse printed in black	—
45.	1956–	50 Kroner, blue green. Ole Romer at left	
		a. Watermarked with crowns	30.00
		b. Watermarked with lines and "50"	—
46.	1961–	100 Kroner, red brown. H. C. Orsted at left	
		a. Watermarked with narrow waves	45.00
		b. Watermarked with "100"	—
47.	1964–	500 Kroner, green. Chr. D. F. Reventlow at left	—

Allierede Overkommando til Brug i Danemark (Issues of the Allied High Command for Denmark)

M1.	(1945)	25 Ore, brown and lilac	4.50
M2.		1 Krone, lilac	5.00
M3.		5 Kroner, green	10.00

138 × 78

M4.	10 Kroner, dark brown	25.00
M5.	50 Kroner, violet	65.00
M6.	100 Kroner, green blue (pattern, not issued)	RR

Danske Krigsministerium, Den Danske Brigade (Danish War Ministry, The Danish Brigade)

Military currency for Danish troops stationed in Germany

M7.	(1945)	5 Ore, blue	2.50
M8.		10 Ore, brown	4.50
M9.		25 Ore, blue	3.50
M10.		1 Krone, brown	7.50
M11.		5 Kroner, blue	16.50

111 × 70

M12.	10 Kroner, brown	35.00

ESTONIA (Eesti)

Estonia was under Danish and then Swedish rule until 1710, when it passed to Russian domination. An independent republic was declared in 1918 which lasted until 1940 when the country was occupied first by the Russians, then by German troops. Estonia was reabsorbed by Russia during World War II.

1 Ruble = 100 Kopecks (1918)
1 Marka = 100 Penni (1919–27)
1 Kroon = 100 Senti (1928)

Eesti Wabariigi 5% Wolakohustus (Obligation notes of the Estonian State bearing 5% interest).

Authorized legal tender

1.	to 1.5.1919, serial letter A	50 Marka, grey	$30.00
2.		100 Marka, grey	35.00
3.		200 Marka, grey	45.00
4.		500 Marka, grey. Both sides printed	65.00
5.		500 Marka, grey. Reverse not printed	65.00
6.		1,000 Marka, grey	125.00
7.	to 1.6.1919, serial letter B	50 Marka, yellow brown. Both sides printed	27.50
8.		50 Marka, yellow brown. Reverse side printed	30.00

208 × 135

9.	100 Marka, yellow brown	25.00

10.		200 Marka, yellow brown. Both sides printed	35.00
11.		200 Marka, yellow. Reverse not printed	40.00
12.		500 Marka, yellow brown	45.00
13.		1,000 Marka, yellow brown	125.00
14.	to 1.7.1919, serial letter D	50 Marka, green	35.00
15.		100 Marka, green	45.00
16.		200 Marka, green. Both sides printed	65.00
17.		200 Marka, green. Reverse not printed	70.00
18.		500 Marka, green. Both sides printed	85.00
19.		500 Marka, green. Reverse not printed	100.00
20.		1,000 Marka, green	250.00
21.	to 1.11.1919	50 Marka, grey	35.00
22.		100 Marka, yellow brown	45.00
23.		200 Marka, orange	65.00
24.		500 Marka, green	70.00
25.	to 1.12.1919	50 Marka, grey	35.00
26.		100 Marka, yellow brown	45.00
27.		200 Marka, orange	65.00
28.		500 Marka, green	70.00
29.	to 1. 1.1920	50 Marka, grey	25.00
30.		50 Marka, green	30.00
31.		100 Marka, grey	25.00
32.		100 Marka, yellow brown	30.00
33.		200 Marka, orange	57.50
34.		500 Marka, grey	50.00
35.		500 Marka, green	100.00
36.		1,000 Marka, green	250.00
37.	to 1. 5.1920	100 Marka, grey	25.00
38.		200 Marka, grey	35.00

Eesti Vabariigi Kassataht (State Loan Office Notes)

39.	(1919)	5 Penni, green	1.25
40.		10 Penni, brown	1.50
41.		20 Penni, yellow. Windmill	1.75
42.	1919	50 Penni, blue	2.25
43.		1 Marka, brown	2.50
		For notes #42 and 43 stamped "Pohjan Pojat Rykmentin," see #M2 and M3.	
44.		3 Marka, green. Agricultural symbol	4.50
45.		5 Marka, blue. Farmer plowing	5.00
46.		10 Marka, brown. Shepherd with horn, cow and sheep	
		a. "Kumme Marka" inserted in black border on reverse	8.50
		b. "Kumme Marka" without black border on reverse	8.50
47.		25 Marka, violet. Potato harvest	10.00

155 × 94

48.		100 Marka, brown. Woman spinning	20.00
49.	(1920–21)	500 Marka, violet on bluish paper. Eagle with arms on reverse. (Notes without series number, Series II and III (A and B) issued in 1920, series D in 1921)	40.00
50.		1,000 Marka, green and brown. "Birth of Freedom" on the reverse. (Notes without series letter issued 1920, series A and B issued 1921)	65.00
51.	1923	100 Marka, green and brown. Bank building (Notes without series letter issued 1923, series A issued 1927)	15.00
52.		500 Marka, brown, blue and yellow, Toompealoss Castle	40.00

Eesti Vabariigi Vahetustaht (Promissory Notes)

53.	1922	10 Marka, red brown	
		a. Watermarked with "E.V." without series letter	16.50
		b. Watermarked, with squares serial letter A (issued 1924)	20.00

145 × 78

| 54. | | 25 Marka, olive and violet (varieties without series letter and series A issued 1926) | 35.00 |

Eesti Pank (Estonian Bank)

Bank notes in mark denominations

| 55. | 1919 | 50 Marka, green. Globe on reverse | 16.50 |

56.	1921	100 Marka, brown. Two blacksmiths	35.00
57.	(1921)	500 Marka, light green and grey	45.00
58.	1922	100 Marka, violet, brown and green. Sailing ship on reverse	18.50
59.	(1922)	1,000 Marka, rose, violet and green. City and harbor of Tallinn (Reval)	45.00
60.	1923	5,000 Marka, blue, brown and green. Bank building on reverse	250.00

Eesti Vabariigi Kassastaht (Treasury Notes)

Notes in kroon denominations

61.	(1928)	1 Kroon, green and brown. Same as #51 with overprint of new value	12.50

Eesti Pank (Estonian Bank)

Bank notes in kroon denominations

62.	1928	10 Krooni, blue. Peasant woman in national costume	20.00
63.	1929	5 Krooni, red brown. Fisherman at rudder	8.50
64.		50 Krooni, brown. Steep coastline of Rannamoisa	12.50
65.	1932	20 Krooni, grey green. Shepherd with horn	10.00

181 × 102

66.	1935	100 Krooni, blue. Blacksmith at anvil	16.50
67.	1937	10 Krooni, blue. Type of #62 but different date and signature	10.00
68.	1940	10 Krooni, blue. Type of #67 (not issued)	RR

"Pohjan Pojat" (Finnish Regiment, Sons of the North)

Finnish and Estonian notes stamped "Pohjan Pojat Rykmentin Rahaston hoitaja"—paymaster of the regiment, Sons of the North—circulated in 1919 in southern Estonia and northern Latvia.

M1.		1 Mark. Same as Finland #19 but overprinted	RR
M2.		50 Penni. Same as Estonia #42 but overprinted	RR
M3.		1 Marka. Same as Estonia #43 but overprinted	RR

FAROE ISLANDS (Faeroerne)

A group of islands in the North Atlantic Ocean that have been under Danish control since 1400.

1 Krone = 100 Ore

Danish notes with red overprint "Kun gyldig paa Faeroerne, Faero Amt, Juni 1940"

1.	June 1940	5 Kroner, blue. Denmark #30 with above overprint. Signature "Hilbert" printed	$75.00
2.		10 Kroner, brown. Denmark #31 with above overprint. Signature "Hilbert" handwritten	150.00

130 × 78

3.		10 Kroner, brown. Type of #2 but signature printed	100.00
4.		50 Kroner, blue. Denmark #32 with above overprint. Signature "Hilbert" printed	175.00
5.		100 Kroner, brown. Denmark #33 with above overprint. Signature "Hilbert" printed	250.00
6.		500 Kroner, grey blue. Denmark #34 with above overprint. Signature "Hilbert" printed	RRR

Faero Amt (Faroe Government Council)

Newly printed notes

7.	1.10.1940	10 Kronur, brown on light brown	175.00
8.		100 Kronur	RR

9.	November 1940	1 Krona, blue and violet	20.00
10.		5 Kronur, green	65.00
11.		10 Kronur, lilac and green	85.00
12.		100 Kronur, green and brown	250.00
13.	12.4.1949	5 Kronur, green. Coins and sheep at left	6.50
14.		10 Kronur, orange. Arms and sheep at left	10.00

155 × 103

15.		100 Kronur, grey green	
		a. Trimmed edge	65.00
		b. Deckle edge left and right	75.00
16.	12.4.1949	100 Kronur, red. V.U. Hammershaimb at left (issued 1967)	—
17.	12.4.1949	50 Kronur, blue green. Nolsoyar Pall at left (issued 1968)	—

FINLAND (Suomi)

Under Swedish control until 1809, Finland was then made a Grand Duchy of Czarist Russia. After the collapse of the Russian Empire in 1917, Finland declared itself an independent republic.

1 Markka = 100 Pennia

Suomen Pankki—Finlands Bank (Bank of Finland)

Notes issued after 1909 are known with numerous signature variations.

Grand Duchy

1.	1897	5 Markkaa, blue. Woman's head in middle. On the reverse, the lower part of the arms shield is round	$15.00
2.		5 Markkaa, blue. Type of #1 but the arms shield on the reverse is pointed	20.00
3.	1898	10 Markkaa, violet. Standing woman at left. Reverse printed in green	30.00
4.		10 Markkaa, violet. Type of #3 but reverse printed in brown	30.00
5.		20 Markkaa, dark green. Woman with youth and globe	45.00
6.		50 Markkaa, blue. Woman with writing tablet at left	85.00
7.		100 Markkaa, violet. Young couple at left	77.50

195 × 111

8.		500 Markkaa, blue. Woman with lion at left	175.00
9.	1909	5 Markkaa, blue. River and river boat on reverse (serial numbers to 19,397,000)	
		a. Watermarked with "FB SP"	3.50
		b. No watermark	4.50
10.		10 Markkaa, lilac. House and two cows on reverse	5.00

11.		20 Markkaa, orange brown. Stylized tree on reverse (serial numbers to 9,927,507)	
		a. Watermarked with "FB SP"	12.50
		b. No watermark	6.50
12.		50 Markkaa, blue. Lighthouse on reverse	16.50
13.		100 Markkaa, violet. Farmer plowing at left and right (serial numbers to 2,775,000)	16.50
14.		500 Markkaa, orange and brown. Two blacksmiths (serial numbers to 170,000)	45.00
15.		1,000 Markkaa, yellow and brown. Two men with caduceus	85.00
16.	1915	1 Markka, red	
		a. Without series letter	6.50
		b. With series letter "A"	2.50
17.	1916	25 Penni, yellow brown (not issued)	125.00
18.		50 Penni, grey blue (not issued)	125.00
19.		1 Markka, dark brown on rose	3.00

For note with overprint "Pohjan Pojat," see Estonia #M1.

Soviet Issue, 1918

20.	1909	5 Markkaa, blue. Type of #9 but serial numbers 19,397,001-20,789,000 (issued 1918)	3.00
21.		20 Markkaa, orange brown. Type of #11 but serial numbers 9,927,508–10,019,000 (issued 1918)	5.00

169 × 102

22.		100 Markkaa, violet. Type of #13 but serial numbers 2,775,001–2,983,000 (issued 1918)	15.00
23.		500 Markkaa, orange and brown. Type of #14 but serial numbers 170,001–262,000 (issued 1918)	35.00

Republic

24.	1909, "Litt. A" (issued 1918)	5 Markkaa, blue. Type of #9 but with "Litt. A"	
		a. Watermarked with "FB SP"	4.50
		b. No watermark	6.50
25.		10 Markkaa, red. Type of #10 but with "Litt. A"	7.75

26.		20 Markkaa, orange brown. Type of #1 but with "Litt. A"	10.00
27.		50 Markkaa, blue. Type of #12 but with "Litt. A"	18.50
28.		100 Markkaa, violet. Type of #13 but with "Litt. A"	25.00
29.		500 Markkaa, orange and brown. Type of #14 but with "Litt. A"	150.00
30.	1909, "Ser. II" (issued 1918)	5 Markkaa, green. Type of #9 but with "Ser. II"	3.00
31.		100 Markkaa, grey green. Type of #13 but with "Ser. II"	25.00
32.		500 Markkaa, yellow. Type of #14 but with "Ser. II"	65.00
33.	1918	25 Penni, dark brown and light brown	1.75
34.		50 Penni, dark brown and blue	2.25
35.		1 Markka, dark brown on rose. Type of #19	2.25
36.		5 Markkaa, green. Type of #9	2.50
37.		10 Markkaa, lilac. Type of #10	3.50

38.		20 Markkaa, blue. Type of #11	6.50
39.		50 Markkaa. Type of #12	16.50
40.		100 Markkaa, light brown on grey. Type of #13	25.00
41.		1,000 Markkaa. Type of #15	100.00

Suomen Pankki (Finlands Bank)

42.	1922	5 Markkaa, green. Spruce tree in middle	2.25
43.		10 Markkaa, brown. Pine tree in middle	3.50
44.		20 Markkaa, violet. Pine tree in middle (issued 1926)	4.50
45.		50 Markkaa, dark blue. Allegorical group of six figures	8.50
46.		100 Markkaa, dark brown. Type of #45 (issued 1923)	12.50
47.		500 Markkaa, brown on green. Allegorical group of 11 figures (issued 1924)	35.00
48.		1,000 Markkaa, brown. Allegorical group of 13 figures (issued 1923)	150.00

118 × 61

49.	1922, "Litt. A"	5	Markkaa, green. Type of #42 but with "Litt. A" (issued 1926)	4.50
50.		10	Markkaa, brown. Type of #43 (issued 1926)	6.50
51.		20	Markkaa, violet. Type of #44 (issued 1927)	10.00
52.		50	Markkaa, dark blue. Type of #45 (issued 1925)	20.00
53.		100	Markkaa, dark brown. Type of #46 (issued 1923)	32.50
54.		500	Markkaa, brown on green. Type of #47 (issued 1930)	65.00
55.		1,000	Markkaa, brown. Type of #48 (issued 1929)	100.00
56.	1922, "Litt. B"	5	Markkaa, green. Type of #42 but with "Litt. B" (issued 1929)	12.50
57.		10	Markkaa, brown. Type of #43 (issued 1929)	18.50
58.		20	Markkaa, violet. Type of #44 (issued 1929)	25.00
59.		50	Markkaa, dark blue. Type of #45 (issued 1929)	35.00
60.		100	Markkaa, dark brown. Type of #46 (issued 1929)	50.00
61.	1922, "Litt. C"	5	Markkaa, green. Type of #42 but with "Litt. C" (issued 1930)	1.75
62.		10	Markkaa, brown. Type of #43 (issued 1930)	4.50

#67

203 × 120

63.		20 Markkaa, red. Type of #44 (issued 1931)	6.50
64.		50 Markkaa, dark blue. Type of #45 (issued 1931)	10.00
65.		100 Markkaa, dark brown. Type of #46 (issued 1931)	16.50
66.		500 Markkaa, brown on green. Type of #47 (issued 1932)	25.00
67.		1,000 Markkaa, brown. Type of #48 (issued 1931)	30.00
68.	1922, "Litt. A"	5,000 Markkaa. Same as #47 with blue overprint (issued 1939)	RRR
69.	1939, "Litt. D"	5 Markkaa, green. Type of #42 (issued 1942)	2.25
70.		10 Markkaa, brown. Type of #43 (issued 1939)	2.50
71.		20 Markkaa, violet. Type of #44 (issued 1939)	3.50
72.		50 Markkaa, dark blue. Type of #45 (issued 1939)	6.50
73.		100 Markkaa, dark brown. Type of #46 (issued 1940)	10.00
74.		1,000 Markkaa, brown. Type of #48 (issued 1939)	65.00
75.	1939	5,000 Markkaa, dark blue and violet. J. V. Snellmann at left	175.00

In 1946, some 500, 1,000 and 5,000 markkaa notes were cut in half. The right halves became a forced loan, the left halves were temporarily valued at half face value as legal tender as follows:

250 Markkaa (left halves of #47, #54 or #66)
500 Markkaa (left halves of #48, #55 or #67)
2,500 Markkaa (left half of #75)

76.	1945, "Litt. A" (issued 1946)	5 Markkaa, yellow. Spruce tree in middle	2.25
77.		10 Markkaa, red. Pine tree in middle	2.50
78.		20 Markkaa, blue. Pine tree in middle	4.50
79.		50 Markkaa, brown. Young couple on reverse	5.30
80.		100 Markkaa, blue green. Woman with lion on reverse	8.50
81.		500 Markkaa, blue. Allegorical group of 11 figures	35.00
82.		1,000 Markkaa, blue violet. Allegorical group of 13 figures	65.00
83.		5,000 Markkaa, dark brown. Type of #75	150.00
84.	1945, "Litt. B" (issued 1948)	5 Markkaa, yellow. Type of #76	1.75
85.		10 Markkaa, red. Type of #77	2.25
86.		20 Markkaa, blue. Type of #78	2.50
87.		50 Markkaa, brown. Type of #79	5.00

120 × 103

88.		100 Markkaa, blue green. Type of #80	7.75
89.		500 Markkaa, blue. Type of #81	20.00
90.		1,000 Markkaa, violet. Type of #82	35.00
91.	1955	100 Markkaa, brown on olive	16.50
92.		500 Markkaa, brown on blue. Conifer tree branch	25.00

140 × 70

93.		1,000 Markkaa, dark green. J. K. Paasikivi at left	16.50
94.		5,000 Markkaa, brown and lilac. K. J. Stahlberg at left	50.00
95.		10,000 Markkaa, lilac. J. V. Snellmann	70.00
96.	1956	500 Markkaa, blue. Conifer tree branch	8.50
97.	1957	100 Markkaa, lilac brown on yellow brown	1.75

Currency Reform, 1963: *100 Old Markkaa = 1 New Markka*

98.	1963	1 Markka, lilac brown on yellow. Type of #97	—
99.		5 Markkaa, blue. Type of #96	—
100.		10 Markkaa, dark green. Type of #93	—
101.		50 Markkaa, brown. Type of #94	—
102.		100 Markkaa, violet. Type of #95	—
103.	1963, "Litt. A" (issued 1969)	10 Markkaa, dark green. Type of #100	—
104.		50 Markkaa, brown. Type of #101	—
105.		100 Markkaa, violet. Type of #101	—
106.	1963, "Litt. B"	50 Markkaa, brown. Type of #101	—

FIUME (Rijeka)

Following the Hungarian revolution of 1919, the Fiume area was occupied by the Italian, Gabriele d'Annunzio. The Treaty of Rapallo (12.11.1920) made Fiume temporarily independent. After World War II, the Fiume area was given to Yugoslavia.

The notes in use were those of the Austro-Hungarian Bank with one of the following stamps or overprints:

1. Round hand stamp "Citta di Fiume,"
2. Round machine stamp "Citta di Fiume,"
3. Square overprint "Instituto di Credito Consiglio Nacionale, Citta di Fiume," size 45 × 58 mm.

Notes with overprint #2 were not known until the 1950's. A large parcel of them was sold at auction, but the authenticity of these notes has not yet been established.

1.	1.12.1916 (issued 1920)	1 Krone, stamp #1	$16.50
2.		1 Krone, stamp #2	8.50
3.		1 Krone, overprint #3	RR
4.		1 Krone, stamp #1. Serial number above 7,000	25.00
5.		1 Krone, stamp #2. Serial number above 7,000	16.50
6.		1 Krone, overprint #3. Serial number above 7,000	RR
7.	5.8.1914 (issued 1920)	2 Kronen, stamp #1	30.00
8.		2 Kronen, stamp #2	16.50
9.		2 Kronen, overprint #3	RR
10.	1.3.1917 (issued 1920)	2 Kronen, stamp #1	16.50
11.		2 Kronen, stamp #2	8.50
12.		2 Kronen, overprint #3	RR
13.		2 Kronen, stamp #1. Serial number above 7,000	25.00
14.		2 Kronen, stamp #2. Serial number above 7,000	16.50
15.		2 Kronen, overprint #3. Serial number above 7,000	RR
16.		2 Kronen, with overprint "Deutsch Osterreich"	100.00
17.	2.1.1904 (issued 1920)	10 Kronen, stamp #1	75.00
18.		10 Kronen, stamp #2	30.00
19.		10 Kronen, overprint #3	RR

149 × 79

20.	2.1.1915 (issued 1920)	10 Kronen, stamp #1	25.00
21.		10 Kronen, stamp #2	10.00
22.		10 Kronen, overprint #3	RR
23.	2.1.1907 (issued 1920)	20 Kronen, stamp #1	125.00
24.		20 Kronen, stamp #2	65.00
25.	2.1.1913 (issued 1920)	20 Kronen, stamp #1	30.00
26.		20 Kronen, stamp #2	12.50
27.		20 Kronen, overprint #3	RR
28.		20 Kronen, "II issue," stamp #1	25.00
29.		20 Kronen, "II issue," stamp #2	12.50
30.		20 Kronen, "II issue," overprint #3	RR
31.	2.1.1902 (issued 1920)	50 Kronen, stamp #1	125.00
32.		50 Kronen, stamp #2	65.00
33.	2.1.1914 (issued 1920)	50 Kronen, stamp #1	35.00
34.		50 Kronen, stamp #2	12.50
35.		50 Kronen, overprint #3	RR
36.	2.1.1910 (issued 1920)	100 Kronen, stamp #1	150.00
37.		100 Kronen, stamp #2	150.00
38.	2.1.1912 (issued 1920)	100 Kronen, stamp #1	35.00
39.		100 Kronen, stamp #2	12.50
40.		100 Kronen, overprint #3	RR
41.	2.1.1902 (issued 1920)	1,000 Kronen, stamp #1	45.00
42.		1,000 Kronen, stamp #2	20.00
43.		1,000 Kronen, overprint #3	RR

FRANCE

France's Third Republic was established in 1871, following the Franco-Prussian War. It ended in 1940 when German troops occupied the country and set up the Vichy regime under the aged Marshal Petain. The Fourth Republic was set up in 1946, the Fifth, under General Charles De Gaulle, in 1958.

1 Franc = 100 Centimes

Most French bank notes carry the date of printing rather than a date of issue which gives rise to many varieties. The dates given in the listings below are the first and last dates of printing known for each type and the valuations given are for the commonest date and signature combinations. The listings below follow the *Catalogue des Billets de la Banque de France* by Maurice Muszynski which is considered authoritative.

Banque de France (Bank of France)

5 Franc notes

1.	1.12.1871–19. 1.1874	5 Francs, blue. Man at left, woman with sword at right. Three figures on reverse	$30.00

126 × 80

2.	2. 1.1912– 2. 2.1917	5 Francs, blue. Type of #1 but ornaments only on reverse	15.00
3.	1.12.1917–14. 9.1933	5 Francs, lilac. Helmeted woman's head at left, "Caissier Principal" (five signature varieties)	2.50
4.	13. 7.1939– 9. 1.1941	5 Francs, lilac. Type of #3 but "Caissier General"	1.00
5.	2. 6.1943–30.10.1947	5 Francs, blue, green and multicolored. Pyrenees herdsman on reverse (two signature varieties)	1.00

10 Franc notes

6.	3. 1.1916–25. 2.1937	10 Francs, blue. Minerva head at left, "Caissier Principal" (five signature varieties)	2.25

7.	2. 2.1939– 5. 3.1942	10 Francs, blue. Type of #6 but "Caissier General"	1.25
8.	11. 9.1941–30. 6.1949	10 Francs, multicolored. Miner at left (two signature varieties)	1.00

20 Franc notes

9.	1. 7.1874–11. 1.1905	20 Francs, blue on ochre. Mercury seated at left, woman seated right. Denomination in black (two signature varieties)	85.00
10.	2. 1.1906–12. 2.1913	20 Francs. Type of #9 but denomination blue (two signature varieties)	45.00
11.	1. 7.1916–21. 2.1919	20 Francs. Head of Bayard at left	20.00
12.	7.12.1939– 8. 1.1942	20 Francs, multicolored. Man and woman (Science and Industry) at right	5.00
13.	12. 2.1942– 9. 2.1950	20 Francs, multicolored. Breton fisherman (two signature varieties)	.75

50 Franc notes to 1945

14.	1. 8.1884– 4. 3.1889	50 Francs, blue. Woman's head at left and right, two cupids above (three signature varieties)	650.00

179 × 124

15.	1. 5.1889–25. 3.1927	50 Francs, blue on lilac. Type of #14 but five heads in medallions in middle (eight signature varieties)	15.00
16.	11. 2.1927–17. 7.1930	50 Francs, multicolored. Three angels, Mercury below. Artist's name, "Luc Olivier-Merson," at bottom on both sides	12.50
17.	24. 7.1930–16. 8.1934	50 Francs, multicolored. Type of #16 but without artist's name (two signature varieties)	8.50

18.	15.11.1934–30. 6.1937	50 Francs, multicolored. Ceres and park at Versailles, with "Caissier Principal"	1.75
19.	5. 8.1937–13. 6.1940	50 Francs, multicolored. Type of #18 but "Caissier General" (two signature varieties)	1.50
20.	13. 6.1940–15. 5.1942	50 Francs, multicolored. Jacques Coeur and underground palace in Bourges at left	1.25

100 Franc notes to 1945

21.	2. 1.1882–11. 9.1888	100 Francs, blue. Two seated women (four signature varieties)	650.00
22.	12. 9.1888–29. 1.1909	100 Francs, blue on rose. Type of #21 but four women's heads in middle (five signature varieties)	65.00
23.	2. 1.1908–10. 5.1908	100 Francs, multicolored. Woman and child at left and right. Bundles of goods inscribed with "L.O.M. 02" at right	65.00
24.	11. 5.1909–29.11.1923	100 Francs, multicolored. Type of #23 but no "L.O.M. 02" (three signature varieties)	4.50
25.	30.11.1923–30. 6.1937	100 Francs, multicolored. Type of #24 but space in frame for serial number measures from 20 to 23 mm wide, with "Caissier Principal"	1.75
26.	9. 9.1937–14. 9.1939	100 Francs, multicolored. Type of #25 but "Caissier General" (two signature varieties)	
		a. Thin paper	1.75
		b. Thick paper	1.75
27.	19. 4.1939–23. 4.1942	100 Francs, multicolored. Woman and child with view of Paris in background	1.25

160 × 91

| 28. | 15. 5.1942–14.12.1944 | 100 Francs, multicolored. Descartes at right | 7.75 |

300 Franc note

| 29. | (1938) | 300 | Francs, multicolored. Ceres at left | 77.50 |

500 Franc notes to 1945

30.	2.11.1888–10. 6.1937	500	Francs, blue on lilac. Woman's head at left, Mercury head at right, with "Caissier Principal" (13 signature varieties)	8.50
31.	5. 8.1937–18. 1.1940	500	Francs, blue on rose. Type of #30 but "Caissier General" (three signature varieties)	6.50
32.	4. 1.1940–19. 4.1945	500	Francs, multicolored. Woman with wreath at left (two signature varieties)	2.50

1,000 Franc notes to 1945

33.	7.11.1889–16. 9.1926	1,000	Francs, blue on lilac. Mercury at left, woman's head in medallion and allegorical figures at right (11 signature varieties)	35.00
34.	11. 2.1927–26. 8.1937	1,000	Francs, ochre, blue and multicolored. Ceres head at left, Mercury at right, two cupids below, with "Caissier Principal" (three signature varieties)	8.50
35.	4.11.1937–25. 7.1940	1,000	Francs, ochre, blue and multicolored. Type of #34 but "Caissier General" (three signature varieties)	7.50

192 × 118

| 36. | 24.10.1940–12.10.1944 | 1,000 | Francs, multicolored. Two women's heads. Blacksmith and Mercury on reverse (two signature varieties) | 15.00 |
| 37. | 28. 5.1942– 6. 4.1944 | 1,000 | Francs, multicolored. Ceres and Hercules. Mercury on reverse | 8.50 |

5,000 Franc notes to 1947

38.	2. 1.1918–29 1.1918 5,000 (Issued 1938)	Francs, multicolored. Seated worker and Mercury at left, cupid and agricultural products at right. View of Paris on reverse	650.00
39.	8.11.1934–11. 7.1935 5,000	Francs, violet and multicolored. Woman with victory statuette and olive branch. Statuette in copper plate print on the reverse. With "Caissier Principal"	250.00
40.	15.10.1938 5,000	Francs, violet and multicolored. Type of #39 but "Caissier General"	300.00
41.	8.12.1938–27. 7.1944 5,000	Francs, violet and multicolored. Type of #40 but reverse not copper plate print	25.00
42.	5. 3.1942– 25.9.1947 5,000	Francs, multicolored. Woman with three natives (two signature varieties)	18.50

Tresor Central (State Notes)

Notes #43 and #46 through 48 were given out on Corsica.

155 × 99

43.	2.10.1943 100	Francs, blue on green and violet. Marianne head in middle (printed in England)	150.00
44.	(1944) 500	Francs, brown. Marianne head at left (printed in England)	85.00
45.	1,000	Francs, green. Marianne head in middle (printed in England, two control number varieties)	25.00
46.	(1945) 500	Francs, blue on green. Note of "Banque de l'Algerie" of October, 1943 overprinted "TRESOR"	600.00
47.	1,000	Francs, multicolored. Note of "Banque de l'Algerie" of 1942–1943 overprinted "TRESOR"	RRR
48.	5,000	Francs, brown violet on rose. Note of "Bank de l'Algerie" of 1943 overprinted "TRESOR" (all notes destroyed, no specimens known)	

State notes, "Freedom Issue, American printing

First Issue—Obverse with "Emis de France," French flag on reverse

| 49. | 1944 | 2 Francs, green | 1.25 |

50.		5 Francs, blue on green	1.50
51.		10 Francs, lilac on green	2.00
52.		50 Francs, lilac on green	12.50
53.		100 Francs, blue on green	15.00
54.		500 Francs, brown on green	250.00
55.		1,000 Francs, red on green	450.00
		5,000 Francs (trial note only)	

Second Issue—Obverse with "France" only, flag inscribed "France" on reverse

156 × 67

56.	1944	50 Francs, lilac on green	3.50
57.		100 Francs, blue on green	4.50
58.		1,000 Francs, red on green	100.00

Banque de France (Bank of France)

Notes issued after 1945 with values in old Francs (also see #5, #8, #13 and #42)

59.	14. 3.1946– 7. 6.1951	50 Francs, multicolored. Head of Leverrier (four signature varieties)	1.75
60.	7.11.1945– 1. 4.1954	100 Francs, multicolored. Farmer with two oxen (four signature varieties)	2.25
61.	19. 7.1945– 2. 7.1953	500 Francs, violet and multicolored. Chateaubriand (three signature varieties)	12.50
62.	7. 1.1954–12. 2.1959	500 Francs, multicolored. Victor Hugo at right (three signature varieties)	7.50
63.	12. 4.1945–29. 6.1950	1,000 Francs, multicolored. Minerva and Hercules (two signature varieties)	20.00
64.	2. 4.1953– 5. 9.1957	1,000 Francs, multicolored. Richelieu at right	18.50

#65
171 × 111

65.	10. 3.1949– 7.11.1957	5,000 Francs, multicolored. Allegorical figures of Land and Sea (four signature varieties)	50.00
66.	7. 2.1957– 5. 3.1959	5,000 Francs, multicolored. Henry IV in middle (two signature varieties)	45.00
67.	27.12.1945– 7. 6.1959	10,000 Francs, multicolored. Young girl with book and globe (four signature varieties)	90.00
68.	1.12.1955–30.10.1958	10,000 Francs, multicolored. Napoleon Bonaparte at right (two signature varieties)	65.00

Currency Reform 1960: *100 Francs = 1 New Franc*

Notes with values overprinted in new francs (NF.), various dates to 1959.

69.	(1960)	5 NF. overprinted on #62	12.50
70.		10 NF. overprinted on #64	16.50
71.		50 NF. overprinted on #66	70.00
72.		100 NF. overprinted on #68	75.00

Newly printed notes with denomination in new francs (NF.)

73.	5 NF., multicolored. Type of #62	5.00
74.	10 NF., multicolored. Type of #64	8.50
75.	50 NF., multicolored. Type of #66	35.00
76.	100 NF., multicolored. Type of #68	60.00
77.	500 NF., multicolored. Moliere	300.00

Notes with denominations in francs (new francs) issued from 1963

78.	5 Francs, multicolored. Louis Pasteur at left	4.50
79.	10 Francs, multicolored. Voltaire at right	—
80.	50 Francs, multicolored. Racine at right	—
81.	100 Francs, multicolored. Pierre Corneille in middle	—
82.	500 Francs, yellow brown and dark brown. Blaise Pascal in middle	—

Regie des Chemins de Fer des Territoires Occupes (Railroad Authority of the occupied territories)

Issued by the French and Belgian railroad administration during the occupation of German territories following the First World War. All notes show a locomotive above, a view of the Rheinland in the background.

R1.	(1923)	0.05 Franc, yellow brown background	.60
R2.		0.10 Franc, light blue background	.60
R3.		0.25 Franc, violet background	.70
R4.		0.50 Franc, green background	.75
R5.		1 Franc, green background	1.50
R6.		5 Francs, grey background	3.50
R7.		10 Francs, grey green background	8.50
R8.		20 Francs, violet background	15.00

180 × 112

| R9. | 50 | Francs, rose background | 65.00 |
| R10. | 100 | Francs, rose background | 125.00 |

French Military Notes

All notes show a woman and child at left, a soldier and a dog at right. Undated, these notes were valid from 1917 until two years after the Armistice.

M1.	50	Centimes, blue	.75
M2.	1	Franc, brown	1.75
M3.	2	Francs, violet	6.50

Undated, these notes were valid from 1919 until four years after the Armistice.

| M4. | 50 | Centimes, blue. Type of M1 | 1.00 |
| M5. | 1 | Franc, brown. Type of M2 | 2.00 |

French Military Notes for German territories occupied after 1945

First Issue with "Tresor Francais"

M6.	(1947)	5	Francs, multicolored. Woman's head	1.75
M7.		10	Francs, multicolored. Woman's head	2.00
M8.		50	Francs, multicolored. Mercury	2.50
M9.		100	Francs, multicolored. Mercury	3.50
M10.		1,000	Francs, multicolored. Mercury	150.00

Second Issue with "Tresor Public"

M11.	(1955)	100	Francs, multicolored. Type of M9	7.50
M12.		1,000	Francs, multicolored. Mercury facing right	85.00
M13.		5,000	Francs, multicolored. Young farm couple	500.00

122 × 80

M14.   (1960)   5 NF., overprinted on 500 francs, multicolored.
                       Mercury   90.00
                       The 500 franc note is not known without the
                       overprint
M15.   50 NF., multicolored. Same as M13 except for over-
                       print   650.00

French Military Notes for the Suez War of 1956

M16.   (1956)   50 Francs, multicolored. Same as M8 but overprinted
                       "Forces Francaises en Mediterranee Orientale"   300.00
M17.   100 Francs, multicolored. Same as M9 but overprinted
                       as M16   325.00
M18.   1,000 Francs, multicolored. Same as M10 but over-
                       printed as M16   650.00

GERMANY (Deutschland)

In 1871, the German States united to form the German Empire (Deutsches Reich) under Wilhelm I of Prussia who ruled until 1888. His son, Emperor Frederick III, died after only 99 days of rule. He was followed by Emperor Wilhelm II (1888–1918). Following the First World War, a republic was formed under President Friedrich Ebert, after whose death Field Marshal Paul von Hindenburg was elected to the office. In 1933, von Hindenburg appointed Adolf Hitler as Reichs Chancellor, Hitler eventually rising to become the dictator of the National Socialist Party. After World War II, the Allied Control set up the four zones of occupation controlled by the Americans, British, French and Russians. In 1949 the Western Zone became the German Federal Republic, the East or Russian Zone became the Communist German Democratic Republic.

1 Taler = 30 Groschen
1 Gulden = 60 Kreuzer
1 Mark = 100 Pfennig (1874–1923)
1 Rentenmark = 100 Rentenpfennig (1923–48)
1 Reichsmark = 100 Reichspfennig (1924–48)
1 Deutsche Mark (West) = 100 Pfennig (since 1948)
1 Deutsche Mark (East) = 100 Deutsche Pfennig (since 1948)

On inflation currency:

1 Million = 1,000,000
1 Milliard = 1,000,000,000
1 Billiard = 1,000,000,000,000

Empire

Reichskassenscheine (Empire Treasury Bank Notes), 1874–1914

1.	11. 7.1874	5 Mark, dark blue and grey blue. Two cupids with oak leaf garland	$1,850.00
2.		20 Mark, green and yellow. Medieval herald	RRR
3.		50 Mark, dark violet, brown and green. Two winged figures (the Military and Agriculture)	RRR
4.	10. 1.1882	5 Mark, dark blue. Knight in armour holding a long sword	300.00
5.		20 Mark, green. Two cupids holding fruit	RRR
6.		50 Mark, dark brown. Winged figure holding hour glass and caduceus	RRR

149 × 99

7.	5. 1.1899	50 Mark, dark green and brown olive. Seated figure of Germania at left	RRR
8.	31.10.1904	5 Mark, blue and blue green. Germania with child and dove at left. Dragon guarding treasure on the reverse	2.25
9.	6.10.1906	10 Mark, dark green and olive green. Woman with palm branch at right (Agriculture)	1.75

Reichsbanknoten (Empire Bank Notes), 1875–1914

10.	1. 1.1876	100 Mark, dark blue and grey blue. Head of Minerva within wreath at right. Two cupids on the reverse	RRR
11.		1,000 Mark, brown. Woman and two children on the reverse (Industry, Trade and Transportation)	RRR

157 × 100

12.	3. 9.1883	100 Mark, blue. Germania head in medallion supported by two women (Industry and Agriculture) on reverse	650.00
13.	2. 1.1884	1,000 Mark, brown. Two female figures (Sailing and Agriculture) on the reverse	RRR
14.	1. 1.1891	1,000 Mark, brown. Type of #13	RRR
15.	1. 5.1891	100 Mark, blue. Type of #12	500.00
16.	1. 3.1895	100 Mark, blue. Type of #12	650.00
17.		1,000 Mark, brown. Type of #13	RRR
18.	10. 4.1896	100 Mark, blue. Type of #12	175.00

19.		1,000 Mark, brown. Type of #13	375.00
20.	1. 7.1898	100 Mark, blue. Type of #12	6.50
21.		1,000 Mark, brown. Type of #13	16.50
22.	17. 4.1903	100 Mark, blue. Type of #12	2.25
23.	10.10.1903	1,000 Mark, brown. Type of #13	8.50
24.	18.12.1905	100 Mark, blue. Type of #12	2.50
25.	10. 3.1906	20 Mark, blue. German eagle at upper right	2.25
26.		50 Mark, green. Head of Germania in medallions at upper left and right	2.25

186 × 110

27.	26. 7.1906	1,000 Mark, brown. Type of #13	10.00
28.	8. 6.1907	20 Mark, blue. Type of #25	1.75
29.		50 Mark, green. Type of #26	100.00
30.		100 Mark, blue. Type of #12	3.00
31.	7. 2.1908	20 Mark, blue. Type of #25	1.25
32.		50 Mark, green. Type of #26	1.25
33.		100 Mark, blue. Type of #12	
		a. Red serial numbers and seal, numbers 29 mm wide	.60
		b. Serial numbers 24 mm wide	2.50
34.		100 Mark, blue. Type of #12 but green control numbers and seal	.75

205 × 101

35.		100 Mark, blue. Mercury head at left, Ceres head at right. Long, narrow format. Germania and naval fleet on reverse	1.25

36.		1,000 Mark, brown. Type of #13	12.50
37.	10. 9.1909	20 Mark, blue. Type of #25	1.50
38.		100 Mark, blue. Type of #35	1.50
39.		1,000 Mark, brown. Type of #13	4.50
40.	21. 4.1910	20 Mark, blue. Type of #25	
		a. No watermark	.60
		b. Watermarked "20"	3.50
41.		50 Mark, green. Type of #26	.60
42.		100 Mark, blue. Type of #35, red serial numbers and seal	.60
43.		100 Mark, blue. Type of #35, green serial numbers and seal	.75
44.		1,000 Mark, brown. Type of #13, red serial numbers and seal	
		a. Six digit serial numbers (to 1916)	2.50
		b. Seven digit serial numbers	.60
45.		1,000 Mark, brown. Type of #13, green serial numbers and seal	.75
46.	19. 2.1914	20 Mark, blue. Type of #25	.60

Darlehnskassenscheine (State Loan Office Treasury Bank Notes), 1914–22

47.	5. 8.1914	5 Mark, grey violet. Bust of Germania in medallions at left and right on reverse	.60
48.		20 Mark, brown and violet. Minerva head at upper left. Mercury head at upper right on reverse	.60
49.		50 Mark, lilac red on grey. Bust of Germania in medallions on reverse	.60
50.	12. 8.1914	1 Mark, light green and lilac. Without background color	.60
51.		1 Mark. Type of #50 but with background printing and red serial numbers and seal	.40
52.		1 Mark. Type of #51 but blue serial numbers and seal	.40
53.		2 Mark, carmine red. Without background color	.60

#54
139 × 90

54.		2 Mark. Type of #53 but with background printing and red serial numbers and seal	.40
55.		2 Mark. Type of #54 but blue serial numbers and seal	.45
56.	1. 8.1917	5 Mark, violet blue. Young girl's head at right	.40
57.	20. 2.1918	20 Mark, dark brown on carmine. Minerva head at left, Mercury head at right. Man and woman (War and Peace) on reverse	.40
58.	1. 3.1920	1 Mark, olive green and blue green	.40
59.		2 Mark, red. Brown serial numbers and seal	.40
60.		2 Mark, brown. Red serial numbers and seal	.40
61.	15. 9.1922	1 Mark, dark green on light green	
		a. Light green paper	.40
		b. Grey paper	25.00
62.		2 Mark, brown on rose	.40

Reichsbanknoten (Reichsbank Notes) 1915–24, with denominations in mark values

Among the inflation notes are many watermark and serial number varieties as well as different grades of paper. Counterfeits of many issues are common.

| 63. | 4.11.1915 | 20 Mark, violet and dark blue. Two men with cornucopias of money. Man and woman (Work and Rest) on reverse | .40 |

139 × 107

64.	20.10.1918	50 Mark, dark brown on grey violet. Dark border lines (known as the "mourning note")	
		a. Watermarked with wavy lines	175.00
		b. Watermarked with spades	250.00
65.	30.11.1918	50 Mark, olive brown. Broad ribbon frame with white oval in middle (known as the "picture frame" or "egg" note)	8.50
66.	24. 6.1919	50 Mark, green on light green. Woman's head in frame at upper right	.40
67.	6. 2.1920	10 Mark, dark green and olive green	.40
		Error: Without underprinting (letters)	125.00

68.	23. 7.1920	50	Mark, dark green and green. Woman's head with flowers and fruit (Autumn) at right. Farmer and worker on reverse	.45
69.	1.11.1920	100	Mark, dark brown and blue green. Head of the Bamberg Knight at upper left and right	.40
70.	19. 1.1922	10,000	Mark, blue green on olive brown. Young man's head at right (from a painting by Albrecht Durer). Rectangular ornaments on reverse (210 × 125 mm)	.45
71.		10,000	Mark. Type of #70 but oval ornament on reverse	.40
72.		10,000	Mark. Type of #71 but smaller format (180 × 100 mm)	.40
73.	27. 3.1922	500	Mark, dark blue and olive green. Bust of a young noble landowner (Junker) at right	.60
74.	7. 7.1922	500	Mark, black on white	
			a. Red serial numbers	.70
			b. Green serial numbers	.40
75.	4. 8.1922	100	Mark, blue black on white	.40
76.	15. 9.1922	1,000	Mark, dark green on green and lilac	
			a. White paper watermarked with hook-pointed stars	.40
			b. Light blue paper watermarked with thorns	.40
			c. Light blue paper watermarked with irregular lines	.40
			d. White paper watermarked with C pattern	.40
			e. White paper watermarked with small quatrefoil design	.40
			f. White paper watermarked with latticework of figure eights	.40
			g. White paper watermarked with figure eight design	.40
			h. Light blue and white paper watermarked with waves	.45
77.	16. 9.1922	5,000	Mark, blue on grey and green. Portrait of Mintmaster Spinelli at right (from a painting by Memling)	2.00

#78
198 × 105

78.	19.11.1922	5,000 Mark, dark brown on brown. Portrait of Treasurer H. Urmiller at left (from a painting by an unknown artist)	.70
79.		50,000 Mark, black on white. At right, paper deep green. Burgomaster Brauweiler at left (from a painting by B. Bruyn)	.40
80.		50,000 Mark. Type of #79 but German eagle printed behind inscription	.40
81.	2.12.1922	5,000 Mark, brown on green and light brown. Portrait of the merchant Imhoff (from a painting by Albrecht Durer) at right	
		a. Watermarked with hook-pointed stars	.40
		b. Watermarked with latticework	.45
		c. Watermarked with thorns	.45
		d. Watermarked with C pattern	.40
		e. Watermarked with waves	.75
82.	15.12.1922	1,000 Mark, black on dark brown. Portrait of Mintmaster Jorg Herz (from a painting by G. Penz) at left (not issued)	5.00
		For note overprinted "1 Milliarde," see #113.	
83.	1. 2.1923	100,000 Mark, dark brown on lilac. At right, paper deep lilac. Portrait of the merchant Gisze (from a painting by Hans Holbein) at left	.40
		Notes with "1" under illustration are several times scarcer.	
84.	3. 2.1923	10,000 Mark, dark blue on green and red (not issued)	125.00
85.	20. 2.1923	20,000 Mark, dark blue on rose and green	
		a. Watermarked with small crosses	.40
		b. Watermarked with hook-pointed stars	.40
		c. Watermarked with latticework of figure eights	.60
		d. Watermarked with thorns	.75
		e. Watermarked with C pattern	1.25
		f. Watermarked with waves	1.75
86.		1,000,000 Mark, dark brown on light brown and dark green	.45
87.	15. 3.1923	5,000 Mark, dark brown on olive brown. Portrait of Treasurer H. Urmiller at left (not issued)	200.00
		For note overprinted "500 Milliarden" see #124.	
88.	1. 5.1923	500,000 Mark, dark green, on lilac and green. Medallion portraits of a bearded man wearing a liberty cap	.60
89.	1. 6.1923	5,000,000 Mark, brown on lilac and green. Woman's head in middle. Paper deep yellow at right edge	.45
90.	23. 7.1923	2,000,000 Mark, dark brown on rose and green. Portraits of the merchant Gisze (from a painting by Hans Holbein) at left and right	.45

91.	25. 7.1923	100,000 Mark, black on green	
		a. Greenish paper watermarked with hook-pointed stars	.40
		b. White paper, watermarked with waves	.60
92.		500,000 Mark, carmine red. Paper deep violet at right edge	.40
93.		1,000,000 Mark, blue on lilac and light brown. Value over printed on 20,000 Mark	.75
94.		1,000,000 Mark, black on white. Paper deep yellow at right edge. Reverse blank	.40
95.		5,000,000 Mark, black on white. Paper blue green at left edge	.40
96.		10,000,000 Mark, black and dark green. Paper yellow at right edge	.40
97.		20,000,000 Mark, black and light blue. Paper lilac at right edge	.40
98.		50,000,000 Mark, black and lilac brown. Paper lilac at right edge	.40
99.	9. 8.1923	50,000 Mark, black on light brown	.60
100.		200,000 Mark, black on grey	.40
101.		1,000,000 Mark, black on white. Paper green at right edge, watermarked with oak leaves	.40
102.		1,000,000 Mark, black and green. Paper green at right edge	
		a. Watermarked with hook-pointed stars	.40
		b. Watermarked with small crosses	.45
		c. Watermarked with lattice work of figure eights	.45
		d. Watermarked with waves	.45
103.		2,000,000 Mark, black on white paper. Paper lilac at right edge, watermarked with oak leaves	.40
104.		2,000,000 Mark, black and lilac. Lilac ornament at right	
		a. Watermarked with hook-pointed stars	.40
		b. Watermarked with small crosses	.40
		c. Watermarked with lattice work of figure eights	.40
		d. Watermarked with waves	.70
105.	20. 8.1923	5,000,000 Mark, black on grey green. Rose paper	.40

#106

125 × 80

106.	22. 8.1923	10,000,000 Mark, black on olive green and blue grey	
		a. Watermarked with hook-pointed stars	.40
		b. Watermarked with small crosses	.40
		c. Watermarked with lattice work of figure eights	.75
		d. Watermarked with waves	.60
107.		100,000,000 Mark, black on blue green and olive brown	
		a. Watermarked with oak leaves	.40
		b. Watermarked with small quatrefoils. Thread fibers in paper on reverse	.60
		c. Watermarked with small quatrefoils. No thread fibers in paper on reverse	.40
		d. Watermarked with hook-pointed stars	.40
		e. Watermarked with small crosses	.40
		f. Watermarked with stars and S	1.50
		g. Watermarked with lozenge shapes	1.25
108.	1. 9.1923	20,000,000 Mark, black on olive brown and green	
		a. Watermarked with small crosses	.40
		b. Watermarked with lozenge shapes	1.50
		c. Watermarked with hook-pointed stars	.40
		d. Watermarked with waves	.45
		e. Watermarked with lattice work of figure eights	.10
		f. Watermarked with stars and S	18.50
109.		50,000,000 Mark, black on grey and lilac	
		a. Watermarked with small quatrefoils, grey paper	.40
		b. Watermarked with hook pointed stars, white paper	.40
		c. Watermarked with small crosses, white paper	.40
		d. Watermarked with lozenge shapes, white paper	2.00
		e. Watermarked with stars and S, white paper	1.25
		f. Watermarked with lattice work of figure eights, white paper	.45
110.		500,000,000 Mark, dark brown on light brown and lilac. With "500" at right edge	
		a. Watermarked with thistle leaves. Paper lilac at right edge	.40
		b. Watermarked with small quatrefoils	.40
		Error: "500" reading up	150.00
		c. Watermarked with hook-pointed stars	.40
		d. Watermarked with small crosses	.40
		e. Watermarked with stars and S	.75
		f. Watermarked with lozenge shapes	50.00
		g. Watermarked with lattice work of figure eights	3.50

111.		500 Milliard Mark, blue, lilac and green (unissued pattern, printed in Vienna)	RRR

180 × 98

112.		1 Billiard Mark, violet and lilac (unissued pattern, printed in Vienna)	RRR
113.	(Sept. 1923)	1 Milliard Mark, black on dark brown. Same as #82 with red overprint	
		a. Watermarked with "1000." White paper with brown threads at right edge	.40
		Error: Overprint inverted	65.00
		Error: Overprint on reverse only	85.00
		b. Watermarked with small quatrefoils, brown paper	.45
		c. Watermarked with small quatrefoils, white paper	2.40
114.	5. 9.1923	1 Milliard Mark, black on dark green, lilac and blue. Paper blue green at right edge	.75
115.	10. 9.1923	5 Milliard Mark, black on olive brown	
		a. Watermarked with oak leaves. Paper lilac at right edge	.70
		b. Watermarked with small quatrefoils	1.25
116.	15. 9.1923	10 Milliard Mark, black on grey lilac and blue green	
		a. Watermarked with thistle leaves. Paper yellow at right edge	.65
		b. Watermarked with small quatrefoils	3.50
117.	1.10.1923	10 Milliard Mark, dark green on lilac and green	
		a. Watermarked with hook-pointed stars	1.75
		b. Watermarked with small crosses	1.75
		c. Watermarked with stars and S	3.50
		d. Watermarked with lozenge shapes	35.00
		e. Watermarked with lattice work of figure eights	2.25
118.		20 Milliard Mark, dark green on blue and orange	
		a. Watermarked with hook-pointed stars	2.50
		Error: "20 Milliarden" on left edge	50.00
		b. Watermarked with small crosses	2.50
		Error: "20 Milliarden" on left edge	50.00
		c. Watermarked with lozenge shapes	4.50

118. (Cont.)		d. Watermarked with lattice work of figure eights	5.00
		e. Watermarked with stars and S	10.00
119.	10.10.1923	50 Milliard Mark, black on orange and blue	
		a. Watermarked with oak leaves. Paper green at right edge	2.50
		b. Watermarked with small quatrefoils, white paper	2.50
		c. Watermarked with small quatrefoils, grey paper (no serial numbers)	1.25
120.		50 Milliard Mark, black on orange, blue and green. Type of #119, white paper, but green rectangles in background at right	
		a. Watermarked with hook-pointed stars	1.75
		b. Watermarked with small crosses	1.75
		c. Watermarked with stars and S	1.75
121.	15.10.1923	200 Milliard Mark, black on violet and green	
		a. Watermarked with hook-pointed stars	4.50
		b. Watermarked with small crosses	6.50
		c. Watermarked with stars and S	20.00
		d. Watermarked with lattice work of figure eights	125.00
122.	20.10.1923	1 Milliard Mark, black on blue green	.75
123.		5 Milliard Mark, black on violet	.75
124.	(Oct. 1923)	500 Milliard Mark, dark brown on olive brown. Same as #87 but overprinted with new value	15.00
		Error: Overprint on reverse only	65.00
125.	26.10.1923	50 Milliard Mark, black on blue green	
		a. Grey paper	.60
		b. Green paper	.75
126.		100 Milliard Mark, dark blue on white. Paper blue at right edge	1.75
127.		500 Milliard Mark, dark brown on white	
		a. Watermarked with oak leaves. Paper green at right edge	5.00
		b. Watermarked "500," paper blue or violet at right edge	4.50
128.		100 Billiard Mark, black on lilac and grey. Paper brown at right edge	450.00
129.	1.11.1923	1 Billiard Mark, brown violet. Paper lilac at right edge	22.50
130.		5 Billiard Mark, black on blue and rose	
		a. Watermarked with thistles, paper yellow at right edge	45.00
		b. Watermarked with small quatrefoils	77.50
131.		10 Billiard Mark, black on green and light brown (format 170 × 85 mm)	
		a. Watermarked with thistles, paper blue green at right edge	70.00
		b. Watermarked with small quatrefoils	87.50

132.		10 Billiard Mark, black on brown and blue green (format 120 × 82 mm)	
		a. Watermarked with hook-pointed stars	70.00
		b. Watermarked with small crosses	77.50
133.	5.11.1923	100 Milliard Mark, red brown on olive and blue green	2.50
134.		1 Billiard Mark, black on violet and brown	22.50
135.		2 Billiard Mark, black on green and rose	
		a. Watermarked with hook-pointed stars	30.00
		b. Watermarked with small crosses	40.00
		c. Watermarked with stars and S	65.00
136.	7.11.1923	5 Billiard Mark, black on blue and rose	
		a. Watermarked with thistles, paper yellow at right edge	77.50
		b. Watermarked with small quatrefoils	375.00
		c. Watermarked with hook-pointed stars	250.00
		d. Watermarked with small crosses	85.00
137.	1. 2.1924	10 Billiard Mark, brown on green. Paper lilac at right edge	65.00
138.	5. 2.1924	20 Billiard Mark, blue green and violet. Portrait of a woman at right (from a painting by Albrecht Durer). Paper violet at right edge	325.00

175 × 95

139.	10. 2.1924	50 Billiard Mark, brown and olive. Portrait of Councilman J. Muffel (from a painting by Albrecht Durer) at right. Paper green at right edge	525.00
140.	15. 2.1924	100 Billiard Mark, red brown and blue. Portrait of Willibald Pirkheimer (from a painting by Albrecht Durer) at right. Paper light blue at right edge	775.00
141.	15. 3.1924	5 Billiard Mark, green and lilac	40.00

Zinskupons der Kriegsanleihen (Interest Coupons of War Loan Bonds)

In October, 1918, all interest coupons due on 2.1.1919 (letter q) were declared legal tender.

142.	Loan Year 1915, 1916, 1917, 1918	2.50 Mark	16.50

143.		5	Mark	25.00

100 × 48

144.	12.50	Mark	30.00
145.	25	Mark	45.00
146.	50	Mark	65.00
147.	125	Mark	100.00

Wertbestandige Anleihestucke (Fixed Value Loan Pieces)

In October, 1923, fractional notes of the Reichsbank issued against exchequer bonds, part pieces of exchequer bonds and whole bonds of the German Government were declared to be legal tender.

FRACTIONAL AND SMALL NOTES OF THE REICHSBANK

148.	23.10.1923	0.42 Goldmark = 1/10 Dollar	16.50
149.		1.05 Goldmark = $\frac{1}{4}$ Dollar. Watermarked "5," reverse blank	65.00
150.		1.05 Goldmark = $\frac{1}{4}$ Dollar. Watermarked "50" large letters on reverse	25.00
151.		2.10 Goldmark = $\frac{1}{2}$ Dollar	57.50

PART PIECES OF EXCHEQUER BONDS

152.	26.10.1923	0.42 Goldmark = 1/10 Dollar	20.00
153.		1.05 Goldmark = $\frac{1}{4}$ Dollar. Watermarked "5"	90.00
154.		1.05 Goldmark = $\frac{1}{4}$ Dollar. Watermarked "10"	50.00
155.		1.05 Goldmark = $\frac{1}{4}$ Dollar. Watermarked "50"	35.00
156.		2.10 Goldmark = $\frac{1}{2}$ Dollar. Watermarked "5"	100.00
157.		2.10 Goldmark = $\frac{1}{2}$ Dollar. Watermarked "20"	65.00

COMPLETE EXCHEQUER BONDS

158.	25. 8.1923	4.20 Goldmark = 1 Dollar	150.00
159.		8.40 Goldmark = 2 Dollar	290.00
160.		21.00 Goldmark = 5 Dollar	290.00

Rentenbankscheine (Land Value Bank Notes from 1923)

1 Billiard Mark = 1 Rentenmark

161.	1.11.1923	1 Rentenmark, olive green	10.00
162.		2 Rentenmark, red and green	18.50
163.		5 Rentenmark, blue green and violet	40.00
164.		10 Rentenmark, lilac and green	77.50
165.		50 Rentenmark, brown and violet	525.00
166.		100 Rentenmark, brown and blue green	375.00
167.		500 Rentenmark, blue grey and green	RRR

154 × 85

168.		1,000	Rentenmark, brown and light green	RRR
169.	20. 3.1925	50	Rentenmark, brown, green and lilac. Head of farmer at right	175.00
170.	3. 7.1925	10	Rentenmark, green and brown. Head of peasant woman at left	275.00
171.	2. 1.1926	5	Rentenmark, dark green and olive. Head of peasant girl at right	10.00
172.	6. 7.1934	50	Rentenmark, dark brown on olive green. Portrait of Baron von Stein at right	52.50
173.	30. 1.1937	1	Rentenmark, olive green	.60
174.		2	Rentenmark, brown	.60

Reichsbanknoten (Government Bank Notes), from 1924

1 Rentenmark = 1 Reichsmark

175.	11.10.1924	10	Reichsmark, dark green and red lilac. Portrait of merchant Diedrich Born (from a painting by Hans Holbein)	77.50

159 × 80

176.		20	Reichsmark, brown and red lilac. Portrait of a woman (from a painting by Hans Holbein)	85.00
177.		50	Reichsmark, brown and dark green. Portrait of a young man (from a painting by Hans Holbein)	35.00
178.		100	Reichsmark, brown and blue green. Portrait of an English Lady (from a painting by Hans Holbein)	27.50
179.		1,000	Reichsmark, brown and blue. Portrait of the nobleman Wedigh (from a painting by Hans Holbein)	70.00

180.	22. 1.1929	10 Reichsmark, green. Portrait of Albrecht Daniel Thaer at right. Female head (Agriculture) on reverse	
		a. Watermarked at left with head of Thaer, letters in background	2.25
		b. Watermarked at left with ornament, no letters (issued 1945)	12.50
		Also see #188.	
181.		20 Reichsmark, brown. Portrait of Werner von Siemens at right. Worker's head (Craftsmanship) on reverse	
		a. Watermarked at left with head of von Siemens, letters in background	2.50
		b. Watermarked at left with ornament, no letters (issued 1945)	12.50
182.	30. 3.1933	50 Reichsmark, green. Portrait of David Hansemann at right. Mercury head on reverse	
		a. Watermarked at left with head of Hansemann, letters in background	2.50
		b. Watermarked at left with ornament, no letters (issued 1945)	7.75
		Also see #189.	
183.	24. 6.1935	100 Reichsmark, blue. Head of Justus von Liebig at right. Head and torch (Knowledge) on reverse	
		a. Watermarked at left with head of von Liebig, letters in background	3.00
		b. Watermarked at left with ornament, no letters (issued 1945)	7.00
		Also see #190.	
184.	22. 2.1936	1,000 Reichsmark, brown. Head of Karl Friedrich Schinkel at right. Head and protractor on reverse (Art)	85.00

160 × 79

185.	16. 6.1939	20 Reichsmark, brown. Young Austrian woman holding edelweiss flower. Mountain scene on reverse	3.50
186.	1. 8.1942	5 Reichsmark, red brown. Youth's head at right. Lion monument in Brunswick on reverse	1.75
		Error: Watermarked "S" inverted	65.00

After the Allied troops' entry into the Eupen-Malmedy district in 1944, the then current German bank notes plus some isolated issues of German Credit Account Notes were stamped by various Belgian communities. These stamped notes were only valid as legal tender in exchange for Belgian notes. Nearly all of these notes are scarce and seldom seen. The values range from $12.50 to more than $50.00.

Reichsbanknoten (National Bank Notes) Emergency Issue of 1944–45

ISSUES FOR THE SUDETENLAND AND LOWER SILESIA (REICHENBERG)
187. 28. 4.1945   20 Reichsmark, brown   3.50

ISSUES OF THE GERMAN NATIONAL BANK AUTHORITY IN GRAZ, LINZ AND SALZBURG

These notes were photo-mechanically reproduced from a specimen of the circulating notes. All notes of any one value have the same control numbers.

188. 22. 1.1929   10 Reichsmark, blue green. Type of #180 but
                      poorly printed, serial number D 02776733   77.50
189. 30. 3.1933   50 Reichsmark, green. Type of #182 but poorly
                      printed, serial number E 06647727   52.50

177 × 95

190. 24. 6.1935   100 Reichsmark, blue. Type of #183 but poorly
                      printed, serial number T 7396475   52.50

Alliierte Militarbehorde (Allied Military Administrative Authority)

The notes issued by the Western Allies show the initial "F" of the printer Forbes. Those of the Russian printing (printing plates acquired from the USA) are without this imprint. These circulated alongside the Reichsmark and Rentenmark issues.

191. 1944   ½ Mark, green on light blue   1.25
192.   1 Mark, blue on light blue   2.25
193.   5 Mark, lilac on light blue   3.00
194.   10 Mark, blue on light blue   4.50
195.   20 Mark, red on light blue   5.30

155 × 68

196.   50 Mark, blue on light blue   10.00
197.   100 Mark, lilac on light blue   10.00
198.   1,000 Mark, green on light blue   100.00

GERMAN FEDERAL REPUBLIC (Bundesrepublik Deutschland)

Currency Reform, 1948: Deutsche Mark introduced 20.6.1948.

Bank notes of 1948

1.	1948	½ Deutsche Mark, green	2.50
2.		1 Deutsche Mark, blue	3.00
3.		2 Deutsche Mark, lilac. Seated female figure at left	5.00
4.		5 Deutsche Mark, brown. Seated man at right (Seafaring)	16.50
5.		10 Deutsche Mark, blue. Three figures (Labor, Justice, Building) in middle	12.50
6.		20 Deutsche Mark, green. Two figures (Industry and Agriculture) at left	20.00

150 × 67

7.		50 Deutsche Mark, violet. Female figure in middle	65.00
8.		100 Deutsche Mark, red brown. Woman reading in center	100.00
9.	(1948)	20 Deutsche Mark, blue. Woman's head in medallion at left.	100.00
10.		50 Deutsche Mark, green blue. Female head in middle (in circulation only a few days)	750.00

Bank Deutscher Lander (Bank of the German Lands)

11.	(1948)	5 Pfennig, green	1.75
12.		10 Pfennig, blue	1.75
13.	9.12.1948	5 Deutsche Mark, black green and yellow. Europa being adbucted on the back of a winged bull	6.50
14.		50 Deutsche Mark, brown and yellow green. Portrait of the merchant Imhoff (from a painting by Albrecht Durer) at right. Imhoff and a medieval trading scene on reverse	35.00
15.		100 Deutsche Mark, light violet and rose on blue. Councilman J. Muffel (from a painting by Albrecht Durer) at right. Muffel and a view of medieval Nuremberg on reverse	60.00

140 × 66

16. 22. 8.1949   10 Deutsche Mark, blue. Type of #5 but with
                       name of bank   10.00
17.   20 Deutsche Mark, green. Type of #6 but with
                       name of bank   18.50
                     Notes #1–10 and 13–17 are also known with a "B" stamp,
                     "B" perforation, or both, as a control mark on currency
                     used in West Berlin as legal tender. Their value is about
                     50% more than the normal notes.

Deutsche Bundesbank (German Government Bank)

18. 2. 1.1960   5 Deutsche Mark, green. Young Venetian girl
                       (from a painting by Albrecht Durer). Oak leaf
                       and acorns on the reverse   —
19.   10 Deutsche Mark, blue. Portrait of a man with
                       long hair. Sailing ships on the reverse   —
20.   20 Deutsche Mark, green. Portrait of Elsbeth
                       Tucher (from a painting by Albrecht Durer).
                       Violin and clarinet on reverse   —
21.   50 Deutsche Mark, brown and green. Portrait of
                       Treasurer H. Urmiller. View of the Holstentor
                       in Lubeck on reverse   —
22.   100 Deutsche Mark, blue. Portrait of Master of Arts
                       S. Munster (from a painting by Christian
                       Amberger)   —
23.   500 Deutsche Mark, brown lilac. Man's head.
                       View of Eltz on reverse   —
24.   1,000 Deutsche Mark, brown. Portrait of the astrono-
                       mer Dr. Schoner (from a painting by Lucas
                       Kranach the Elder). Limburg cathedral on
                       reverse   —

25.	2. 1.1970	5 Deutsche Mark, green. Type of #18 but with different signatures and penalty notice	—
26.		10 Deutsche Mark, blue. Type of #19	—
27.		20 Deutsche Mark, green. Type of #20	—
28.		50 Deutsche Mark, brown. Type of #21	—
29.		100 Deutsche Mark, blue. Type of #22	—

GERMAN DEMOCRATIC REPUBLIC

Currency Reform, 1948: East German Mark introduced.

Provisional issue created by pasting gummed, perforated stamps on to old Rentenmark and Reichsbank notes. The stamps carry the date and value.

1.	1948	1 Deutsche Mark. Blue control stamp on #173 1 Rentenmark of 30.1.1937	$2.25
2.		2 Deutsche Mark. Green control stamp on #174, 2 Rentenmark of 30.1.1937	3.50
3.		5 Deutsche Mark. Brown control stamp on #186, 5 Reichsmark of 1.8.1942	4.50
4.		10 Deutsche Mark. Lilac control stamp on #180, 10 Reichsmark of 22.1.1929	6.50

160 × 80

5.	20 Deutsche Mark. Brown control stamp on #181, 20 Reichsmark of 22.1.1929, or #185, 20 Reichsmark of 16.6.1939	8.50
6.	50 Deutsche Mark. Blue control stamp on #182, 50 Reichsmark of 30.3.1933	20.00
7.	100 Deutsche Mark. Green blue control stamp on #183, 100 Reichsmark of 24.6.1935	35.00

Stamps are also found on 5 Rentenmark notes of 2.1.1926 (#171) and 50 Rentenmark notes of 6.7.1934 (#172). They were not, however, officially affixed.

Deutsche Notenbank (German Note Bank)

8.	1948	50 Deutsche Pfennig, blue	1.75
9.		1 Deutsche Mark, olive	1.75
10.		2 Deutsche Mark, brown	2.50
11.		5 Deutsche Mark, brown	3.50
12.		10 Deutsche Mark, green	3.50
13.		20 Deutsche Mark, brown	3.25
14.		50 Deutsche Mark, green	2.50
15.		100 Deutsche Mark, blue	6.50

191 × 97

16.		1,000 Deutsche Mark, brown	65.00
17.	1955	5 Deutsche Mark, grey blue	5.00
18.		10 Deutsche Mark, violet and lilac	8.50
19.		20 Deutsche Mark, blue violet	16.50
20.		50 Deutsche Mark, red brown	35.00
21.		100 Deutsche Mark, brown	50.00
22.	1964	5 Deutsche Mark, brown. Alexander von Humboldt at right	—
23.		10 Deutsche Mark, green. Friedrich von Schiller at right	—
24.		20 Deutsche Mark, red brown. Johann Wolfgang von Goethe at right	—
25.		50 Deutsche Mark, blue green. Friedrich Engels at right	—
26.		100 Deutsche Mark, blue. Karl Marx at right	—

GERMAN REGIONAL BANK NOTES

Of the numerous note-issuing banks of the old German States, only those mentioned below produced paper money after 1900. During the war of 1914–1918 and in the following years of inflation, many local banks and governments issued paper money most of which was not recognized as legal tender. The exceptions were the notes issued by the *Badischen Bank* (Baden), the *Bayerischen Notenbank* (Bavaria), the *Sachsischen Bank* (Saxony) and the *Wurttembergische Notenbank* (Wurttemberg) which did not lose their right to print paper money until 1935.

Baden

Badische Bank (Bank of Baden)

Notes R1 through R6 carry the same allegorical designs. On the obverse at left and right is a woman with two children; on the reverse is a river god (the Rhine) and a goddess (the Neckar).

R1.	1.12.1870	10 Gulden, black and green on grey brown	450.00

171 × 115

R2.	1. 7.1871	50 Gulden, black and blue on yellow brown	650.00
R3.	1. 1.1874	100 Mark, black on blue and yellow brown	375.00
R4.	1. 1.1890	100 Mark	RRR
R5.	1.10.1902	100 Mark, black and blue on light blue	7.50
R6.	1. 1.1907	100 Mark, black and blue on light blue	
		a. With printer's name	4.50
		b. Without printer's name	3.50
R7.	15.12.1918	100 Mark, blue and blue green	1.75
R8.	1. 8.1922	500 Mark, violet on grey green	1.25
R9.	1.12.1922	5,000 Mark, brown on violet and yellow	1.25
R10.	1. 4.1923	10,000 Mark, brown, blue and green	.75
R11.	1. 8.1923	500,000 Mark, dark brown on grey brown and violet	.75
R12.	7. 8.1923	1 Million Mark, black on violet	.75
R13.	25. 9.1923	2 Milliard overprint on 20 Million Mark, dark brown on grey green. Red overprint	1.00
R14.	30.10.1923	100 Milliard Mark, dark brown on brown violet and light blue	4.50
R15.	11.10.1923	50 Reichsmark. J. Peter Hebel	500.00

The bank's right to issue paper money expired in 1935.

Bavaria

Bayerische Notenbank (Bavarian Note-issuing Bank)

R16.	3.11.1875	100 Mark, black on blue. Four allegorical figures	375.00
R17.	1. 1.1900	100 Mark, black on blue and brown. Type of R16	1.00
R18.	1. 1.1922	100 Mark, multicolored	.75
R19.	1.10.1922	1,000 Mark, blue black on blue and brown	.75
R20.	1.12.1922	5,000 Mark, multicolored	.75
R21.	1. 3.1923	20,000 Mark, multicolored	.75
R22.	15. 3.1923	50,000 Mark, multicolored	1.00
R23.	15. 6.1923	100,000 Mark, multicolored	1.00
R24.	15. 8.1923	1,000,000 Mark, blue black on brown and blue	1.00
R25.	18. 8.1923	500,000 Mark, violet and lilac	1.25
R26.	20. 8.1923	1,000,000 Mark, dark brown on yellow and green	1.25
R27.		5,000,000 Mark, dark brown on green and red brown	1.25
R28.		25,000,000 Mark, blue and brown	1.50
R29.		50,000,000 Mark, light olive and red brown	1.50
R30.	1. 9.1923	10,000,000 Mark, blue and brown	1.25
R31.	1.10.1923	1 Milliard Mark, dark brown and violet	1.75
R32.	10.10.1923	5 Milliard Mark, lilac and grey blue	2.50
R33.	24.10.1923	50 Milliard Mark, dark green	3.50
R34.	Old date: 1. 8.1923	500 Milliard overprint on 100 milliard Mark, multicolored. Red-brown overprint	45.00
R35.	11.10.1924	50 Reichsmark	500.00
R36.		100 Reichsmark	450.00

170 × 84

R37.	1. 9.1925	50 Reichsmark. H. Holzschuher (from a painting by Durer) at right	400.00

The bank's right to issue paper money expired in 1935.

Brunswick

Braunschweigische Bank (Brunswick Bank)

R38.	1. 5.1854	10 Taler	450.00
R39.	1. 6.1856	10 Taler	500.00
R40.	1. 1.1869	10 Taler, black on brown. Bank building	375.00
R41.	1. 7.1874	100 Mark	400.00

The bank relinquished its right to print paper money in 1905.

Frankfurt

Frankfurter Bank (Bank of Frankfurt)

R42.	1. 1.1855	5 Gulden, brown and blue. Crowned female bust at left and right	250.00
R43.		10 Gulden. Type of R42	375.00
R44.		35 Gulden. Type of R42	450.00
R45.		50 Gulden. Type of R42	500.00
R46.		100 Gulden. Type of R42	650.00
R47.		500 Gulden. Type of R42	650.00
R48.	25. 7.1870	500 Gulden (deposit note)	RRR
R49.	1. 1.1874	100 Mark, brown and blue. Crowned female bust at left and right	450.00
R50.		500 Mark. Type of R49	500.00

214
×
137

R51.		1,000 Mark. Type of R49	650.00
R52.	1. 8.1890	100 Mark. Type of R49	375.00
R53.		1,000 Mark, dark brown and brown. Type of R49	450.00

The bank relinquished its right to print paper money in 1901.

Hesse

Bank fur Suddeutschland (Bank for South Germany)

R54.	1. 7.1856	10 Gulden	375.00
R55.		10 Taler	RRR
R56.	1.12.1856	25 Gulden	RRR
R57.		50 Gulden	RRR
R58.		100 Gulden	RRR
R59.		25 Taler	RRR
R60.		50 Taler	RRR
R61.		100 Taler	RRR

R62.	20. 3.1857	10	Taler	RRR
R63.	2. 1.1870	10	Gulden, black on green	375.00
R64.		25	Gulden	RRR
R65.	1. 1.1874	100	Mark	375.00

The bank relinquished its right to print paper money in 1902.

Saxony

Landstandische Bank des kgl. Sachs. Markgraftums Oberlausitz (People's Bank of the Kingdom of Saxony and the Margraviate of Oberlausitz) in Bautzen

R66.	1860	5	Taler	RRR
R67.	1861	10	Taler	RRR
R68.	10.10.1868	10	Taler	375.00
R69.	1. 1.1875	100	Mark, green and red	375.00

The bank relinquished its right to print paper money in 1906.

Sachsische Bank (Bank of Saxony) in Dresden

R70.	15. 1.1866	10	Taler	RRR
R71.		20	Taler	RRR
R72.		50	Taler	RRR
R73.		100	Taler	RRR

171 × 102

R74.	1. 1.1874	100	Mark, black on green. Woman's head at left, Mercury head at right	85.00
R75.		500	Mark	RRR
R76.	15. 6.1890	100	Mark, black on blue and brown. Type of R74	10.00
R77.		500	Mark, black on red brown and blue. Type of R74	15.00
R78.	2. 1.1911	100	Mark. Type of R76	3.50
R79.		500	Mark. Type of R77	4.50
R80.	1. 7.1922	500	Mark. Type of R77	2.00
R81.	12. 9.1922	500	Mark, blue on yellow	1.75
R82.		1,000	Mark, dark olive on light olive	2.25

R83.	1. 3.1923	10,000 Mark, green and rose	.75
R84.	12. 3.1923	5,000 Mark, green blue on green	.75
R85.	2. 7.1923	100,000 Mark, green and rose	1.00
R86.	25. 7.1923	50,000 Mark, blue on green and brown	.75
R87.	12. 8.1923	5,000,000 Mark, dark brown and grey green	1.00
R88.	15. 8.1923	500,000 Mark, black on green and violet	.75
R89.	18. 8.1923	1,000,000 Mark, brown and light blue	.75
R90.	1. 9.1923	2,000,000 Mark, brown olive	.75
R91.	1.10.1923	100,000,000 Mark, multicolored	1.00
R92.	20.10.1923	20 Milliard Mark, brown violet and green	6.50
R93.		100 Milliard Mark, brown violet and light brown	16.50
R.94	15.11.1923	1 Billiard Mark, green and olive	45.00
R95.		10 Billiard Mark, lilac and blue	65.00
R96.	11.10.1924	50 Reichsmark. Leibniz	500.00
R97.		100 Reichsmark, dark blue and brown. Lessing at left	500.00

The bank's right to print paper money expired in 1935.

Wurttemberg

Wurttembergische Notenbank (Wurttemberg Note-issuing Bank)

Notes R98–R101 display three cupids at right and left.

| R98. | 15.11.1871 | 10 Gulden | 450.00 |

159 × 107

R99.		35 Gulden	500.00
R100.	1. 1.1874	100 Mark, dark brown on light brown and blue	300.00
R101.	1. 1.1875	100 Mark, blue and light brown	250.00
R102.	1. 1.1890	100 Mark. Type of R101	175.00
R103.	1. 1.1902	100 Mark. Type of R101	85.00
R104.	1. 1.1911	100 Mark. Type of R101 (two signature varieties)	4.50
R104a.	15.12.1918	100 Mark, dark green and olive brown. Without imprint "50 Md" (known only as a proof)	250.00

R105.	1. 9.1922	1,000	Mark, blue on grey violet	3.50
R106.	20. 2.1923	10,000	Mark, dark blue and yellow brown	.75
R107.	10. 6.1923	50,000	Mark, green and red brown on lilac	.75
R108.	15. 6.1923	20,000	Mark, dark green and red on light brown	.75
R109.		100,000	Mark, dark green and blue on brown	.75
R110.		1	Million Mark, blue and red brown on brown	.75
R111.	1. 8.1923	1	Million Mark, red and blue on orange. Man's head in middle	.75
R112.		5	Million Mark, carmine	1.25
R113.		100	Million Mark, dark blue	2.25
R114.	15.10.1923	10	Milliard Mark	
			a. Until 30.11.1923	3.50
			b. Until 31.12.1923	3.50
R115.	Old date:			
	15.12.1918	50	Milliard Mark on 100 Million Mark	8.50
R116.	20.11.1923	500	Milliard Mark	65.00
R117.	11.10.1924	50	Reichsmark	450.00
R118.		100	Reichsmark	500.00
R119.	1. 8.1925	50	Reichsmark. Schubart	500.00

The bank's right to print paper money expired in 1935.

NOTES FOR GERMAN OCCUPIED TERRITORIES

Ostbank fur Handel und Gewerbe, Darlehnskasse Ost (Eastern Bank for Trade and Industry, Eastern State Loan Office) in Posen

Notes circulating in Lithuania from 1919

R120.	17. 4.1916	20 Kopecks, blue green	$1.25
R121.		50 Kopecks, red brown and blue green	
		a. Small letters in reverse text, reads "Aiſdewu" at right	1.75
		b. Larger letters in reverse text	2.25
		c. As R121a but text at right reads "Aiſdewu"	1.00
		d. As R121b but text at right reads "Aiſdewu"	1.25
R122.		1 Ruble, blue and brown	
		a. Reverse as R121a	1.75
		b. Reverse as R121b	1.75
		c. Reverse as R121c	1.50
		d. Reverse as R121d	1.50
R123.		3 Rubles, brown on green	
		a. Reverse text reads "Aiſdewu . . ." at right	5.30
		b. Reverse text reads "Aiſdewu . . ." at right	4.50
R124.		10 Rubles, red brown and green	6.50
R125.		25 Rubles, blue and lilac	16.50

171 × 107

R126.	100 Rubles, blue. Woman's head at left, helmeted man's head at right	25.00

Darlehnskasse Ost (Eastern State Loan Office) in Kowno

As R120–R126, the following notes circulated in Lithuania from 1919.

R127.	½ Mark, lilac and light brown	1.75
R128.	1 Mark, brown and green	2.50

R129.	2 Mark, red brown and lilac	3.75
R130.	5 Mark, brown and blue	4.50
R131.	20 Mark, red brown on green and rose	8.50
R132.	50 Mark, dark blue on grey violet	16.50
R133.	100 Mark, brown. Woman's head at left, helmeted man's head at right	25.00
R134.	1,000 Mark, green. Mercury and youth in armor at right	20.00

Reichskreditkassenscheine (German Government Loan Office Notes)

Established as legal tender in the various countries occupied by German troops during World War II.

R135. (1939–45)	50 Reichspfennig, green	2.00
R136.	1 Reichsmark, brown	
	a. With embossing	2.00
	b. Without embossing (starting with "Series 481")	.75
R137.	2 Reichsmark, dark green and brown	
	a. With embossing (seven digit serial number)	1.75
	b. Without embossing (eight digit serial number)	.75
R138.	5 Reichsmark, dark blue. Man's head at left and right	
	a. With embossing (seven digit serial number)	2.00
	b. Without embossing (eight digit serial number)	.75
R139.	20 Reichsmark, brown on red brown and olive. "Der Baumeister" ("The Master Builder" from a painting by Durer)	2.50
R140.	50 Reichsmark, dark blue on violet. Reverse Farmer's wife at right	4.50

At the end of World War II, the 5, 20 and 50 reichsmark notes of the government loan office issues were declared legal tender in the British Zone of Occupation when officially stamped by an office of the Reichsbank. All notes bearing any of the various stamps on them are quite scarce and seldom seen. Values range upward from $25.00.

German Military Notes

Etappen Inspektion I

Notes stamped to indicate control check by communications commander of the First Army. Issued for use in occupied French territories. All have "1915" printed, balance of date handwritten.

M1.	1915	50 Centimes	65.00
M2.		1 Franc	65.00
M3.		2 Francs	65.00
M4.		5 Francs	65.00

Etappen Kommandantur

Notes stamped to indicate control check by the communications command. Issued for use in occupied French territories.

M5.	1915	50 Centimes. Type of M1	65.00
M6.		1 Franc	65.00
M7.		2 Francs	65.00
M8.		5 Francs	65.00

Etappen Inspektion 2

Notes stamped to indicate control check by communications command of the Second Army. Issued for use in occupied French territories. These are the so-called "Deichmann-Bons" notes with stamps of various French communities.

M9.	1914–15	5 Francs	100.00
M10.		10 Francs	100.00
M11.		20 Francs	100.00

174 × 100

M12.		50 Francs	100.00
M13.		100 Francs	100.00

Etappen Kommandantur

Issued in occupied French territories, "Deichmann-Bons" issue

M14.	1914–15	5 Francs. Type of M9	100.00

M15.	10 Francs	100.00
M16.	20 Francs	100.00
M17.	50 Francs	100.00
M18.	100 Francs	100.00

Etappen Inspektion 3

Control check by communications command of Third Army. Issued for use in occupied French territories.

M19.	1915	1 Franc	65.00
M20.		2 Francs	65.00
M21.		3 Francs	65.00
M22.		5 Francs	65.00
M23.		10 Francs	65.00
M24.		25 Francs	65.00
M25.		50 Francs	65.00
M26.		100 Francs	65.00

Reichsmarine des Ostseebereichs (German Navy, Eastern Sea Command) in Kiel

M27.	27.10.1923	1 Milliard Mark	20.00
M28.		5 Milliard Mark	25.00
M29.		20 Milliard Mark	10.00
M30.		50 Milliard Mark	12.50

Behelfszahlungsmittel fur die Deutsche Wehrmacht (Auxiliary Payment Certificates for use by the German Army)

During World War II, currency was the responsibility of the military. The face value of the following notes was only 1/10 of their actual value. A 1 pfennig note thus had the purchasing power of 10 pfennig.

100 × 50

M31.	(1940)	1 Reichspfennig, lilac brown. Swastika in middle background	37.50
M32.	(1942)	1 Reichspfennig, blue. Small swastika and eagle in background	2.25
M33.		5 Reichspfennig, red	2.50
M34.		10 Reichspfennig, green	3.50
M35.		50 Reichpfennig, red	4.50
M36.		1 Reichsmark, ochre	7.70
M37.		2 Reichsmark, lilac	18.50

Also see Greece M20–M22.

Verrechnungsscheine fur die Deutsche Wehrmacht (Accounting Notes for the German Army)

Near the end of 1944, the actual value of the military paper money was about the same as the face value stated on the note as legal tender.

M38.	15.9.1944	1 Reichsmark, green		1.00
M39.		5 Reichsmark, blue		1.50
M40.		10 Reichsmark, red		2.40
M41.		50 Reichsmark, lilac brown		3.75

GIBRALTAR

A peninsula on the southern coast of Spain, Gibraltar has been under British control since 1704.

1 Pound = 20 Shillings

Government notes with the embossed seal of the "Anglo-Egyptian Bank, Ltd. Gibraltar"

1.	5.8.1914, Series A	2 Shillings, red	$150.00
2.		10 Shillings, blue	200.00
3.		1 Pound, black on yellowish paper	250.00
4.		5 Pounds, black on bluish paper	RR
5.		50 Pounds, black on bluish paper	RRR
6.	6.8.1914, Series B	2 Shillings, green on rose	150.00
7.		10 Shillings, lilac on rose	200.00
8.		1 Pound, blue on green	250.00
9.		5 Pounds, brown on green	RR
10.		50 Pounds, rose on green	RRR

2 Shilling notes with the date 3.8.1938 (Series C) were printed but not issued. They were destroyed in 1968.

Government of Gibraltar, "Currency Note Ordinance 1927"

11.	1.10.1927	10 Shillings, blue on yellow brown. Cliffs of Gibraltar at right	65.00
12.		1 Pound, green on yellow brown. Cliffs of Gibraltar in middle	85.00
13.		5 Pounds, brown. Cliffs of Gibraltar in middle	150.00

Government of Gibraltar, "Currency Note Ordinance of 1934"

Printed by Waterlow and Sons Ltd. Various date varieties

14.		10 Shillings, blue on yellow brown. Type of #11 (two control number and four signature varieties)	—

145 × 94

15.		1 Pound, green on yellow brown. Type of #12 (two control number and five signature varieties)	—

16.		5 Pounds, brown. Type of #13 (two control number and four signature varieties)	—

Printed by Thomas de la Rue & Co. Ltd.

17.	1.5.1965	10 Shillings. Type of #11	—
18.		1 Pound. Type of #12	—
19.		5 Pounds. Type of #13	—

GREAT BRITAIN

The kingdom of Great Britain is composed of England, Wales, Scotland with its off-shore islands, the Isle of Man, the Channel Islands of Jersey and Guernsey and Northern Ireland. Queen Victoria ruled from 1837 to 1901 followed by King Edward VII, 1901–10; George V, 1910–36; Edward VIII, January to December, 1936; George VI, 1936–52; and Elizabeth II, from 1952.

1 Pound = 20 Shillings = 100 New Pence
1 Shilling = 12 Pence

Bank of England

The note type introduced in 1870 has black printing on only one side of watermarked paper. Each note carries two control or serial numbers. A third small control number below the signature was added in 1903. All types have various date and signature (Chief Cashier) varieties. Through 1939, notes were issued at various cities besides London.

1.	London, dates to 1945	5 Pounds, black. Paper without silver thread	$45.00
2.	1945–48	5 Pounds. Type of #1 but thick paper with silver thread	57.50
3.	1948–57	5 Pounds. Type of #2 but thinner paper	45.00
4.	dates to 1943	10 Pounds, black	85.00
5.	dates to 1943	20 Pounds, black	150.00
6.	dates to 1943	50 Pounds, black	RR
7.	dates to 1943	100 Pounds, black	RRR
8.	dates to 1928	200 Pounds, black	RRR
9.	dates to 1943	500 Pounds, black	RRR
10.		1,000 Pounds, black	RRR

During the Second World War, "perfect" counterfeits of 5-, 10-, 20- and 50-pound notes were produced. They are known with various dates.

11.	Birmingham, dates to 1939	5 Pounds. Type of #1	50.00
12.		10 Pounds, black	50.00
13.		20 Pounds, black	RR
14.		50 Pounds, black	RR
15.		100 Pounds, black	RRR
16.		500 Pounds, black	RRR
17.		1,000 Pounds, black	RRR
18.	dates to 1928	200 Pounds, black	RRR
19.	Bristol, dates to 1939	5 Pounds. Type of #1	85.00
20.		10 Pounds, black	85.00
21.		20 Pounds, black	RR

22.	Bristol, dates to 1939	50 Pounds, black	RR
23.		100 Pounds, black	RRR
24.		500 Pounds, black	RRR
25.		1,000 Pounds, black	RRR
26.	dates to 1928	200 Pounds, black	RRR
27.	Hull, dates to 1939	5 Pounds. Type of #1	85.00
28.		10 Pounds, black	85.00
29.		20 Pounds, black	RR
30.		50 Pounds, black	RR
31.		100 Pounds, black	RRR
32.		500 Pounds, black	RRR
33.		1,000 Pounds, black	RRR
34.	dates to 1928	200 Pounds, black	RRR
35.	Leeds, dates to 1939	5 Pounds. Type of #1	70.00
36.		10 Pounds, black	70.00
37.		20 Pounds, black	RR
38.		50 Pounds, black	RR
39.		100 Pounds, black	RRR
40.		500 Pounds, black	RRR
41.		1,000 Pounds, black	RRR
42.	dates to 1928	200 Pounds, black	RRR
43.	Liverpool, dates to 1939	5 Pounds. Type of #1	50.00
44.		10 Pounds, black	50.00
45.		20 Pounds, black	RR
46.		50 Pounds, black	RR
47.		100 Pounds, black	RRR
48.		500 Pounds, black	RRR
49.		1,000 Pounds, black	RRR
50.	dates to 1928	200 Pounds, black	RRR
51.	Manchester, dates to 1939	5 Pounds. Type of #1	50.00
52.		10 Pounds, black	50.00
53.		20 Pounds, black	RR
54.		50 Pounds, black	RR
55.		100 Pounds, black	RRR
56.		500 Pounds, black	RRR
57.		1,000 Pounds, black	RRR
58.	dates to 1928	200 Pounds, black	RRR
59.	Newcastle-on-Tyne, dates to 1939	5 Pounds. Type of #1	50.00
60.		10 Pounds, black	50.00
61.		20 Pounds, black	RR
62.		50 Pounds, black	RR
63.		100 Pounds, black	RRR
64.		500 Pounds, black	RRR
65.		1,000 Pounds, black	RRR
66.	dates to 1928	200 Pounds, black	RRR
67.	Plymouth, dates to 1939	5 Pounds. Type of #1	70.00
68.		10 Pounds, black	70.00
69.		20 Pounds, black	RR
70.		50 Pounds, black	RR
71.		100 Pounds, black	RRR

72.	Plymouth, dates to 1939	500 Pounds, black	RRR
73.		1,000 Pounds, black	RRR
74.	dates to 1928	200 Pounds, black	RRR
75.	Portsmouth, dates to 1939	5 Pounds. Type of #1	70.00
76.		10 Pounds, black	70.00
77.		20 Pounds, black	RR
78.		50 Pounds, black	RR
79.		100 Pounds, black	RRR
80.		500 Pounds, black	RRR
81.		1,000 Pounds, black	RRR
82.	dates to 1928	200 Pounds, black	RRR

Treasury Notes

130 × 63

83.	(August 1914)	10 Shillings, red. Head of George V at left. Signature "John Bradbury" (1st issue), three control number varieties (format 130 × 63 mm)	125.00
84.		1 Pound, black. Head of George V at left. Signature "John Bradbury" (1st issue), seven control number varieties (format 130 × 63 mm)	150.00
85.	(January 1915)	10 Shillings, red. Head of George V at left, St. George at right. Signature "John Bradbury" (2nd issue, format 138 × 80 mm)	65.00
86.	(October 1914)	1 Pound, black. Head of George V at left, St. George at right. Signature "John Bradbury" (2nd issue, format 140 × 80 mm)	50.00
87.	(November 1918)	10 Shillings, green. Britannia at left, head of George V at right. Inscribed "United Kingdom of Great Britain and Ireland." Signature "John Bradbury" (3rd issue), red or black control numbers	50.00
88.	(February 1917)	1 Pound, brown. St. George and dragon at left, head of George V at right. Inscription as #87. Signature "John Bradbury" (3rd issue)	45.00
89.	(1919–20)	2 Shillings 6 Pence (2/6) (not released, entire printing destroyed). Proof printings exist	RRR
90.		5 Shillings, lilac and green. Signature "John Bradbury" or "Warren Fisher" (issue withdrawn after two days)	RRR
91.	(October 1919)	10 Shillings, green. Type of #87 but signature "N. F. Warren Fisher" (1st issue), control numbers with "No."	37.50

92.	(October 1919)	1 Pound, brown. Type of #88 but signature "N. F. Warren Fisher" (1st issue). Watermarked at top and bottom "One Pound" in one line	22.50
93.	(1922–23)	10 Shillings, green. Type of #91 with signature "N. F. Warren Fisher" (2nd issue) but control numbers without "No."	27.50
94.		1 Pound, brown. Type of #92 with signature "N. F. Warren Fisher" (2nd issue) but watermark "One Pound" in two lines	22.50
95.	(1928)	10 Shillings, green. Britannia at left, head of George V at right. Inscribed "United Kingdom of Great Britain and Northern Ireland." Signature "N. F. Warren Fisher" (3rd issue)	25.00
96.		1 Pound, brown. St. George and dragon at left, head of George V at right. Inscription as #95. Signature "N. F. Warren Fisher" (3rd issue)	22.50

Bank of England

97.	(1928–48)	10 Shillings, brown. Britannia at left. Paper without metallic thread	
		a. Signature "C. P. Mahon" (1928–29)	65.00
		b. Signature "B. G. Gatterns" (1929–34)	32.50
		c. Signature "K. O. Peppiatt" (1934–48)	25.00
98.		1 Pound, green. Britannia at left. Paper without metallic thread	
		a. Signature "C. P. Mahon" (1928–29)	32.50
		b. Signature "B. G. Gatterns" (1929–34)	25.00
		c. Signature "K. O. Peppiatt" (1934–48)	16.50
99.	(1939)	2 Shillings 6 Pence (2/6), light blue (not issued)	RRR
100.		5 Shillings, rose (not issued)	RRR
101.	(1940–48)	10 Shillings, violet. Britannia at left. Paper with metallic threads. Signature "K. O. Peppiatt"	12.50
102.		1 Pound, light or dark blue. Britannia at left. Paper with metallic threads. Signature "K. O. Peppiatt"	10.00
103.	(1948–60)	10 Shillings, brown. Type of #97 but paper with metallic threads	
		a. Signature "K. O. Peppiatt" (1948–49)	11.50
		b. Signature "P. S. Beale" (1949–55)	10.00
		c. Signature "L. K. O'Brien" (1955–60)	6.50
104.		1 Pound, green. Type of #98 but paper with metallic threads	
		a. Signature "K. O. Peppiatt" (1948–49)	12.50
		b. Signature "P. S. Beale" (1949–55)	8.50
		c. Signature "L. K. O'Brien" (1955–60)	6.50

105.	(1957–61)	5 Pounds, blue and multicolored. Britannia head at left, St. George and dragon in middle. Value "£5" in blue on reverse	25.00
106.	(1961–63)	5 Pounds, blue and multicolored. Type of #105 but reverse value in white outline figure	25.00
107.	(1960–70)	10 Shillings, brown. Queen Elizabeth at right	
		a. Signature "L. K. O'Brien" (1960–61)	6.50
		b. Signature "J. Q. Hollom" (1962–66)	5.00
		c. Signature "J. S. Fforde" (1966–70)	2.50
108.	(from 1960)	1 Pound, green. Queen Elizabeth at right	
		a. Signature "L. K. O'Brien" (1960–61)	8.50
		b. Signature "J. Q. Hollom" (1962–66)	7.50
		c. Signature "J. S. Fforde" (1966–70)	4.50
		d. Signature "J. B. Page" (from 1970)	—
109.	(1963–72)	5 Pounds, blue. Queen Elizabeth at right	
		a. Signature "J. Q. Hollom" (1963–66)	18.50
		b. Signature "J. S. Fforde" (1966–70)	17.50
		c. Signature "J. B. Page" (1970–72)	16.50
110.	(from 1964)	10 Pounds, brown. Queen Elizabeth at right	
		a. Signature "J. Q. Hollom" (1964–66)	40.00
		b. Signature "J. S. Fforde" (1966–70)	37.50
		c. Signature "J. B. Page" (from 1970)	—
111.	(from 1970)	20 Pounds, lilac. Queen Elizabeth at right	
		a. Signature "J. S. Fforde" (1970)	65.00
		b. Signature "J. B. Page" (from 1970)	—
112.	(from 1971)	5 Pounds, blue. New portrait of Queen at right. Signature "J. B. Page" (format 145 × 78 mm)	—

Local Bank Issues

Many local banks in Britain once had the right to issue paper money. The Bank Charter Act of 1844 drastically reduced their number. Notes of the following banks were in circulation in 1900 and later:

Ashford Bank, Pomfret, Burra & Co. (until 1902)
Aylesbury Old Bank, Cobb Bartlett & Co. (until 1902)
Banbury Bank, Gillet & Co. (until 1918)
Banbury Old Bank, T. R. Cobb & Sons (until 1902)
Bank of Whitehaven Ltd. (until 1916)
Bedford Bank, Thomas Barnard & Co. (until 1915)
Bicester & Oxfordshire Bank—Tibb & Co. (until 1920)
Bradford Banking Co. Ltd. (until 1910)
Bradford Commercial Banking Co. Ltd. (until 1904)
Buckingham Bank—Bartlett & Co. (until 1902)
Cambridge & Cambridgeshire Bank Ltd.—Fosters (until 1904)
Canterbury Bank, Hammand, Plumptre, Hilton, McMaster & Furley (until 1903)
Carlisle & Cumberland Banking Co. Ltd. (until 1911)
City Bank, Exeter—Milford, Snow & Co. (until 1901)
Cumberland Union Banking Co. Ltd. (until 1901)

Derby Bank, Samuel Smith & Co. (until 1902)
East Riding Bank, Beckett & Co., York (until 1920)
Exeter Bank—Sanders & Co. (until 1901)
Faversham Bank, Hilton, Rigden & Rigden (until 1902)
Halifax Commercial Bank Ltd. (until 1919)
Halifax & Huddersfield Union Bank Ltd. (until 1910)
Hull & Kingston-upon-Hull, Samuel Smith (until 1902)
Ipswich Bank, Bacon Cobbold & Co. (until 1904)
Kington & Radnorshire Bank Ltd.—Davies Bank & Co. (until 1910)
Knaresborough & Claro Banking Co. Ltd. (until 1903)
Lancaster Banking Co. Ltd. (until 1907)
Leeds Bank, Beckett & Co. Leeds (until 1920)
Leeds Union Bank, William Williams, Brown & Co. (until 1900)
Leicestershire Banking Co. Ltd. (until 1900)
Lincoln Bank, Smith, Ellison & Co. (until 1902)
Lincoln & Lindsey Banking Co. Ltd. (until 1913)
Llandovery & Llandilo Bank—David Jones & Co. (until 1909)
Moore & Robinsons, Notts Banking Co. Ltd. (until 1901)
Naval Bank, Plymouth, Harris, Bulteel & Co. (until 1914)
Newark Bank, Samuel Smith & Co. (until 1902)
Newark & Sleaford Bank, Peacock, Wilson & Co. (until 1912)
Newmarket Bank, Hammand & Co. (until 1905)
North & South Wales Bank Ltd. (until 1908)
Nottingham Bank, Samuel Smith & Co. (until 1902)
Nottingham and Nottinghamshire Banking Co. Ltd. (until 1919)
Oxford Old Bank, Parsons Thomson & Co. (until 1900)
Oxfordshire Witney Bank, Gillett & Co. (until 1918)
Pares' Leicestershire Banking Co. Ltd. (until 1902)
Reading Bank, Simonds & Co. (until 1913)
Richmond Bank, Yorkshire, Roper & Priestman (until 1902)
Sheffield Banking Co. Ltd. (until 1905)
Sheffield & Hallamshire Bank, Ltd. (until 1913)
Sheffield & Rotherham Joint Stock Banking Co. Ltd. (until 1907)
Stamford, Spalding & Boston Banking Co. Ltd. (until 1907)
Stuckeys Banking Co. Ltd. (until 1909)
Tring Bank & Chesham Bank, Thomas Butcher & Sons (until 1900)
Uxbridge Old Bank—Woodbridge, Lacy, Hartland, Hibbert & Co. (until 1900)
Wakefield & Barnsley Union Bank Ltd. (until 1906)
Wallingford Bank, Hedges Wells & Co. (until 1905)
Wellington, Somerset Bank, Fox, Fowler & Co. (until 1920)
West Riding Bank, Leathem Tew & Co. (until 1906)
West Riding Union Banking Co. Ltd.(until 1902)
West Yorkshire Banking Co. Ltd. (until 1919)
Whitehaven Joint Stock Banking Co. Ltd. (until 1908)
Wilts & Dorset Banking Co. Ltd. (until 1914)
Worcester Old Bank, Berwick Lechmere & Co. (until 1905)
Yarmouth, Norfolk & Suffolk Bank Ltd.—Lancons, Youell & Kemp (until 1901)
York City & County Banking Co. Ltd. (until 1909)
Yorkshire Banking Co. Ltd. (until 1901)
York Union Banking Co. Ltd. (until 1902)

Scotland

All notes are known with various dates and signatures. The dates in parenthesis are examples from notes actually observed. The following local banks had the right to print paper money:

Aberdeen Town and County Bank (until 1903)
Caledonian Banking Company, Inverness (until 1903)

Bank of Scotland

SA1.	dates from 1900	1 Pound. Format 175 × 128 mm (20.6.1919)	45.00
SA2.		5 Pounds	125.00
SA3.		10 Pounds	RR
SA4.		20 Pounds	RR
SA5.		50 Pounds	RRR
SA6.		100 Pounds	RRR
SA7.	dates from 1929	1 Pound, yellow brown and grey blue. Medallion in middle (Fortuna with cornucopia), regal arms at left (format 152 × 85 mm) (14.11.1929; 11.3.1930; 6.8.1931; 10.10.1932)	20.00
SA8.	dates from 1935	1 Pound, yellow brown and grey blue. Type of SA7 but arms of the bank at left (15.1.1935; 15.9.1937; 8.3.1937; 5.1.1939; 12.1.1939; 20.4.1939; 24.8.1939; 4.7.1940; 1.3.1941; 4.1.1945)	18.50
SA9.	dates from 1945	1 Pound, yellow and grey. Medallion in middle, no arms at left. Arms on reverse (29.3.1945; 11.12.1945; 11.12.1946; 28.1.1947; 5.1.1948; 10.2.1949; 4.10.1950; 5.1.1951; 17.9.1952; 16.10.1953; 4.3.1955)	15.00
SA10.		5 Pounds, grey and light brown. Arms on reverse (format 177 × 102 mm) (18.1.1951; 11.5.1951)	35.00

150 × 85

SA11.	dates from 1956	1 Pound, light brown and light blue. Similar to SA9 but sailing ship on the reverse (13.9.1956; 9.5.1957; 25.8.1958; 1.12.1959; 30.11.1960)	12.50

Great Britain • 125

SA12.		5 Pounds, blue and light brown. Similar to SA10 but arms and ship on reverse. Double line numeral of value (format 139 × 84 mm) (11.6.1958; 14.9.1961)	25.00
SA13.	dates from 1961	1 Pound, light brown and light blue. Medallion in middle. Date at bottom (format 150 × 71 mm) (20.11.1961; 3.12.1962)	12.50
SA14.	dates from 1966	1 Pound, light brown and light blue. Similar to SA13 but date in middle on reverse (1.6.1966)	11.00
SA15.	dates from 1967	1 Pound, light brown and light blue. Similar to SA14 but with dark stripes on reverse for mechanical sorting (3.3.1967)	10.00
SA16.		5 Pounds, blue and light brown. Similar to SA12 but solid numeral of value (format 139 × 84 mm) (1.2.1967)	20.00
SA17.	dates from 1968	1 Pound, ochre and multicolored. Arms and two women. "Edinburgh" 19 or 24 mm long (format 135 × 66 mm) (17.7.1968; 18.8.1969)	8.50
SA18.		5 Pounds, green and multicolored. Arms and two women (format 145 × 77 mm) (1.11.1968)	16.50
SA19.	dates from 1970	1 Pound, green and multicolored. Sir Walter Scott at right (10.8.1970; 31.8.1971)	—
SA20.		5 Pounds, blue and multicolored. Sir Walter Scott at right (10.8.1970)	—
SA21.		20 Pounds, purple. Sir Walter Scott at right (1.10.1970)	—
SA22.		100 Pounds, red. Sir Walter Scott at right	—

The British Linen Bank (until 1906, the British Linen Co.). The dominant color of all notes is blue.

SB1.	dates from 1900	1 Pound, blue and red	250.00
SB2.		5 Pounds	250.00
SB3.		10 Pounds	RR
SB4.		20 Pounds	RRR
SB5.		100 Pounds	RRR
SB6.	dates from 1906	1 Pound, blue and red. Type of SB1 but new bank name. Blank reverse	250.00
SB7.		5 Pounds	250.00
SB8.		10 Pounds	RR
SB9.		20 Pounds	RR
SB10.		100 Pounds	RRR
SB11.	dates from 1914	1 Pound. Printed reverse	RR
SB12.	dates from 1915	5 Pounds. Printed reverse	250.00
SB13.		10 Pounds	RR
SB14.		20 Pounds	RR
SB15.		100 Pounds	RRR

SB16.	dates from 1927	1 Pound, Regal arms (format 150 × 84 mm) (4.10.1927; 31.10.1928; 2.12.1929; 30.11.1931; 8.2.1932; 26.1.1933)	35.00
SB17.	dates from 1937	1 Pound. Similar to SB16 but arms of bank. Printed by Waterlow (9.2.1937; 3.10.1939; 7.3.1940; 23.6.1941; 3.1.1944; 7.7.1947; 5.8.1950; 28.8.1958; 15.4.1960)	12.50
SB18.	dates from 1944	5 Pounds. Smaller format 184 × 99 mm (2.7.1959)	32.50

150 × 84

SB19.	dates from 1961	1 Pound. Similar to SB17 but printed by Thomas De La Rue (30.9.1961)	12.50
SB20.	dates from 1961/62	1 Pound. Type of SB19 but format 150 × 72 mm (31.2.1962; 4.5.1964)	11.50
SB21.		5 Pounds. Type of SB18 but format 159 × 90 mm (2.1.1961)	25.00
SB22.		5 Pounds Sir Walter Scott at right (format 140 × 85 mm) (21.9.1962)	25.00
SB23.	dates from 1967	1 Pound. Type of SB20 but different design on reverse, with stripes for mechanical sorting (format 150 × 72 mm) (13.6.1967)	8.50
SB24.	dates from 1968	1 Pound. Sir Walter Scott at right (format 135 × 67 mm) (29.2.1968; 5.11.1969; 20.7.1970)	—
SB25.		5 Pounds. Type of SB22 but different format (145 × 78 mm) (22.3.1968)	—

Clydesdale Bank Ltd. (United with North of Scotland Bank in 1950)

SC1.	dates from 1900	1 Pound	RR
SC2.		5 Pounds	RR
SC3.		20 Pounds	RR
SC4.		100 Pounds	RRR
SC5.	dates from 1922	1 Pound. New type	RR
SC6.		5 Pounds	RR
SC7.		20 Pounds	RR
SC8.		100 Pounds	RRR
SC9.	dates from 1927	1 Pound, blue and orange. Industry and Agriculture at left and right (format 150 × 85 mm) (3.1.1927; 8.8.1934; 30.6.1937; 19.3.1941; 24.10.1945; 14.12.1949)	25.00

151 × 85

SC10.	dates from 1950	1 Pound, blue, yellow and orange. Port and field at left and right, with new name, "Clydesdale & North of Scotland Bank" (format 151 × 85 mm) (1.11.1950; 1.11.1956; 1.11.1960)	18.50
SC11.		5 Pounds, violet. Arms on reverse (format 180 × 97 mm) (2.5.1951; 1.2.1958)	35.00
SC12.		20 Pounds, green (2.5.1951)	100.00
SC13.		100 Pounds, blue (2.5.1951)	RRR
SC14.	dates from 1961	1 Pound, green. Arms at right (format 152 × 71 mm) (1.5.1961; 2.5.1962; 1.2.1963)	15.00
SC15.		5 Pounds, blue (format 140 × 85 mm) (20.9.1961)	25.00
SC16.	dates from 1963	1 Pound. Type of SC14 but bank name "Clydesdale Bank Ltd." (2.9.1963)	12.50
SC17.		5 Pounds, blue and violet. Type of SC15 but bank name "Clydesdale Bank Ltd." (format 140 × 85 mm) (2.9.1963)	20.00
SC18.		10 Pounds, brown. Arms at right (20.4.1964)	40.00
SC19.		20 Pounds, carmine red. Inscribed "Clydesdale Bank Ltd." (19.11.1964)	77.50
SC20.		100 Pounds, violet. Inscribed "Clydesdale Bank Ltd." (29.4.1965; 1.2.1968)	RRR
SC21.	dates from 1967	1 Pound, greenish. Type of SC16 but stripes for mechanical sorting on reverse (format 152 × 71 mm) (3.4.1967; 1.9.1969)	8.50
SC22.		5 Pounds, blue and violet. Type of SC17 but with stripes for mechanical sorting on reverse (format 140 × 85 mm) (1.5.1967)	16.50
SC23.	dates from 1971/72	1 Pound, green. Robert the Bruce at left (format 134 × 66 mm) (1.3.1971)	—
SC24.		5 Pounds, blue. Robert Burns at left (1.3.1971)	—
SC25.		10 Pounds, brown and light violet. David Livingston at left (1.3.1972)	—
SC26.		20 Pounds, lilac. Lord Kelvin at left (1.3.1972)	—
SC27.		100 Pounds, red. Lord Kelvin at left (1.3.1972)	—

Commercial Bank of Scotland (merged with the National Bank of Scotland in 1959)

SD1.	dates from 1900	1 Pound	RR
SD2.		5 Pounds	RR
SD3.		20 Pounds	RR
SD4.		100 Pounds	RRR
SD5.	dates from 1907	1 Pound, blue on yellow. Allegorical figures. Black or red control numbers (2.1.1909; 2.1.1918)	25.00
SD6.		5 Pounds	RR
SD7.		20 Pounds	RR
SD8.		100 Pounds	RR
SD9.	dates from 1925	1 Pound, blue on yellow and orange. Portrait (format 160 × 118 mm) (1.11.1926)	30.00
SD10.		5 Pounds	100.00
SD11.		20 Pounds	RR
SD12.		100 Pounds	RRR
SD13.	dates from 1927	1 Pound, blue on yellow and orange. Similar to SD9 but format 150 × 85 mm (1.12.1927; 31.5.1932; 6.8.1940; 2.12.1944)	20.00
SD14.	dates from 1947	1 Pound, lilac. Portrait of Lord Cockburn at right (2.1.1947; 3.1.1950; 2.1.1953)	12.50
SD15.	dates from 1951	5 Pounds, violet. Portrait of Lord Cockburn in middle (3.1.1951)	25.00
SD16.		20 Pounds, blue (3.1.1951)	100.00
SD17.		100 Pounds, green (3.1.1951)	R

SD18.	dates from 1954	1 Pound, blue (2.1.1958)	15.00

National Bank of Scotland (merged with the Commercial Bank of Scotland in 1959 under the new name of National Commercial Bank of Scotland)

SE1.	dates from 1900	1 Pound	RR
SE2.		5 Pounds	RR
SE3.		20 Pounds	RR
SE4.		100 Pounds	RRR
SE5.	dates from 1907	1 Pound, blue on yellow and brown. Portrait of Marquis of Lothian (12.11.1917)	35.00
SE6.		5 Pounds	RR
SE7.		20 Pounds	RR
SE8.		100 Pounds	RRR

SE9.	dates from 1927	1 Pound, black on orange brown and yellow. Regal arms in middle. Printed by Waterlow. Smaller format (150 × 85 mm) (1.11.1929)	30.00
SE10.	dates from 1931	1 Pound. Similar to SE9 but printed by W. and A. K. Johnston (2.2.1931; 11.11.1932; 11.11.1933)	18.50
SE11.	dates from 1934	1 Pound. Similar to SE10 but arms of bank in middle. Printed by W. and A. K. Johnston with "Cashier" or "General Manager" (12.11.1934; 2.1.1937; 31.7.1940; 1.5.1941; 1.11.1947; 1.10.1954)	12.50
SE12.	dates from 1955	1 Pound. Similar to SE11 but printed by W. and A. K. Johnston and G. W. Bacon with "GENERAL MANAGER" or "General Manager" (1.3.1955; 28.3.1957; 2.2.1959)	10.00
SE13.	dates from 1957	5 Pounds, green. Bridge on reverse (format 179 × 102 mm) (1.11.1957)	27.50
SE14.		20 Pounds, red. Bridge on reverse (format 179 × 102 mm) (1.11.1957)	125.00
SE15.		100 Pounds, blue. Bridge on reverse (format 179 × 102 mm) (1.11.1957)	R
SE16.	dates from 1959	1 Pound, blue. Bridge. New name "National Commercial Bank of Scotland" (format 152 × 85 mm) (16.9.1959)	10.00
SE17.		5 Pounds, green. Bridge on reverse. New name "National Commercial Bank of Scotland" (format 179 × 102 mm) (16.9.1959)	27.50
SE18.		20 Pounds, red. Type of SE17	—
SE19.		100 Pounds, violet. Type of SE17	—
SE20.	dates from 1961	1 Pound, green. Type of SE16 but smaller format (151 × 77 mm) (1.11.1961; 1.11.1962; 1.10.1964; 4.1.1966)	8.50
SE21.		5 Pounds, green. Type of SE17 but smaller format (179 × 102 mm) (3.1.1961)	25.00
SE22.	dates from 1963	5 Pounds, blue. Landscape with buildings on reverse (format 141 × 85 mm) (2.1.1963)	—
SE23.	dates from 1966	10 Pounds, brown. Bridge on reverse (format 151 × 94 mm) (16.8.1966)	—

SE24
150 × 72

| SE24. | dates from 1967 | 1 Pound, green. Type of SE20 but stripes for mechanical sorting on reverse (format 150 × 72 mm) (4.1.1967) | 7.50 |
| SE25. | dates from 1968 | 1 Pound, green. As SE24 but smaller format (136 × 67 mm) (4.1.1968) | — |

North of Scotland Bank (united with Clydesdale Bank in 1950)

SF1.		1 Pound. Large format	85.00
SF2.		5 Pounds	50.00
SF3.		20 Pounds	100.00
SF4.		100 Pounds	RRR
SF5.	dates from 1926	1 Pound, blue on yellow. Marishal College of Aberdeen in middle. Printed by Bradbury (format 155 × 85 mm) (1.3.1926; 1.3.1932; 1.3.1935)	27.50
SF6.	dates from 1938	1 Pound, blue on yellow. Kings College in middle. Printed by Thomas De La Rue (format 155 × 85 mm) (1.7.1938; 1.7.1945; 1.7.1949)	16.50

Royal Bank of Scotland

SG1.		1 Pound, blue. Allegorical figures at left and right (format 165 × 125 mm) (24.1.1921)	50.00
SG2.		5 Pounds	RR
SG3.		10 Pounds	RR
SG4.		20 Pounds	RR
SG5.		100 Pounds	RRR
SG6.	dates from 1927	1 Pound, blue. Printed by W. & A. K. Johnston (format 150 × 83 mm) (2.2.1927; 11.11.1931; 1.12.1938; 1.7.1942; 1.4.1953)	18.50

150 × 83

SG7.	dates from 1953	1 Pound, dark blue on yellow and brown. Printed by W. & A. K. Johnston (format 150 × 83 mm) (1.12.1953; 1.2.1956; 1.10.1962; 2.9.1963; 1.7.1964)	15.00
SG8.	dates from 1964	1 Pound, dark blue on yellow and brown. Similar to SG7 but format 150 × 71 mm (1.8.1964; 2.8.1965; 1.7.1967)	10.00
SG9.		5 Pounds, dark blue, brown and yellow (format 140 × 85 mm) (2.11.1964; 2.8.1965)	30.00

SG10.	dates from 1967	1 Pound, green. David Dale at left (1.9.1967)	8.50
SG11.	dates from 1966	5 Pounds, blue (1.11.1966)	20.00
SG12.	dates from 1969	1 Pound, green. Bridge (19.3.1969; 15.7.1970)	7.50
SG13.		5 Pounds, blue. Arms at left (19.3.1969)	18.50
SG14.		10 Pounds, brown. Arms in middle. Bridge on reverse (format 152 × 85 mm) (19.3.1969)	40.00
SG15.		20 Pounds, violet (format 161 × 90 mm) (19.3.1969)	200.00
SG16.		100 Pounds, red (format 161 × 90 mm) (19.3.1969)	RRR
SG17.	dates from 1972	1 Pound, green. Arms at right (5.1.1972)	—
SG18.		5 Pounds, blue (5.1.1972)	—
SG19.		10 Pounds, brown. Castle on reverse (5.1.1972)	—
SG20.		20 Pounds, violet (5.1.1972)	—
SG21.		100 Pounds, red (5.1.1972)	—

Union Bank of Scotland (merged with the Bank of Scotland in 1955)

SH1.	1 Pound (large format)	RR
SH2.	5 Pounds	RR
SH3.	10 Pounds	RR
SH4.	20 Pounds	RR
SH5.	100 Pounds	RRR

151 × 84

SH6.	dates from 1927	1 Pound, blue on red orange. Equestrian statues at lower left and right (format 151 × 84 mm) (3.10.1927; 1.6.1933; 1.8.1940; 1.6.1948)	18.50
SH7.	dates from 1949	1 Pound, blue on red orange. Arms at left, ship at right (1.3.1949; 17.10.1949; 1.6.1954)	16.50
SH8.		5 Pounds, blue on red orange. Arms at left, ship at right (5.6.1951)	30.00
SH9.		20 Pounds, blue on red orange. Arms at left, ship at right (1.9.1950)	85.00
SH10.		100 Pounds, blue on red orange. Arms at left, ship at right (9.10.1950)	RRR

Northern Ireland

Until 1928, the notes of private banks circulated throughout all of Ireland. After the founding of the Irish Free State (see separate listing under "Ireland"), the private notes were only valid in Northern Ireland. The Irish notes all have date and signature varieties.

Bank of Ireland

NA1.	dates from 1928	1 Pound, green underprinting. "One" in middle, Dublin (20.1.1925)	30.00
NA2.		5 Pounds, black and red. Dublin (format 225 × 130 mm) (25.4.1914)	65.00
NA3.		10 Pounds	RR
NA4.		20 Pounds	RR
NA5.	dates from 1928	1 Pound, green underprinting. Similar to NA1 but Belfast (9.3.1936)	20.00
NA6.		5 Pounds, red and ochre. Woman's head in middle (20.12.1946)	35.00
NA7.		10 Pounds, blue and green (20.1.1942)	RR
NA8.		20 Pounds, brown and green (9.5.1929)	RR

152 × 82

NA9.	dates from 1939	1 Pound, blue underprinting. Woman's head in middle (23.2.1942; 24.8.1942; 15.11.1943)	8.50
NA10.	(from 1966)	1 Pound, brown lilac. Woman's head at left	—
NA11.		5 Pounds, blue violet	—
NA12.		10 Pounds, brown and yellow	—
NA13.		20 Pounds	—

Belfast Banking Company

NB1.	dates from 1900	1 Pound	45.00
NB2.		5 Pounds, brown underprinting. Arms at left and middle (format 197 × 110 mm) (3.12.1913)	65.00
NB3.		10 Pounds	RR
NB4.		20 Pounds	RR
NB5.		50 Pounds	RR
NB6.		100 Pounds	RRR

NB7.	dates from 1922	1 Pound, blue underprinting. Arms in middle, control number varieties (4.4.1924; 9.11.1939)	15.00
NB8.		5 Pounds	45.00
NB9.		10 Pounds	R
NB10.		20 Pounds	RR
NB11.		50 Pounds	RR
NB12.		100 Pounds	RRR

National Bank Ltd.

NC1.	dates from 1900	1 Pound. Woman with harp	45.00
NC2.		5 Pounds, blue on brown (5.6.1923)	65.00
NC3.		10 Pounds, green on brown	100.00
NC4.		20 Pounds	RR
NC5.	dates from 1928	1 Pound, black on green. Arms in middle (1.8.1933)	16.50
NC6.		5 Pounds, blue on brown (6.5.1929)	35.00
NC7.		10 Pounds, green on brown (6.5.1929)	50.00
NC8.		20 Pounds, brown on blue (6.5.1929)	RR
NC9.	dates from 1937	1 Pound, black and green. Woman with harp (1.9.1937; 2.10.1939)	10.00
NC10.		5 Pounds, blue and brown (2.5.1949)	—
NC11.		10 Pounds, green and light brown (1.8.1942)	—
NC12.		20 Pounds, brown and green (1.1.1949)	—

Northern Bank Ltd.

ND1.	dates from 1900	1 Pound	R
ND2.		5 Pounds	R
ND3.		10 Pounds	R
ND4.		20 Pounds	RR
ND5.		50 Pounds	RR
ND6.		100 Pounds	RRR

150 × 81

ND7.	dates from 1928	1 Pound, blue underprinting. Sailing ship, red or black control numbers (6.5.1929; 1.1.1940)	7.50
ND8.		5 Pounds	65.00
ND9.		10 Pounds	RR
ND10.		20 Pounds	RR
ND11.		50 Pounds	RR
ND12.		100 Pounds	RR

ND13.	dates from 1970	1 Pound, green on rose. Cows at left, shipyard in middle, textiles at right (1.7.1970)	—
ND14.		5 Pounds, light blue (1.7.1970)	—
ND15.		10 Pounds, brown (1.7.1970)	—
ND16.		20 Pounds, violet (1.7.1970)	—
ND17.		100 Pounds, red (1.7.1970)	—

Provincial Bank of Ireland

NE1.	dates from 1900	1 Pound, green (format 157 × 90 mm) (1.12.1926)	45.00
NE2.		5 Pounds	75.00
NE3.		10 Pounds, blue (format 203 × 122 mm) (10.7.1915)	100.00
NE4.		20 Pounds	RR
NE5.		50 Pounds	RR
NE6.		100 Pounds	RRR
NE7.	dates from 1928	1 Pound, green underprinting, blue reverse. Building in middle (format 148 × 85 mm) (1.4.1933)	20.00
NE8.		1 Pound. Type of NE7 but reverse green (1.5.1939; 1.9.1942)	16.50
NE9.		5 Pounds, grey on brown and rose (format 151 × 89 mm) (5.4.1952)	45.00
NE10.		10 Pounds	85.00
NE11.		20 Pounds	RR
NE12.	dates from 1954	1 Pound. Woman's head in middle (format 150 × 84 mm)	
		a. Printed by Waterlow (1.10.1954)	15.00
		b. Printed by De La Rue (1.12.1965)	12.50
NE13.		5 Pounds. Type of NE12	35.00
NE14.	dates from 1966	1 Pound. Type of NE12 but smaller format (150 × 71 mm)	—
NE15.		5 Pounds. Type of NE13 but smaller format (139 × 84 mm)	—

Ulster Bank

NF1.	dates from 1900	1 Pound	RR
NF2.		5 Pounds	RR
NF3.		10 Pounds	RR
NF4.		20 Pounds	RR
NF5.		50 Pounds	RR
NF6.		100 Pounds	RRR
NF7.	dates from 1928	1 Pound, blue underprinting. Sailing ship (1.12.1929)	45.00
NF8.		5 Pounds	65.00
NF9.		10 Pounds	RR
NF10.		20 Pounds	RR
NF11.		50 Pounds	RR
NF12.		100 Pounds	RRR

NF13.	dates from 1966	1 Pound. Smaller format (150 $\times$ 72 mm) (4.10.1966)	7.50
NF14.		5 Pounds. Smaller format (138 $\times$ 84 mm) (4.10.1966)	—
NF15.		10 Pounds (4.10.1966)	—
NF16.	dates from 1971	1 Pound, dark blue. As NF13 but format 135 $\times$ 66 mm (15.2.1971)	—

Isle of Man

All Manx bank notes have date and signature varieties. Treasury bills issued after 1961 are undated.

Barclays Bank Ltd.

MA1.	dates from 1924	1 Pound, brown and green (7.6.1924; 16.4.1935; 30.3.1960)	45.00

Isle of Man Bank Ltd. (The Isle of Man Banking Co. Ltd. prior to 1926)

MA2.	dates from 1900	1 Pound, black and brown. Printed by Johnston (format 168 × 120 mm)	RR
MA3.		5 Pounds, black and blue (format 203 × 112 mm)	RR
MA4.	dates from 1926	1 Pound, black and rose. Printed by W. & A. K. Johnston (format 158 × 90 mm) (1.12.1926; 4.9.1933)	RR
MA5.	dates from 1927	5 Pounds, blue, green and rose (format 176 × 92 mm) (1.11.1927; 3.1.1945)	RR
MA6.	dates from 1934	1 Pound, blue, brown and green (1.10.1934; 2.12.1935; 5.5.1937; 20.5.1940; 17.3.1958)	35.00

Lancashire & Yorkshire Bank Ltd.

MA7.	1904/1920	1 Pound. Mountain in middle, "Manx Bank, Branch of the Lancashire & Yorkshire Bank Ltd." (format 167 × 120 mm) (10.11.1904; 30.10.1920)	RR
MA8.	1920/1927	1 Pound. Arms at left, mountain at right, "Lancashire & Yorkshire Bank Ltd." (format 165 × 85 mm) (13.12.1920; 28.12.1927)	RR
MA9.	1919/1921	1 Pound, black and green without underprinting (format 156 × 114 mm) (23.4.1919; 10.12.1920)	RR
MA10.	1921/1929	1 Pound. Type of MA9 but rose underprinting "One Pound" (23.3.1921; 21.1.1927)	RR
MA11.	1929/1935	1 Pound, black and green on rose. Words "Incorporated in England" behind one another (format 150 × 84 mm) (1.8.1929; 14.2.1934)	RR

| MA12. | 1935/1954 | 1 Pound. Type of MA11 but words divided. Bank name on reverse in shaded letters (28.1.1935; 20.2.1953) | 85.00 |
| MA13. | 1954/1961 | 1 Pound. Type of MA12 but bank name in solid letters (2.1.1955; 14.3.1961) | 75.00 |

London County Westminster & Paris Bank Ltd. (Westminster Bank after 1923)

MA14.	1918	1 Pound. Note of Paris Bank overprinted with new bank's name (22.11.1918)	RR
MA15.	1919/21	1 Pound. Type of MA14 but new bank name printed (format 157 × 118 mm) (25.11.1921)	RR
MA16.	1923/29	1 Pound. Type of MA15 but name "Westminster Bank"	RR
MA17.	dates from 1929	1 Pound, black on light yellow (format 150 × 84 mm) (9.1.1929; 18.2.1947; 30.3.1955)	35.00

Manx Bank Ltd. (taken over by the Mercantile Bank of Lancashire Ltd. in 1901)

| MA18. | 1882/1900 | 1 Pound. Mountain in middle (11.11.1882; 30.5.1900) | RR |

Martins Bank Ltd.

| MA19. | 1928/1929 | 1 Pound. Note of the Lancashire and Yorkshire Bank Ltd. overprinted "Martins Bank" | RRR |
| MA20. | 1929/1946 | 1 Pound, black. Bird on dark field in shield of arms at left (2.4.1929; 1.8.1934; 1.10.1938) | 85.00 |

#MA21
151 × 84

MA21.　1946/1961　　　1 Pound, black. Bird on light field in shield of
　　　　　　　　　　　　　　arms at left (1.3.1946; 1.5.1953; 1.2.1957)　　35.00

Mercantile Bank of Lancashire Ltd. (taken over by the Lancashire and Yorkshire
Bank in 1904)

MA22.　1901/1904　　　1 Pound. Mountain in middle, similar to
　　　　　　　　　　　　　　MA18 (13.6.1901; 6.9.1902)　　　　　　　　RR

Paris Bank Ltd. (merged with the London County & Westminster Bank in 1918)

MA23.　1900/1918　　　1 Pound, grey (format 157 × 118 mm)
　　　　　　　　　　　　　　(20.8.1900; 10.11.1916)　　　　　　　　　　RR

Government Notes

MA24.　(from 1961)　　10 Shillings, red. Queen Elizabeth at right.
　　　　　　　　　　　　　　Two signature varieties　　　　　　　　　　10.00
MA25.　　　　　　　　　1 Pound, violet. Type of MA24 (format
　　　　　　　　　　　　　　151 × 71 mm)　　　　　　　　　　　　　　8.50
MA26.　　　　　　　　　5 Pounds, green and blue. Type of MA24
　　　　　　　　　　　　　　(format 140 × 85 mm)　　　　　　　　　　25.00
MA27.　(from 1969)　　50 New Pence, blue. Queen Elizabeth at right
　　　　　　　　　　　　　　(format 139 × 66 mm)　　　　　　　　　　3.50
MA28.　(from 1972)　　50 New Pence, blue. New portrait of Queen
　　　　　　　　　　　　　　Elizabeth at right (format 127 × 62 mm)　　—
MA29.　　　　　　　　　1 Pound, violet (format 135 × 66 mm)　　　—
MA30.　　　　　　　　　5 Pounds, blue and lilac brown (format
　　　　　　　　　　　　　　146 × 77 mm)　　　　　　　　　　　　　　—
MA31.　　　　　　　　　10 Pounds, brown and green　　　　　　　　—

Guernsey

Notes #1, #2, #10–16 and #42–46 have date and signature varieties.

The States of Guernsey, Government Notes

1.	dates from 1900	1 Pound	RRR
2.		5 Pounds	RRR
3.	5. 8.1914	5 Shillings	RRR
4.		10 Shillings	RRR
5.	1. 9.1914	5 Shillings = 6 Francs	RRR
6.		10 Shillings = 12 Francs	RRR
7.		1 Pound	RRR
8.	(1921)	5 Shillings. Same as #5 but overprinted "British"	RRR
9.		10 Shillings. Same as #6 but overprinted "British"	RRR
10.	1. 3.1921–19.11.1932	10 Shillings, black and grey. No numerals in middle (17.5.1924)	200.00
11.	1. 3.1921–6.12.1926	1 Pound, black and grey on orange. No numerals in middle (17.5.1924)	RR
12.	22. 7.1927–2.12.1932	1 Pound, black and grey on red. Value "£1" in middle (6.12.1927)	RR
13.	3. 1.1933–18.11.1933	10 Shillings, light blue and brown. Value "10/–" in middle. One signature only. English text on reverse (18.11.1933)	175.00
14.		1 Pound, grey on red. Type of #12 but only one signature. English text on reverse	200.00
15.	from 29.3.1934	10 Shillings, light blue and brown. Type of #13 but text "s'BALLIVIE INSULE DEGERNEREYE" on reverse	175.00
16.		1 Pound, grey. Type of #14 but reverse text as #15	250.00
17.	March 1940	1 Pound	65.00
18.	25. 3.1941	2 Shillings 6 Pence (2/6), blue and orange	45.00
19.		5 Shillings, black and red	50.00
20.	17. 5.1941	2 Shillings 6 Pence (2/6)	45.00
21.		5 Shillings	45.00
22.	16.10.1941	6 Pence (6d), violet and rose	45.00
23.		1 Shilling 3 Pence (1/3), black and yellow	45.00
24.	1. 1.1942	6 Pence (6d)	45.00
25.		1 Shilling 3 Pence (1/3)	50.00
26.	18. 7.1942	1 Shilling 3 Pence (1/3)	50.00
27.		1 Shilling overprinted on 1 Shilling 3 Pence. Same as #26 with overprint	65.00
28.	1. 1.1943	1 Shilling overprinted on 6 pence. Same as #24 with overprint	85.00
29.		1 Shilling overprinted on 1 Shilling 3 Pence. Same as #26 with overprint	85.00
30.		2 Shillings 6 Pence (2/6)	65.00
31.		5 Shillings (5/–)	65.00
32.		10 Shillings (10/–), blue	65.00

149 × 88

33.		1 Pound, black	85.00

Notes #18–33 were issued during the German occupation in World War II.

34.	1. 1.1945	5 Shillings. Text reads "Backed by Guernsey Notes." Printed on French paper	RRR
35.		10 Shillings	RRR
36.		1 Pound	RRR
37.		5 Pounds	RRR
38.		5 Shillings. Text reads "Backed by British Notes"	RRR
39.		10 Shillings	RRR
40.		1 Pound	RRR
41.		5 Pounds	RRR
42.	dates from 1945	10 Shillings, lilac and light green (1.8.1945; 1.1.1950; 1.5.1953; 1.6.1959)	12.50
43.		1 Pound, violet and green (1.8.1945; 1.1.1950; 1.5.1953; 1.2.1955)	25.00
44.		5 Pounds, green and blue (1.12.1956)	65.00
45.	(1969)	1 Pound, olive and yellow	—
46.		5 Pounds, violet and light brown	—

Guernsey Banking Co. Ltd.

R1.	dates to 1914	1 Pound	RRR

The bank's right to print paper money expired in 1914 but the notes continued to circulate until the bank's merger with the National Provincial Bank in 1923.

Guernsey Commercial Banking Co. Ltd.

R2.	dates to 1914	1 Pound	RRR

The bank's right to print paper money expired in 1914 but the notes continued to circulate until the bank's merger with the Westminster Bank Ltd. in 1923.

Jersey

The States of Jersey, Government Notes

1.	(1941–42)	6 Pence, dark brown and carmine	25.00
2.		1 Shilling, dark brown and blue	35.00
3.		2 Shillings, blue and light brown. Picture on reverse	45.00
4.		2 Shillings, violet and light brown. No picture on reverse	40.00

128 × 84

5.		10 Shillings, green	45.00
6.		1 Pound, violet and green	50.00

Notes #1–6 were issued during the German occupation in World War II.

7.	(1963)	10 Shillings, brown. Queen Elizabeth	—
8.		1 Pound, green. Queen Elizabeth	—
9.		5 Pounds, dark red. Queen Elizabeth	—

Private bank notes of 1 pound denomination were issued by the Banque Massoit Cie., Barclays Bank, Ltd., Capital and Countries Bank, Lloyds Bank Ltd., Midland Bank Ltd. and the National Provincial Bank.

Military Notes

British Military Authority

Issued 1943–45 for use in North Africa and Greece, all notes show the British lion and crown.

M1.	(1943–45)	6 Pence (6d), lilac brown	6.50
M2.		1 Shilling, grey on violet	5.00
M3.		2 Shillings 6 Pence (2/6), green on rose	6.50
M4.		5 Shillings, brown on blue and green	8.50
M5.		10 Shillings, blue on olive and lilac	18.50
M6.		1 Pound, violet on light brown	45.00

British Armed Forces Special Vouchers

Issued for the British troops in Germany and Austria. All are multicolored and only the dominant color is listed below.

M7.	(1945–46)	$\frac{1}{2}$ Pence ($\frac{1}{2}$d). Round, imprinted disc of brown plastic	6.50
M8.		1 Pence (1d). Type of M7	6.50
M9.		3 Pence (3d), lilac	1.75
M10.		6 Pence (6d), brown	2.25
M11.		1 Shilling, grey blue	2.50
M12.		2 Shillings 6 Pence (2/6), red	3.50
M13.		5 Shillings, green	12.50
M14.		10 Shillings, violet	16.50

139 × 70

M15.		1 Pound, blue	25.00
M16.	(1950) "2nd Series"	3 Pence (3d), brown	1.75
M17.		6 Pence (6d), blue	2.25
M18.		1 Shilling, grey blue	2.50
M19.		2 Shillings 6 Pence (2/6), lilac brown	3.50
M20.		5 Shillings, violet	8.50
M21.		10 Shillings, green	12.50
M22.		1 Pound, lilac	20.00
M23.		5 Pounds, dark blue	50.00

GREECE

From 1456 until the beginning of the 19th century, Greece was under Turkish control. An independent kingdom was set up in 1822 and was ruled in turn by Otto I, 1832–62; George I, 1863–1913; Constantine I, 1913–17, 1920–22; Alexander, 1917–20; and George II, 1922–23. Greece was declared a republic in 1924 but King George II was returned to the throne in 1935. During World War II, German and Italian troops occupied the nation and, after their retreat, a civil war raged until 1949. Greece became a kingdom once again in 1947 under Paul I, followed by his son, Constantine II in 1964.

1 Drachma = 100 Lepta

All banknotes issued until 1932 display the portrait of the first Bank Governor, Georgios Stavros. The single type note carries various dates and different issues can be distinguished by an inscription in Greek letters on the reverse. The number of the issue can be determined by referring to the table below. The cardinal numeral follows " *ΕΚΔΟΣΙΣ* ," the Greek word for "issue." The dates in parenthesis are examples taken from notes actually observed.

1st   = *ΠΡΩΤΗ*
2nd = *ΔΕΥΤΕΡΑ*
3rd   = *ΤΡΙΤΗ*
4th   = *ΤΕΤΑΡΤΗ*
5th   = *ΠΕΜΠΤΗ*
6th   = *ΕΚΤΗ*
7th   = *ΕΒΔΟΜΗ*
8th   = *ΟΓΔΟΗ*
9th   = *ΕΝΑΤΗ*
10th = *ΔΕΚΑΤΗ*
11th = *ΕΝΔΕΚΑΤΗ*
12th = *ΔΩΔΕΚΑΤΗ*
13th = *ΔΕΚΑΤΗ ΤΡΙΤΗ*
14th = *ΔΕΚΑΤΗ ΤΕΤΑΡΤΗ*

(National Bank of Greece) *ΕΘΝΙΚΗ ΤΡΑΓΕΖΑ ΤΗΣ ΕΛΛΑΔΟ*

Notes to 1922

1.	5 Drachmai, 1st issue (designation not on note). Printed by Bradbury (2.10.1897; 12.12.1897)	$20.00
2.	5 Drachmai, 2nd issue. Printed by American Bank Note Company (many dates between 1905 and 1919)	10.00
3.	10 Drachmai, 2nd issue (1st issue of this denomination not issued). Printed by American Bank Note Company	25.00
4.	10 Drachmai, 3rd issue	25.00

5.	10 Drachmai, 4th issue	25.00
6.	10 Drachmai, 5th issue	25.00
7.	10 Drachmai, 6th issue (designation not on note). Printed by Bradbury (1.6.1900)	16.50
8.	10 Drachmai, 7th issue (dates to 1907)	16.50
9.	10 Drachmai, 8th issue (designation not on note). Printed by American Bank Note Company	16.50
10.	10 Drachmai, 9th issue. Printed by American Bank Note Company (1.10.1912; 20.3.1913; 8.1.1914; 15.4.1914)	10.00
11.	25 Drachmai, 1st issue (designation not on note). Printed by Bradbury	45.00
12.	25 Drachmai, 2nd issue. Printed by American Bank Note Company	35.00
13.	25 Drachmai, 3rd issue	35.00
14.	25 Drachmai, 4th issue	35.00
15.	25 Drachmai, 5th issue	35.00
16.	25 Drachmai, 6th issue (designation not on note). Printed by Bradbury	35.00
17.	25 Drachmai, 7th issue (dates to 1909)	35.00
18.	24 Drachmai, 8th issue (designation not on note). Printed by American Bank Note Company (3.8.1903)	20.00

167 × 87

19.	25 Drachmai, 9th issue. Printed by American Bank Note Company (10.3.1912; 1.9.1913; 15.7.1917; 10.8.1917)	16.50
20.	50 Drachmai, 1st issue (designation not on note). Printed by Bradbury	50.00
21.	50 Drachmai, 2nd issue. Printed by American Bank Note Company (dates to 1907)	45.00
22.	100 Drachmai, 1st issue (designation not on note). Printed by Bradbury	65.00
23.	100 Drachmai, 2nd issue. Printed by American Bank Note Company	50.00
24.	100 Drachmai, 3rd issue	50.00
25.	100 Drachmai, 4th issue	50.00
26.	100 Drachmai, 5th issue	50.00
27.	100 Drachmai, 6th issue (designation not on note). Printed by Bradbury	45.00
28.	100 Drachmai, 7th issue (dates to 1907)	45.00

29.	100 Drachmai, 8th issue. Printed by American Bank Note Company (dates to 1926)	45.00
30.	100 Drachmai, 9th issue. Printed by American Bank Note Company (7.1.1912; 12.11.1917; 25.2.1918)	25.00
31.	100 Drachmai, 10th issue. Printed by American Bank Note Company (date to 1926)	25.00
32.	500 Drachmai, 1st issue (designation not on note). Printed by Bradbury	85.00
33.	500 Drachmai, 2nd issue. Printed by American Bank Note Company (dates to 1907)	75.00
34.	500 Drachmai, 5th issue (dates to 1917)	65.00
	Third and fourth issues of this denomination not issued.	
35.	500 Drachmai, 6th issue (designation not on note). Printed by Bradbury	65.00
36.	500 Drachmai, 7th issue	65.00
37.	1,000 Drachmai, 8th issue (designation not on note)	150.00

The law of 25.3.1922 decreed a forced loan to the government, based on the bank-notes then in circulation. The notes were cut into halves with the left part continuing to circulate as legal tender at half the former face value (until 1927). The right part had to be held as a loan certificate, also for half of the note's former par-value. The following issues are known to have been halved:

```
    5 Drachmai, 2nd issue
   10 Drachmai, 6th, 8th and 9th issues
   25 Drachmai, 8th and 9th issues
  100 Drachmai, 8th, 9th and 10th issues
  500 Drachmai, 6th and 7th issues
1,000 Drachmai, 1st issue
```

(State Notes of the Finance Ministry) *ΒΑΣΙΛΕΙΟΝ ΤΗΣ ΕΛΛΑΔΟΣ*

38.	1917	1 Drachma, blue and brown (old date 21.12.1885). Head of Athene at left. Printed by Bradbury. Brown overprint *ΝΟΜΟΣ* 991 and *ΤΟΥ* 1917	4.50
39.		2 Drachmai, blue and brown (old date 21.12.1885). Hermes head at right. Printed by Bradbury. Brown overprint as #38	6.50
40.	27.10.1917	1 Drachma, brown. Seated Hermes in middle. Printed by Aspiotis Freres	2.25

66 × 40

41.		1 Drachma, violet and green. Head of Homer in middle. Printed by Bradbury	2.25
42.		1 Drachma, blue on lilac and olive. Seated Hermes at right. Printed by Bradbury	2.50

43.		2 Drachmai, blue green and brown. Type of #40. Printed by Aspiotis Freres	3.50
44.		2 Drachmai, blue on rose and light blue. Statue of Zeus at left. Printed by Bradbury	2.50
45.		2 Drachmai, red brown. Lyre player in middle. Printed by Bradbury	3.00
46.	(1918)	1 Drachma, brown. Pericles at right. Printed by Aspiotis Freres	6.50
47.		2 Drachmai, light blue and yellow. Pericles at left. Printed by Aspiotis Freres	8.50
48.	(1920)	10 Lepta, brown. Hermes head. Postage stamp of 1911–1921 issue printed on cardboard (Scott #202, Michel #162)	
		a. Dark brown, punched	2.50
		b. Light brown, perforated	4.50
49.		50 Lepta, blue. Standing Athena in middle. Printed by Aspiotis Freres	1.75

(National Bank of Greece) *ΕΘΝΙΚΗ ΤΡΑΓΕΖΑ ΤΗΣ ΕΛΛΑΔΟΣ*

Notes issued from March 1922 to 1926 without overprint

50.	5 Drachmai, 3rd issue	25.00
51.	5 Drachmai, green, 4th issue. Printed by Bradbury (24.3.1923)	16.50
52.	5 Drachmai, black on rose and multicolored, 5th issue. Printed by American Bank Note Company (26.4.1923)	15.00
53.	10 Drachmai, blue, 10th issue. Printed by American Bank Note Company (15.7.1926)	16.50
54.	25 Drachmai, 10th issue	20.00
55.	50 Drachmai, 3rd issue	25.00
56.	100 Drachmai, 11th issue	25.00
57.	500 Drachmai, 8th issue	45.00
58.	1,000 Drachmai, 2nd issue	125.00

(National Bank of Greece) *ΕΘΝΙΚΗ ΤΡΑΓΕΖΑ ΤΗΣ ΕΛΛΑΔΟΣ*

Issue of 1926–27

By the law of 23.1.1926, older notes of denominations higher than 25 Drachmai were divided into a three-quarter left side piece and one-quarter right side piece. The left-hand parts were worth three-quarters of their reduced ($\frac{3}{4}$) value toward bank notes and one-quarter of their lowered value toward obligations of the Forced Loan exchange. The right quarter of the original note was likewise exchangeable toward the loan obligations.

The following notes have been encountered as three-quarter pieces:

      50 Drachmai, 4th issue
     100 Drachmai, 8th, 9th, 10th and 12th issues
     500 Drachmai, 6th, 7th and 9th issues
   1,000 Drachmai, 1st, 3rd and 4th issues

The following notes have been encountered as three-quarter pieces with a red overprint "Neon" (new):

    50 Drachmai, 3rd and 4th issues
    100 Drachmai, 11th and 12th issues
    500 Drachmai, 8th and 9th issues
    1,000 Drachmai, 3rd and 4th issues

The following notes are only known divided into parts:

59.	50 Drachmai, 4th issue	
60.	100 Drachmai, 12th issue	
61.	500 Drachmai, 9th issue	
62.	1,000 Drachmai, 3rd issue	
63.	1,000 Drachmai, 4th issue	

New issue without overprint

64.   25 Drachmai, brown, 11th issue. Printed by Bradbury (5.3.1923)   20.00

New printing of undivided notes with red overprint "Neon 1926" (some carry dates prior to 1926)

65.   5 Drachmai, red brown, 6th issue. Printed by American Bank
        Note Company (17.12.1926)   16.50
66.   50 Drachmai, rose and green, 5th issue. Printed by Bradbury
        (6.5.1923)   20.00

157 × 77

67.   100 Drachmai, green. 13th issue. Printed by Bradbury
        (20.4.1923)   16.50
68.   500 Drachmai, brown, 10th issue. Printed by Bradbury
        (12.4.1923)   35.00
69.   1,000 Drachmai, 2nd issue   65.00

(Bank of Greece) ΤΡΑΠΕΖΑ ΤΗΣ ΕΛΛΑΔΟΣ

Provisional issues from 1928

Notes inscribed with the old bank name and dates, without the overprint "Neon" and with no overprint of the new bank name (Reprints of #51, #52, #53 and #64 were also released at this time)

70.   5 Drachmai, 6th issue. Printed by the American Bank Note
        Company (24.5.1927)   8.50
71.   25 Drachmai, multicolored 12th issue. Printed by American
        Bank Note Company (15.4.1923)   10.00

72.   100 Drachmai, green on violet and brown, 14th issue. Printed by
       American Bank Note Company (26.5.1927)   8.50
73.   500 Drachmai, violet, 11th issue. Printed by American Bank
       Note Company (12.11.1926)   25.00

Notes with the old bank name and dates overprinted "Neon"

74.   5 Drachmai, multicolored, 3rd issue. Printed by American
         Bank Note Company (29.7.1918; 26.8.1918; 20.10.1918;
         23.10.1918)   6.50
75.   25 Drachmai, 10th issue (10.1.1918; 25.1.1919)   10.00

Notes overprinted with the new bank name but not "Neon"

76.   5 Drachmai, brown and multicolored, 6th issue. Printed by
         American Bank Note Company (17.9.1926; 17.12.1926)   5.00
77.   20 Drachmai, brown, 1st issue. Printed by American Bank Note
        Company (19.10.1926)   6.50
78.   25 Drachmai, brown, 11th issue. Printed by Bradbury
        (5.3.1923)   10.00
79.   25 Drachmai, 12th issue. Printed by American Bank Note
        Company (15.4.1923)   16.50
80.   50 Drachmai, 3rd issue   25.00
81.   50 Drachmai, rose and green, 5th issue. Printed by Bradbury 20.00
82.   50 Drachmai, olive green, 6th issue. Printed by American Bank
        Note Company (30.4.1927; 13.5.1927; 24.5.1927)   8.50
83.   100 Drachmai, green, 14th issue. Printed by American Bank
       Note Company (6.1.1927; 14.6.1927; 25.5.1927)   8.50
84.   1,000 Drachmai, green, 5th issue. Printed by American Bank Note
        Company (15.10.1926; 4.11.1926)   6.50
85.   5,000 Drachmai, brown, 1st issue. Printed by American Bank Note
        Company (5.10.1926)   65.00

Note overprinted with the new bank name and "Neon"

86.   50 Drachmai, 3rd issue   20.00

Notes with the old bank name overprinted "Neon 1926" (Reprints of re-issue of
#66 and #67 were also released at this time)

87.   25 Drachmai, 11th issue   15.00
88.   25 Drachmai, 12th issue   12.50
89.   500 Drachmai, 11th issue   35.00

Notes overprinted with the new bank name and "Neon 1926"

90.   25 Drachmai, 11th issue   16.50
91.   25 Drachmai, 12th issue   20.00
92.   50 Drachmai, brown, 5th issue. Printed by Bradbury (6.5.1923) 12.50
93.   100 Drachmai, 13th issue. Printed by Bradbury   12.50
94.   500 Drachmai, 11th issue   35.00

(Bank of Greece) *ΤΡΑΠΕΖΑ ΤΗΣ ΕΛΛΑΔΟΣ*

Issues of 1932–1944

| 95. | 1. 9.1932 | 5,000 Drachmai, brown. Athena in middle. Printed by American Bank Note Company | 6.50 |
| 96. | 1.10.1932 | 500 Drachmai, multicolored. Athena in middle. Printed by American Bank Note Company | 4.50 |

204 × 100

97.	1. 5.1935	1,000 Drachmai, multicolored. Young girl in costume holding jug (French printing)	8.50
98.	1. 9.1935	50 Drachmai, multicolored. Young girl with sheaf at left (French printing)	5.00
99.		100 Drachmai, multicolored. Mercury in middle (French printing)	6.50
100.	1. 1.1939	50 Drachmai, green. The poet Hesiod	1.25
101.		100 Drachmai, green and yellow. Two peasant women	45.00
102.		500 Drachmai, blue violet and lilac. Woman in costume at left	3.50
		Error: "*ENI*" instead of "*ΕΠΙ*"	20.00
103.		1,000 Drachmai, green. Woman in costume at right	3.75
104.		1,000 Drachmai on 100 Drachmai, green. Same as #101 but overprinted with new value	2.25
		For 50 drachmai note dated 1.1.1941, see #134.	
105.	10. 7.1941	100 Drachmai, brown. Reverse Kapnikarea church	1.00
106.	1.10.1941	1,000 Drachmai, blue and brown. Coin of Alexander the Great	
		a. Picture name in illustration	4.50
		b. Picture name in field	1.50
107.	20. 6.1942	5,000 Drachmai, brown, red and green. Statue of Victory of Samothrace	1.50
108.	21. 8.1942	1,000 Drachmai, blue and brown. Head of young girl of Thasos	1.00
109.	29.12.1942	10,000 Drachmai, brown. Young peasant couple from Delphi	
		a. Picture name in illustration on reverse	4.50
		b. Picture name in field on reverse	1.25
110.	1. 2.1943	50 Drachmai, brown. Young girl	.75

111.	19. 7.1943	5,000 Drachmai, green, blue and brown. Head of Athena	1.00
112.	12. 8.1943	25,000 Drachmai, brown and green. The nymph Deidamia	1.00
113.	14. 1.1944	50,000 Drachmai, blue. Athlete's head	1.25
114.	21. 1.1944	100,000 Drachmai, green and brown. Ancient Greek coins at left and right	1.00
115.	20. 3.1944	500,000 Drachmai, brown. The Zeus of Mylasa	.75
116.	29. 6.1944	1,000,000 Drachmai, green and brown. Youth of Antikythera	.75
117.	20. 7.1944	5,000,000 Drachmai, green and brown. Head of Arethusa on an ancient coin	.60
118.	29. 7.1944	10,000,000 Drachmai, brown	.60
119.	10. 8.1944	25,000,000 Drachmai, green. Ancient Greek coins at left and right	.75
120.	9. 9.1944	200,000,000 Drachmai, brown and red brown. Section of Parthenon frieze	.60
121.	1.10.1944	500,000,000 Drachmai, blue. The Apollo of Olympia	1.25
122.	11.10.1944	2,000,000,000 Drachmai, green. Section of Parthenon frieze	.75
123.	20.10.1944	10,000,000,000 Drachmai, blue and brown. Head of Arethusa on an ancient coin	2.00
124.	3.11.1944	100,000,000,000 Drachmai, brown. The Nymph Deidamia	8.50

(Treasury bills of the branch office at Patras) *ΥΠΟΚΑΤΑΣΤΗΜΑ ΠΑΤΡΩΝ*

125.	7.10.1944	100,000,000 Drachmai, brown. Ancient Greek coin at left	25.00
126.		500,000,000 Drachmai, blue. Ancient Greek coin in middle	35.00

(Treasury bills of the branch office at Kerkyras) *ΥΠΟΚΑΤΑΣΤΗΜΑ ΚΕΡΚΥΡΑΣ*

139 × 69

127.	7.10.1944	100,000,000 Drachmai, green and olive	35.00

(Treasury bills of the branch office at Kalamata) *ΚΑΛΑΜΑΤΑ*

127a.	20. 9.1944	25,000,000 Drachmai, brown. Flags at left and right	65.00
127b.		100,000,000 Drachmai, blue	65.00
127c.	5.10.1944	200,000,000 Drachmai, orange	65.00

(Government Notes, Kingdom of Greece) *ΒΑΣΙΛΕΙΟΝ ΤΗΣ ΕΛΛΑΔΟΣ*

128.	6. 4.1940	10 Drachmai, blue, brown and green. Head of Demeter at left	.60
129.		20 Drachmai, green and brown. Head of Poseidon on coin	.60

(Greek State Notes) *ΕΛΛΗΝΙΚΗ ΠΟΛΙΤΕΙΑ*

130.	18. 6.1941	50 Lepta, red and light green. Statue of Victory of Samothrace	1.25
131.		1 Drachma, lilac and blue. Statue of Aristotle	.60
132.		2 Drachmai, blue and grey brown. Coin of Alexander the Great	.60
133.		5 Drachmai, brown lilac. Three women (from a wall fresco)	.40

(Bank of Greece) *ΤΡΑΠΕΖΑ ΤΗΣ ΕΛΛΑΔΟΣ*

Currency reform, notes in new values issued from November 1944 to 1953

134.	1. 1.1941 (issued 1944)	50 Drachmai, red brown. Type of #100	1.25
135.	9.11.1944	50 Drachmai, light brown and blue. Statue of Victory of Samothrace	15.00
136.		100 Drachmai, blue. Canaris	8.50
137.		500 Drachmai, green. Count Capo D'Istria (president of 1828–31 republic) at left	8.50
138.		1,000 Drachmai, brown. Freedom fighter Kolokotronis at left (format 161 × 80 mm)	8.50
139.		5,000 Drachmai, red. Woman with children in middle (format 170 × 84 mm)	12.50
140.		5,000 Drachmai, red. Type of #139 but smaller format (153 × 80 mm)	20.00
141.		5,000 Drachmai, blue. Type of #139 but larger format (180 × 90 mm)	20.00
142.		5,000 Drachmai, violet. Type of #140 (format 153 × 80 mm)	12.50
143.		5,000 Drachmai, brown. Type of #140 (format 153 × 80 mm)	16.50

#145
179 × 89

144.		10,000 Drachmai, orange. Head of old man at left (format 180 × 90 mm)	16.50
145.		10,000 Drachmai, blue. Type of #144	12.50
146.		10,000 Drachmai, orange. Type of #144 but smaller format (153 × 80 mm)	12.50
147.		20,000 Drachmai, dark green. Athena (format 180 × 90 mm)	15.00
148.		20,000 Drachmai, dark green. Type of #147 but smaller format (153 × 80 mm)	8.50
149.	9. 1.1947	1,000 Drachmai, brown. Freedom fighter Kolokotronis. Type of #138 but smaller format (145 × 75 mm)	5.00
149a.		5,000 Drachmai, brown violet. Type of #142 (format 153 × 80 mm)	10.00
150.	14.11.1947	1,000 Drachmai, brown. Type of #149	6.50
151.	29.12.1947	10,000 Drachmai, orange. Head of old man at left. Type of #144 but smaller format (150 × 79 mm)	8.50
152.	29.12.1949	20,000 Drachmai, blue. Athena at left. Type of #146 but smaller format (147 × 78 mm)	10.00
153.	28.10.1950	5,000 Drachmai, orange	20.00
154.		5,000 Drachmai, brown. Rev. Battle of Missolonghi (format 151 × 78 mm)	10.00
155.		10,000 Drachmai, dark green	20.00
156.	2.11.1950	20,000 Drachmai, dark green (format 154 × 81 mm)	20.00
157.	1.12.1950	50,000 Drachmai, multicolored. Woman's head at left (format 152 × 80 mm)	16.50

(State Notes, Kingdom of Greece) *ΒΑΣΙΛΕΙΟΝ ΤΗΣ ΕΛΛΑΔΟΣ*

New values from November, 1944

158.	9.11.1944	1 Drachma, blue	1.75
159.		10 Drachmai, brown and green	2.25

87 × 62

160.		20 Drachmai, blue	2.25
161.	15. 1.1945	5 Drachmai, brown	1.75
162.	10. 7.1950	100 Drachmai, blue. Man's head in middle	1.50
163.		500 Drachmai, green. Ancient Greek coins at left and right	2.00
164.		1,000 Drachmai, brown. Type of #163	1.75
165.	1.11.1953	100 Drachmai, blue. Type of #162	1.75
166.		500 Drachmai, green. Type of #163	2.25
167.		1,000 Drachmai, brown. Type of #164	3.50

(Bank of Greece) *ΤΡΑΠΕΖΑ ΤΗΣ ΕΛΛΑΔΟΣ*

Notes in new values from 1954

168.	15. 1.1954	10 Drachmai, orange. Head of old man at left	15.00
169.		20 Drachmai, blue. Head of Athena at left	18.50
170.		50 Drachmai, multicolored. Woman's head at left	25.00
171.	31. 3.1954	100 Drachmai, dark red. Themistocles at left	25.00
172.	15. 5.1954	10 Drachmai, orange. King Paul at left	5.00
173.	1. 3.1955	10 Drachmai, orange. Type of #172	6.50
174.		20 Drachmai, blue. Democritos at left	8.50
175.		50 Drachmai, dark green. Pericles in center	10.00
176.	1. 7.1955	100 Drachmai, dark red. Type of #170	10.00
177.	8. 8.1955	500 Drachmai, green. Socrates in center	35.00
178.	16. 4.1956	1,000 Drachmai, brown. Alexander the Great at left	60.00
179.	1.10.1964	50 Drachmai, blue and green. Head of Arethusa	—
180.	1. 7.1966	100 Drachmai, brown. Democritos at left	—
181.	1.10.1967	100 Drachmai, brown. Type of #180	—
182.	1.11.1968	500 Drachmai, olive. Relief of Eleusis	—
183.	1.11.1970	1,000 Drachmai, brown. Head of Zeus at left	
		a. Watermarked with profile head of Ephebus of Anticythera (issued 1970)	—
		b. Watermarked with half-profile head of Aphrodite of Cnidus (issued 1972)	—

Regional Banks

(Epirus-Thessaly Bank) *ΤΡΑΠΕΖΑ ΗΠΕΙΡΟ — ΘΕΣΣΑΛΙΑΣ*

R1.	dates to 1905	1 Drachma	45.00
R2.		2 Drachmai	100.00
R3.		10 Drachmai	250.00
R4.		25 Drachmai	RR
R5.		100 Drachmai	RRR

The Epirus-Thessaly Bank was taken over by the National Bank in 1899 but its notes continued to circulate until 1905.

(Ionian Bank) *ΙΟΝΙΚΗ ΤΡΑΠΕΖΑ*

R6.	dates to 1920	1 Drachma	35.00
R7.		2 Drachmai	65.00
R8.		10 Drachmai	175.00
R9.		25 Drachmai	RR
R10.		100 Drachmai	RRR

The Bank's right to issue paper money expired in 1920.

(Bank of Crete)

R11.	dates to 1929	10 Drachmai	RRR
R12.		25 Drachmai	RRR
R13.		100 Drachmai	RRR

The Bank of Crete was founded in 1899. Its right to issue paper money expired in 1929.

Occupation Issues

Cassa Mediterranea di Credito per la Grecia (World War II Italian issues for Greece)

M1.	(1940)	5 Dracme, green	$6.50
M2.		10 Dracme, red	7.50
M3.		50 Dracme, blue	10.00
M4.		100 Dracme, brown	10.00
M5.		500 Dracme, dark green	15.00
M6.		1,000 Dracme, light brown	25.00
M7.		5,000 Dracme, lilac	35.00
M8.		10,000 Dracme, grey	50.00

195 × 93

M9.	20,000 Dracme, blue	85.00

Notes previously listed as M10 and M11 have not been verified.

Biglietti a corso legale per le Isole Ionie (Italian issue for the Ionian Islands)

M12.	(1940)	1 Dracma, dark green	4.50
M13.		5 Dracme, red	8.50
M14.		10 Dracme, green	8.50
M15.		50 Dracme, brown	6.50
M16.		100 Dracme, blue	6.50
M17.		500 Dracme, lilac	16.50
M18.		1,000 Dracme, brown	20.00
M19.		5,000 Dracme, blue	10.00

Notes M17–M19 are also known bearing Greek military stamps.

Behelfszahlungsmittel fur die Deutsche Wehrmacht (Emergency Currency for the German Army)

German notes with a German stamp "Saloniki-Agais" and a Greek stamp on the reverse

M20.	1 Pfennig, blue. Same as Germany M32 but stamped	12.50
M21.	5 Pfennig, red. Same as Germany M33 but stamped	18.50
M22.	10 Pfennig, green. Same as Germany M34 but stamped	40.00
M22a.	50 Pfennig, red. Same as Germany M35 but stamped	150.00

(Civil Union for National Freedom) *ΠΟΛΙΤΙΚΗ ΕΠΙΤΡΟΠΗ ΕΘΝΙΚΗΣ*
ΑΠΕΛΕΥΘΕΡΩΣΗΣ

Notes of the Markos Partisans in northern Greece

M23.	5. 6.1944	5 Drachmai, green and light brown. Soldier in middle, burning houses at left, peasants at right	35.00
M24.		25 Drachmai, green and light brown. Type of M23	85.00

M23 is also known with various stampings. It is quite likely that there were issues of 100 and 500 Drachmai denomination.

GREENLAND (Gronland)

The world's largest island, Greenland is an integral part of Denmark.

1 Krone = 100 Ore

Government notes with Copenhagen as place of issue

1.	1888	50 Ore, brown	$175.00
2.	1892	25 Ore, black	100.00
3.	1897	1 Krone, blue	250.00

102 × 68

4.	1905	25 Ore, red	85.00
5.		1 Krone, blue	150.00
6.	(1911)	1 Krone, blue. Note #5 overprinted "Den Kgl. Gronlandske Handel"	RR

Den Kongelige Gronlandske Handel (Royal Greenland Commerce)

7.	1911	25 Ore, red. Bird	20.00
8.		50 Ore, brown. Sea lion	35.00
9.		1 Krone, blue	45.00
10.		5 Kroner, green. Polar bear	50.00

#15
125 × 85

11.	(from 1913)	25 Ore, red. Bird	12.50
12.		50 Ore, brown. Sea lion	25.00
13.		1 Krone, blue	35.00
14.		5 Kroner, green. Polar bear	50.00

Gronlands Styrelse (Government of Greenland)

15.	(from 1926)	5 Kroner, green. Polar bear	
		a. Paper unwatermarked	45.00
		b. Paper watermarked with wavy lines	45.00

132 × 85

16.		10 Kroner, brown. Whale	
		a. Paper unwatermarked	50.00
		b. Paper watermarked with wavy lines	50.00
17.		50 Kroner, lilac. Sailing ship	
		a. Paper unwatermarked	85.00
		b. Paper watermarked with wavy lines	85.00

Den Kongelige Gronlandske Handel (Royal Greenland Commerce)

18.	(from 1953)	5 Kroner, green. Type of #15	40.00
19.		10 Kroner, brown. Type of #16	45.00
20.		50 Kroner, lilac. Type of #17	65.00
21.	16.1.1953	100 Kroner, orange and green blue. K. Rasmussen at left	100.00

Since 1968, only regular Danish notes have been in circulation.

Greenland Administration, Trade Certificates

Notes issued for use by American troops stationed in Greenland during World War II.

Notes M1–M4 are perforated narrow pieces of cardboard with "Grl. Adm" and value.

M1.	1 Ore, brown	12.50
M2.	2 Ore, yellow	12.50
M3.	5 Ore, violet	12.50
M4.	10 Ore, white	20.00

M5.	(1941)	1 Skilling, red. Embossed stamp at left	100.00
M6.		5 Skilling, blue. Embossed stamp at left	125.00
M7.		20 Skilling, green. Embossed stamp at left	125.00
M8.	(1942)	1 Skilling, red. Type of M5 but black stamp at left	50.00
M9.		5 Skilling, blue. Type of M6 but black stamp at left	50.00
M10.		20 Skilling, green. Type of M7 but black stamp at left	50.00

HUNGARY (Magyarorszag)

In 1867, Hungary became a partner in the dual monarchy of the Austro-Hungarian Empire which collapsed at the end of World War I. A republic formed in 1918 was taken over by a communist regime in 1919. In 1920 the kingdom was re-established under the control of a regent. Following World War II, Hungary became a Peoples Republic.

1 Korona = 100 Filler (to 1926)
1 Pengo = 100 Filler (1926–46)
1 Forint = 100 Filler (from 1946)

Except for the special issues of 1914–18 listed below, the paper money used in Hungary was that of Austria-Hungary catalogued under Austria.

Magyar Kiralyi Hadi Kolcsonpenztar-jegy (Kingdom of Hungary, War Loan Office)

1.	27. 9.1914	250 Korona	$100.00
2.		2,000 Korona	100.00
3.		10,000 Korona	100.00

Osztrak-Magyar Bank (Austro-Hungarian Bank)

Non-interest bearing treasury notes of Hungarian branches. Text is printed in Hungarian and there are many date varieties (ended in 1918).

4.	Kolozsvar	1,000 Korona	RRR
5.		5,000 Korona	RRR
6.		10,000 Korona	RRR
7.	Szatmarnemet	1,000 Korona	RRR
8.		5,000 Korona	RRR
9.		10,000 Korona	RRR

Osterreich-Ungarische Bank (Austro-Hungarian Bank)

Notes printed in Budapest in 1919 are variations of the issues regularly printed in Austria.

10.	(1919)	1 Korona, red. Same as Austria #20 but serial number over 7,000. Note dated 1.12.1916	2.25
11.	(1919)	2 Korona, red. Same as Austria #21 but serial number over 7,000. Note dated 1.3.1917	2.25
		Error: Reads "Genenalsekretar"	16.50
12.	(1919)	25 Korona, blue and light brown. Same as Austria #23 but serial number over 3,000. Note dated 27.10.1918. Reverse blank (two control number varieties)	8.50
13.		25 Korona, blue and light brown. Type of #12 but with wavy lines on reverse (three control number varieties)	9.00
14.		200 Korona, green on red brown. Same as Austria #24 but serial numbers to A 2,000	12.50

15.		200 Korona, green on red brown. Type of #14 but serial numbers over A 2,000. Reverse blank	6.50
16.		200 Korona, green on red brown. Type of #15 but with wavy lines on reverse	6.50

Österreich-Ungarische Bank, Treasury Note of the Budapest Branch

| 17. | 3.11.1918 | 200 Korona, Hungarian text (known only as specimens) | RR |

Osztrak-Magyar Bank (Austro-Hungarian Bank)

Notes with a red, stamp-like overprint reading "Magyarorszag" around the Hungarian coat-of-arms were issued as state notes. The seal is upright or turned to the left (less scarce on the 1,000 and 10,000 Korona notes). Notes with seal turned to the right are R.

18.	2.1.1904 (1920)	10 Korona. Dated 2.1.1904. Austria #9 with overprint	15.00
19.		10 Korona. Dated 2.1.1915. Austria #19 with overprint	2.25
20.		20 Korona, Dated 2.1.1913. Austria #13 with overprint	2.25
21.		20 Korona. Dated 2.1.1913, "II Auflage." Austria #14 with overprint	2.25
22.		25 Korona. Dated 27.10.1918. Serial numbers to 3,000. Austria #23 with overprint	18.50
23.		25 Korona. Dated 27.10.1918. Serial numbers over 3,000. Note #12 with overprint	25.00
24.		50 Korona. Dated 2.1.1902. Austria #6 with overprint	150.00
25.		50 Korona. Dated 2.1.1914. Austria #15 with overprint	2.25

163 × 109

26.		100 Korona. Dated 2.1.1910. Austria #11 with overprint	RR
27.		100 Korona. Dated 2.1.1912. Austria #12 with overprint	2.25
28.		200 Korona. Dated 27.10.1918. Serial numbers over A 2,000. Note #15 with overprint	100.00

29.		200 Korona. Dated 27.10.1918. Serial letter B. Austria #24 with overprint	150.00
30.		200 Korona. Dated 27.10.1918. Six digit serial number	150.00
31.		1,000 Korona. Dated 2.1.1902. Austria #8 with overprint	6.50
32.		10,000 Korona. Dated 2.11.1918. Austria #25 with overprint	25.00

Notes #18–32 are known with additional South Slavic or Rumanian stamps. Notes with an unofficial overprint of a Balkan cross in black (#18–23, #25, #27–32) and a Hungarian text stamp of the State Printing Office (#26, #31, #32) are also known.

Magyar Postatakarekpenztar (Hungarian Postal Savings Notes)

33.	1. 5.1919	5 Korona (specimen note, not issued)	
34.	15. 5.1919	5 Korona, blue on green. Man sowing seeds at right. Text reads "Az Osztrak—Magyar Bank Bankjegyeire"	2.50
35.		5 Korona, blue on green. Type of #34 but text reads "Mas Torrenyes Penznemekre"	2.25
36.		10 Korona (specimen, not issued)	RR
37.	15.7.1919	10 Korona, blue on green blue. Woman with cap	2.50
38.		20 Korona, dark blue on olive. Woman's head and two cupids in middle (two control number varieties)	2.40
39.		100 Korona (specimen, not issued)	RR
40.	9. 8.1919	5 Korona (specimen, not issued)	RR
41.		10 Korona, grey blue on brown. Head of woman without cap (three control number varieties)	3.00

143 × 90

42.		20 Korona, dark blue on green and rose. Woman's head and two cupids in middle	3.00
43.	2.10.1920	20 Filler, brown	.40
44.		50 Filler, blue	.40
45.	1. 5.1921	10,000,000 Korona (specimen, not issued)	RR

Magyar Nemzeti Bank (Hungarian National Bank)

Unissued specimen notes

46.	15. 3.1919	50	Korona	RR
47.		1,000	Korona	RR
48.	2. 5.1919	25	Korona	RR
49.	2. 6.1919	2	Korona	RR
50.		20	Korona	RR
51.	1. 8.1919	10	Korona	RR
52.	15. 8.1919	100	Korona	RR
53.		1,000	Korona	RR

Penzugyminiszterium (State Notes of the Finance Ministry)

54.	1920	50	Filler. Round format (unissued proof)	RR
55.		1	Korona. Type of #54	RR
56.		2	Korona. Type of #54	RR
57.	1. 1.1920	1	Korona, blue. Woman's head at right	.40
58.		2	Korona, red. Peasant mowing at right (two control number varieties)	.40
59.		5	Korona (unissued proof)	RR
60.		10	Korona, brown and green. Bridge with city view in middle	.40
61.		20	Korona, green and brown. Church at right (two control number varieties)	.40
62.		50	Korona, brown on yellow brown. Franz Rakoczy at right	.60
63.		100	Korona, brown on light brown. Laureate head of man at right. Format 155 × 100 mm.	.70
64.		100	Korona. Format 119 × 70 mm. (unissued proof)	RR
65.		500	Korona, dark green on olive brown. Helmeted head of man at right	.75
66.		1,000	Korona, dark brown on brown. Head of bearded man at right	1.25
67.		5,000	Korona, dark brown on green and grey. Crowned head of woman at right	2.25
68.		10,000	Korona, dark green and violet. "Patrona Hungariae" at right	3.50
69.	15. 8.1922	25,000	Korona, violet. "Patrona Hungariae" at right	
			a. Paper without silk thread	16.50
			b. Paper with silk thread	75.00
70.		50,000	Korona (unissued proof)	RR
71.	1. 5.1923	50,000	Korona, red. Young man's head at right	
			a. Printed by Orell Fussli	25.00
			b. No printer's imprint	30.00
72.		100,000	Korona, dark blue. Young man's head at right	
			a. Printed by Orell Fussli	50.00
			b. Printed by Magyar Penzjegynyomda	65.00
73.	1. 7.1923	100	Korona, brown. Laureate head of man at right	

#69
212 × 144

73. (Cont.)
a. Printed by Magyar Penzjegynyomda   1.00
b. No printer's imprint   .75

74.   500 Korona, green. Helmeted head of man at right
a. Printed by Magyar Penzjegynyomda   1.50
b. No printer's imprint   1.25

75.   1,000 Korona, dark brown. Head of bearded man at right
a. Printed by Magyar Penzjegynyomda   1.25
b. No printer's imprint   1.25

76.   5,000 Korona, dark brown. Crowned head of woman at right
a. Printed by Magyar Penzjegynyomda   2.00
b. No printer's imprint   2.75

77.   10,000 Korona, dark green. "Patrona Hungariae" at right
a. Printed by Magyar Penzjegynyomda   2.00
b. No printer's imprint   2.75
c. Printed by Orell Fussli   2.40

78.   25,000 Korona, violet. Crowned head of man   25.00

79. 500,000 Korona, violet on brown. Wreathed head of woman at right
a. Printed by Magyar Penzjegynyomda   125.00
b. Printed by Orell Fussli   175.00

#80
184 × 84

80. 4. 9.1923 1,000,000 Korona, blue on green. Wreathed head of
                woman at right
                a. Printed by Magyar Penzjegynyomda   RR
                b. No printer's imprint   RR

A series of notes are believed to have been printed by the authority of the State Bond
Division (5, 10, 50 and 100 million kronen, dated 14.7.1923) but none has ever
been seen.

Currency Reform, 1925: *12,500 old Korona = 1 Pengo*

Notes overprinted with new values

81.   8 Filler on 1,000 Korona. Note #75 overprinted with new
           value
           a. Printed by Magyar Penzjegynyomda   16.50
           b. No printer's imprint   10.00
82.   40 Filler on 5,000 Korona. Note #76 overprinted with new
           value
           a. Printed by Magyar Penzjegynyomda   20.00
           b. No printer's imprint   12.50
83.   80 Filler on 10,000 Korona. Note #77 overprinted with new
           value
           a. Printed by Magyar Penzjegynyomda   25.00
           b. No printer's imprint   25.00
           c. Printed by Orell Fussli   35.00
84.   2 Pengo on 25,000 Korona. Note #78 overprinted with new
           value   65.00
85.   4 Pengo on 50,000 Korona. Note #71 overprinted with new
           value
           a. Printed by Orell Fussli   85.00
           b. No printer's imprint   85.00
86.   8 Pengo on 100,000 Korona. Note #72 overprinted with new
           value
           a. Printed by Orell Fussli   150.00
           b. Printed by Magyar Penzjegynyomda   125.00
87.   40 Pengo on 500,000 Korona. Note #79 overprinted with new
           value
           a. Printed by Magyar Penzjegynyomda   RR
           b. No printer's imprint   RR
88.   80 Pengo on 1,000,000 Korona #80
           a. Printed by Magyar Penzjegynyomda   RRR
           b. No printer's imprint   RRR

Magyar Nemzeti Bank (Hungarian National Bank)

89. 1. 3.1926   5 Pengo, brown. Count Stephan Szechenyi at
                      right   27.50
90.   10 Pengo, green. Franz Deak at right   35.00

91.		20 Pengo, brown on green. Lajos Kossuth at right	45.00
92.		50 Pengo, blue. Franz Rakoczi at right	65.00
93.		100 Pengo, brown lilac. King Mathias at right	90.00

192 × 111

94.	1. 7.1927	1,000 Pengo, blue, green and red. Head of Hungaria at right	200.00
95.	1. 8.1928	5 Pengo, blue. Count Stephan Szechenyi at right	18.50
96.	1. 2.1929	10 Pengo, green. Franz Deak at right	20.00
97.	2. 1.1930	20 Pengo, dark blue. Lajos Kossuth at right	4.50
98.	1. 7.1930	100 Pengo, lilac. King Mathias at right, serial number without *	1.75
99.	1.10.1932	50 Pengo, red brown. Alexander Petofi at right	2.00
100.	22.12.1936	10 Pengo, green. Madonna with Christ child at left, girl's head at right, serial number without *	1.00
101.	15. 1.1938	50 Filler (unissued proof)	RR
102.		1 Pengo, blue on brown. Girl's head at right, serial number without *	2.50
103.		2 Pengo (specimen, not issued)	53.00
104.		5 Pengo, brown on green. Girl's head at right	45.00
105.		20 Pengo on 50 Filler (specimen, not issued)	RR
106.	25.10.1939	5 Pengo, brown. Girl's head at right	3.50
107.		100 Pengo on 5 Pengo (specimen, not issued)	RR
108.	15. 7.1940	2 Pengo, green. Girl's head at right	6.50
109.	15. 1.1941	20 Pengo, blue. Girl in national costume at right	1.00
110.	5. 4.1945	50 Pengo, brown on green. Franz Rakoczy at right	2.50
111.		100 Pengo, lilac. King Mathias at right	2.25

Magyar Nemzeti Bank (Hungarian National Bank)

Issues of the Szalasi regime in Veszprem (1944–45)

112.	1. 7.1930	100 Pengo, lilac. Type of #98 with * in serial number	2.50

160 × 80

113.	22.12.1936	10 Pengo, green. Type of #100 with * in serial number	8.50
114.	15. 1.1938	1 Pengo, blue on brown. Type of #102 with * in serial number	12.50
115.	24. 2.1943	100 Pengo, lilac brown on light brown. Young man with fruit and pigeons at left, girl's head at right	
		a. Both sides printed	65.00
		b. Printed on reverse only	25.00
116.		1,000 Pengo, lilac brown. Head of Hungaria at right	2.50

Magyar Nemzeti Bank (Hungarian National Bank)

Post-war notes in pengo values

117.	15. 5.1945	500 Pengo, blue. Wreathed head of woman at right	1.25
		Error: in reverse text ИЯТЬСОТ	8.50
118.	15. 7.1945	1,000 Pengo, dark green on red brown. Head of woman with flowers at right	
		a. No stamp attached	1.50
		b. With red adhesive stamp attached	1.75
119.		10,000 Pengo, lilac brown on green. Woman's head at right	
		a. No stamp attached	1.25
		b. With brown adhesive stamp attached	1.75

#121

177 × 79

120.	23.10.1945	100,000 Pengo, brown on green blue. Woman in costume at right	1.25
121.		100,000 Pengo, blue. Type of #120	
		a. No stamp attached	150.00
		b. With green adhesive stamp attached	150.00
122.	16.11.1945	1,000,000 Pengo, blue. Lajos Kossuth at right	1.25
123.		10,000,000 Pengo, dark green. Lajos Kossuth at right	1.25
124.	18. 3.1946	100,000,000 Pengo, brown and green. Woman's head with scarf at right	1.25
125.		1,000,000,000 Pengo, lilac and brown. Girl's head at right	1.25

1 Milpengo = 1 Million Pengo

126.	29. 4.1946	10,000 Milpengo, dark blue. Girl's head at right	1.50
127.		100,000 Milpengo, dark green. Woman in costume at right	1.50
128.	24. 5.1946	1,000,000 Milpengo, brown on yellow. Lajos Kossuth at right	1.25
129.		10,000,000 Milpengo, brown on blue. Lajos Kossuth at right	1.25
130.	3. 6.1946	100,000,000 Milpengo, green. Woman's head with cover-cloth at right	1.50
131.		1,000,000,000 Milpengo, blue. Girl's head at right	1.75

1 B.-Pengo = 1,000,000,000 Pengo

132.		10,000 B.-Pengo, brown on lilac. Woman's head at right	1.75
133.		100,000 B.-Pengo, red brown. Woman in costume at right	2.25
134.		1,000,000 B.-Pengo, dark brown. Lajos Kossuth at right	2.50
135.		10,000,000 B.-Pengo, violet. Lajos Kossuth at right	5.30
136.		100,000,000 B.-Pengo, blue. Woman's head with cover cloth at right	8.50
137.		1,000,000,000 B.-Pengo, green. Girl's head at right	16.50

Finance Ministry Notes

1 Adopengo = 2 trillion Pengo (2,000,000,000,000)

138.	25. 5.1946	50,000 (otvenezer) Adopengo, green	
		a. Grey paper with watermark and control numbers	3.50
		b. Grey paper with watermark but no control numbers	4.50
		c. White paper without watermark or control numbers	3.50

139.	500,000 (otszazezer) Adopengo, dark blue	
	a. Grey paper with watermark and control numbers	3.50
	b. White paper without watermark or control numbers	3.50
140.	1 Million (egymillio) Adopengo, red on grey	
	a. Grey paper with watermark and control numbers	3.50
	b. As #140a but arms in background inverted (cross at left)	6.50
	c. White paper without watermark or control numbers	10.00
141.	10 Million (tizmillio) Adopengo, blue on yellow	
	a. White paper without watermark or control numbers	5.00
	b. As #141a but arms in background inverted (cross at left)	10.00
	c. Grey paper with watermark but without control numbers. Arms in background inverted (cross at left)	10.00

134 × 82

142.	100 Million (szazmillio) Adopengo, grey blue on rose	
	a. White paper without watermark or control numbers	5.00
	b. As #142a but arms in background inverted (cross at left)	15.00
143. 28. 5.1946	10,000 (tizezer) Adopengo, brown	
	a. Grey paper with watermark and control numbers. Reverse inscribed "5970/1946 M.E."	3.50
	b. Grey paper with watermark but no control number	3.50
	c. White paper without watermark or control numbers. Reverse inscribed "5600/1946 M.E."	35.00

144.   100,000 (egyszazezer) Adopengo, brown lilac
                        a. Grey paper with watermark and control
                           numbers. Reverse inscribed "5970/1946
                           M.E."   3.50
                        b. Grey paper with watermark but no control
                           numbers   3.50
                        c. As #144a but arms in background in-
                           verted (cross at left)   35.00
                        d. Grey paper with watermark and control
                           numbers. Reverse inscribed "5600/1946
                           M.E."   35.00
                        e. White paper without watermark or control
                           numbers. Reverse inscribed "5600/1946
                           M.E."   10.00

The Finance Ministry decreed that the stamps used on various promissory notes, tax
credits, duties, deeds, judgements, accounts etc. were to circulate as legal tender.

Magyar Nemzeti Bank (Hungarian National Bank)

Notes in forint values

145.	3. 6.1946	10 Forint, green. Young man with hammer at left	20.00
146.		100 Forint, blue. Young woman with sickle and sheaf at left	25.00
147.	27. 2.1947	10 Forint, green. A. Petofi at right	25.00
148.		20 Forint, lilac. G. Dozsa at right	35.00
149.		100 Forint, red brown. Lajos Kossuth at right	25.00
150.	24.10.1949	10 Forint, green. Type of #147 but arms with a star	12.50
151.		20 Forint, blue. Type of #148 but arms with a star	16.50
152.		100 Forint, red brown. Type of #149 but arms with a star	16.50
153.	1. 9.1951	50 Forint, brown. Franz Rakoczy at right	8.50
154.	23.5.1957	10 Forint, green. Type of #150 but arms without hammer and sheaf	6.50
155.		20 Forint, blue. Type of #151 but arms without hammer and sheaf	8.50
156.		100 Forint, red brown. Type of #152 but arms without hammer and sheaf	15.00
157.	24. 8.1960	10 Forint, green. Type of #154 but different signature	—
158.		20 Forint, blue. Type of #155 but different signature	—
159.		100 Forint, red brown. Type of #156 but different signature	—

160.	12.10.1962	10 Forint, green. Type of #157 but different signature	—
161.		20 Forint, blue. Type of #158 but different signature	—
162.		100 Forint, red-brown. Type of #159 but different signature	—
163.	3. 9.1965	20 Forint, blue. Type of #161 but different signatures	—
164.		50 Forint. Type of #153 but different arms	—
165.	24.10.1968	100 Forint, red brown. Type of #162 but different signatures	—
166.	30. 6.1969	10 Forint. Type of #160 but different signatures	—
167.		20 Forint	—
168.		500 Forint	—

Russian Red Army occupation issues of World War II. Many variations of the printing colors exist.

M1.	1944	1 Pengo, blue on brown. Printed area on date side 106 × 49 mm.	
		a. Horizontal waves in background	6.50
		b. Vertical waves in background	6.50

129 × 67

M2.		1 Pengo, blue on brown. Printed area on date side 118 × 54 mm.	
		a. Without control numbers, horizontal waves	1.25
		b. Without control numbers, vertical waves	1.25
		c. With control numbers	45.00
M3.		2 Pengo, blue on green	1.75
M4.		5 Pengo, lilac on light blue	1.75
M5.		10 Pengo, green and lilac	2.00
M6.		20 Pengo, grey	
		a. Without control numbers	50.00
		b. With control numbers (two varieties)	2.40
M7.		50 Pengo, olive (two control number varieties)	2.50
M8.		100 Pengo, dark brown (two control number varieties)	2.50
M9.		1,000 Pengo, red	25.00

ICELAND (Island)

Norwegian refugees settled the island in the 9th century. With the separation of Norway from Denmark in 1814, Iceland elected to remain with Denmark. In 1918 it became a free state under the personal direction of the Danish king. Iceland became an independent republic in 1944.

1 Krone = 100 Aurar

Landssjodur Islands

1.	18. 9.1885	5 Kronur, grey. Profile head of King Christian IX at left	RR
2.		10 Kronur, blue. Type of #1	RR
3.		50 Kronur, grey green and light brown. Type of #1	RRR

120 × 72

4.	18. 9.1885–12. 1.1900	5 Kronur, brown and grey. Facing head of King Christian IX at left	RR
5.		10 Kronur, blue and brown. Type of #4	RR
6.		50 Kronur, grey green and light brown. Head of King Frederick VIII at left	RR
7.		5 Kronur, brown and grey green. Head of King Christian X at left, facing left	RR
8.		10 Kronur, blue and brown. Type of #7	RR
9.		50 Kronur, grey green and light brown. Type of #7	RRR

Islands Banki (Bank of Iceland)

10.	1904	5 Kronur, grey on lilac. King Christian IX at left	$175.00
11.		10 Kronur, dark blue. Type of #10	250.00
12.		50 Kronur, blue and grey. Type of #10	RR
13.		100 Kronur	RRR
14.	1919	100 Kronur, printed on reverse of 5 kronur (#1), blue and grey	RRR

#11
121 × 70

| 15. | 1920 | 5 Kronur, grey on lilac. Geyser at left | 150.00 |
| 16. | | 10 Kronur, dark blue. Landscape and river at left | 250.00 |

Rikissjodur Islands (Government Notes)

17.	18. 9.1885–12. 1.1900	1 Krona, dark blue. Background of circles	25.00
18.		1 Krona, dark blue. Background of double circles	25.00
19.		5 Kronur, brown on green. Type of #7 but with "Fyrir Rikissjod Islands"	150.00
20.		10 Kronur, dark green on green. Type of #8 but with "Fyrir Rikissjod Islands"	175.00
21.		50 Kronur, grey green and light brown. Type of #9 but with "Fyrir Rikissjod Islands"	RR
22.	1941	1 Krona	
		a. Green on greenish paper	15.00
		b. Blue green on white paper	15.00
		c. Blue on white paper	15.00
		d. Blue on yellowish paper	15.00
		e. Light blue on white paper	15.00
		f. Blue violet on white paper	15.00
		g. Brown to dark brown	15.00

Landsbanki Islands (National Bank of Iceland)

All notes have varieties of the signature at right.

23.	15. 4.1928 (Issued 1929)	5 Kronur, brown on green. Type of #19 but with "Landsbanki Islands"	125.00
24.		10 Kronur, dark blue on light blue. Type of #20 but with "Landsbanki Islands"	150.00
25.		50 Kronur, grey green on light brown. Type of #21 but with "Landsbanki Islands"	250.00
26.		100 Kronur, grey blue on grey. King Christian X at left	RR

27.	15. 4.1928 (Issued 1935)	5	Kronur, brown and lilac. Jon Eriksson at left	4.50
28.		10	Kronur, blue. Jon Sigurdsson at left	6.50
29.		50	Kronur, violet. Type of # 27	25.00

151 × 99

30.		100	Kronur, red. Type of #28	50.00
31.		500	Kronur, green. Type of #28	125.00
32.	15. 4.1928 (Issued 1945)	5	Kronur, green. Type of #27	2.25

120 × 70

33.		10	Kronur, red. Type of #28	3.50
34.		50	Kronur, green. Type of #29	12.50
35.		100	Kronur, blue. Type of #30	20.00
36.		500	Kronur, brown. Type of #31	65.00

Landsbanki Islands—Sedlabankinn

37.	21. 6.1957	5	Kronur, red brown. Viking Ingolfur Arnason at left	3.50
38.		10	Kronur, violet brown and green. Jon Eriksson at left	6.50
39.		25	Kronur, violet. Magnus Stephensen at left	8.50
40.		100	Kronur, green blue. Tryggvi Gunnarsson at left	12.50
41.		1,000	Kronur, blue and green. Jon Sigurdsson at right	25.00

Sedlabanki Islands

42.	29. 3.1961	10 Kronur, violet brown and green. Type of #38	—
43.		25 Kronur, violet. Type of #39	—
44.		100 Kronur, green blue. Type of #40	—
45.		500 Kronur, green. Hannes Hafstein at left	—
46.		1,000 Kronur, blue and green. Type of #41	—
47.		5,000 Kronur, brown. Einar Benediktsson at left	—

IRELAND (Eire)

A free state, the Irish Republic was formed in 1921. Northern Ireland remained a part of the United Kingdom.

1 Pound (Punt) = 20 Shillings (Scilling)

Currency Commission—*Coimisiun Airgid Reatha*

All notes show a young Irish girl at the left, with various printing dates from 10.9.1928 to 1942.

1.   10 Shillings, red orange $25.00

151 × 84

2.	1 Pound, green	45.00
3.	5 Pounds, brown	100.00
4.	10 Pounds, blue	175.00
5.	20 Pounds, red	RRR
6.	50 Pounds, violet	RRR
7.	100 Pounds, green	RRR

Currency Commission, Consolidated Bank Notes

A standardized design appears on the notes of all eight "shareholding banks." Only the bank names and signatures vary. All notes show a farmer with a plough and horses. The reverse scenes are different on the various denominations. The issue dates are from 1927 to 1942. The notes circulated until 1953.

Bank of Ireland

8.	1 Pound	16.50
9.	5 Pounds	45.00
10.	10 Pounds	85.00
11.	20 Pounds	250.00
12.	50 Pounds	RR
13.	100 Pounds	RRR

Hibernian Bank

14.	1 Pound	16.50
15.	5 Pounds	45.00
16.	10 Pounds	85.00
17.	20 Pounds	250.00
18.	50 Pounds	RR
19.	100 Pounds	RRR

Munster and Leinster Bank

151 × 83

20.	1 Pound	16.50
21.	5 Pounds	45.00
22.	10 Pounds	85.00
23.	20 Pounds	250.00
24.	50 Pounds	RR
25.	100 Pounds	RRR

National Bank

26.	1 Pound	16.50
27.	5 Pounds	45.00
28.	10 Pounds	85.00
29.	20 Pounds	250.00
30.	50 Pounds	RR
31.	100 Pounds	RRR

Northern Bank

32.	1 Pound	16.50
33.	5 Pounds	45.00
34.	10 Pounds	85.00
35.	20 Pounds	250.00
36.	50 Pounds	RR
37.	100 Pounds	RRR

Provincial Bank of Ireland

38.	1 Pound	16.50

39.	5 Pounds	45.00
40.	10 Pounds	85.00
41.	20 Pounds	250.00
42.	50 Pounds	RR
43.	100 Pounds	RRR

Royal Bank of Ireland

44.	1 Pound	46.50
45.	5 Pounds	45.00
46.	10 Pounds	85.00
47.	20 Pounds	250.00
48.	50 Pounds	RR
49.	100 Pounds	RRR

Ulster Bank

50.	1 Pound	16.50
51.	5 Pounds	45.00
52.	10 Pounds	85.00
53.	20 Pounds	250.00
54.	50 Pounds	RR
55.	100 Pounds	RRR

Central Bank of Ireland—*Banc Ceannais Na Eireann*

Notes are the same as those of the Currency Commission (#1–7) but with "Central Bank of Ireland." Panel at bottom reads "Payable to bearer on demand in London."

138 × 78

56.	dates from 1943	10 Shillings, red orange	8.50
57.		1 Pound, green	12.50
58.		5 Pounds, brown	—
59.		10 Pounds, blue	—
60.		20 Pounds, red	—
61.		50 Pounds, violet	—
62.		100 Pounds, green	—

Notes #63–69 are similar to #56–62 but do not read "Payable in London."

63.	dates from 1962	10 Shillings, red orange	—
64.		1 Pound, green	—
65.		5 Pounds, brown	—
66.		10 Pounds, blue	—
67.		20 Pounds, red	—
68.		50 Pounds, violet	—
69.		100 Pounds, green	—

ITALY (Italia)

King Victor Emmanuel II became king of a unified Italy in 1861. He was followed by Humbert I in 1878 and Victor Emmanuel III who ruled from 1900 until 1946 when Italy became a republic.

1 Lira = 100 Centesimi

Banca d'Italia (Bank of Italy)

The classification of Italian paper money is difficult since several dates appear on most notes—authorization date, dates of various decrees and the actual issue date (the most recent of those on the note). Since arrangement by dates is confusing, the notes have been divided by denomination. Individual listings are based on design differences and variations in the national emblem. The first and last known issue dates are indicated for each type. The following abbreviations refer to the national emblem:

E1. Without national emblem. Reverse text reads "Decreto . . . " (until 18.5.1926).
E2. With fasces emblem (19.5.1926 to 6.8.1943).
E3. With "B.I." (from 7.8.1943).
E4. With head of Italia emblem.
E5. With Medusa head emblem (from 14.8.1947).

The Italian notes are also differentiated by the names of the printing firms, the place of issue "Roma" or "L'Aquila" (1942–44) and the watermarks in the paper. The valuations are for the commonest date and signature variety of each listing.

25 Lire Notes

1. 24. 9.1918–12. 5.1919   25 Lire, brown. Head of Italia at right with eagle above. Paper watermarked with head of Minerva (two signature varieties) $30.00

50 Lire Notes

2. 12. 9.1896– 5. 8.1926   50 Lire, green. Type I with edge imprint, large "L" and woman with three children at left. Female figure on reverse, E1 (five signature varieties)   45.00

Some Italian notes were arranged in sheets with a tall, thin design imprint between pairs of notes. As the notes were separated, the imprint was cut through with a portion remaining on one edge of each note (see left edge of illustration of note #3). The term for this edge imprint is "talon" in German, "matrice" in Italian.

172 × 110

3.	8. 4.1926–17. 3.1936	50 Lire, green. As #2 but reverse E2 (three signature varieties)	20.00
4.	31. 3.1943	50 Lire, green. Type I without edge imprint, large "L" and woman with three children at left. Head of Italia on reverse, E2	12.50
5.	11. 8.1943–30.11.1944	50 Lire, green. As #4 but reverse E3	15.00
6.	16. 6.1915– 4. 1.1920	50 Lire. Type II, seated Italia at right. Farmer with oxen on reverse, E1. Paper watermarked with head of Dante Alighieri (two signature varieties)	65.00
7.	11.10.1933–18. 7.1942	50 Lire, blue violet and yellow brown. Type III, she wolf with Romulus and Remus at right. "Roma" on reverse, E2. Paper watermarked with head of Caesar (two signature varieties)	1.50
8.	28. 2.1942– 6. 8.1943	50 Lire, blue violet and yellow brown. As #7 but with "L'Aquila" on reverse	2.25
9.	23. 8.1943– 1. 2.1944	50 Lire, blue violet and yellow brown. As #7 but reverse E3	2.50
10.	10.12.1944 and 20.4.1946	50 Lire, green. Type IV, head of Italia at left. Paper watermarked with "50" (two signature varieties)	.60

100 Lire Notes

11.	30.10.1897– 6. 3.1926	100 Lire, brown and rose. Type I with edge imprint, large "B" and woman with cupids at left. Reverse E1. Paper watermarked with head of Mercury (four signature varieties)	25.00
12.	18. 6.1926–17.11.1930	100 Lire, brown and rose. As #11 but reverse E2	16.50

13.	2. 2.1926– 4. 5.1926	100 Lire, blue. Type I without edge imprint, large "B" and woman with cupids at left. Reverse E1. Paper watermarked with head of Italia	45.00
14.	8. 8.1926–17.10.1934	100 Lire, blue. As #13 but reverse E2	35.00
15.	9.12.1942–15. 3.1943	100 Lire, brown and rose. As #14 except color	2.50
16.	23. 8.1943–20.12.1944	100 Lire, yellow. As #13 but reverse E3 (two signature varieties)	2.50

185 × 109

17.	5.10.1931–11. 6.1942	100 Lire, olive green and brown. Type II, Roma and she wolf. "Roma" on reverse, E2. Paper watermarked with heads of Italia and Dante (two signature varieties)	.75
18.	28. 8.1942–17. 5.1943	100 Lire, olive green and brown. As #17 but with "L'Aquila" on reverse	1.50
19.	23. 8.1943– 8.10.1943	100 Lire, olive green and brown. As #18 but reverse E.3	4.50
20.	10.12.1944 and 20.4.1946	100 Lire, red. Type III, head of Italia at left. Paper watermarked with "100" (two signature varieties)	.60

500 Lire Notes

21.	25.10.1898–Feb. 1921	500 Lire, rose brown. Type I with edge imprint, oval ornaments with allegorical figures. Reverse E1. Paper watermarked with head of Roma (three signature varieties)	85.00
22.	31. 3.1943	500 Lire, red. Type I without edge imprint, oval ornaments with allegorical figures. Reverse E2	35.00
23.	23. 8.1943–19. 2.1947	500 Lire, red. As #22 but reverse E3 (three signature varieties)	12.50

24.	14.11.1950	500 Lire, red. As #22 but reverse E5	30.00
25.	16. 7.1919–13. 4.1926	500 Lire, lilac and olive brown. Type II, peasant woman with sickle and sheaf at right. Reverse E1. Paper watermarked with head of Leonardo da Vinci	45.00
26.	6.12.1926–23. 3.1942	500 Lire, lilac and olive brown. As #25 but reverse E2 and "Roma" (four signature varieties)	15.00
27.	21.10.1942–17. 5.1943	500 Lire, lilac and olive brown. As #25 but with "L'Aquila" on reverse	16.50
28.	23. 8.1943– 8.10.1943	500 Lire, lilac and olive brown. As #25 but reverse E3	20.00
28a.	10.12.1944	500 Lire. Head of Italia at left (not issued, single specimen known)	—
29.	20. 3.1947–23. 3.1961	500 Lire, lilac and brown. Type III, bust of Italia at left. Paper watermarked with head of Italia (two signature varieties)	2.50

1,000 Lire Notes

30.	6.12.1897–August 1920	1,000 Lire, lilac brown and brown. Type I with edge imprint, large "M" at left. Reverse E1. Paper watermarked with head of Italia at right, "1000" at left (four signature varieties)	125.00
31.	19. 8.1921–13. 4.1926	1,000 Lire, lilac brown and brown. Type I without edge imprint, large "M" at left. Reverse E1. Paper watermarked with head of Italia at right, Banca d'Italia at left	125.00

#32
244
×
148

32.	29. 6.1926– 6. 2.1943	1,000 Lire, lilac brown and brown. As #31 but reverse E2 (four signature varieties)
		16.50
33.	11. 8.1943–12. 7.1947	1,000 Lire, lilac brown and brown. As #31 but reverse E3 (three signature varieties)
		6.50
34.	22.11.1947–14.11.1950	1,000 Lire, lilac brown and brown. As #31 but reverse E5 (two signature varieties)
		8.50
35.	7. 7.1930–15. 3.1943	1,000 Lire, blue and brown. Type II, two seated women (Venice and Genoa). Reverse E2 with "Roma." Paper watermarked with head of Columbus at right, head of Italia at left (three signature varieties)
		16.50
36.	17. 5.1943– 6. 8.1943	1,000 Lire, blue and brown. As #35 but with "L'Aquila" on reverse
		12.50
37.	23. 8.1943– 8.10.1943	1,000 Lire, blue and brown. As #36 but reverse E3
		20.00
37a.	10.12.1944	1,000 Lire, blue. Head of Italia at left (only a few specimens known)
		RRR
38.	20. 3.1947	1,000 Lire, violet and brown. Type III, head of Italia at left, E3. Paper watermarked with head of Italia
		3.50
39.	1948–25.12.1961	1,000 Lire, violet and brown. As #38 but E5 on obverse
		3.50

5,000 Lire Notes

40.	4. 8.1945–12. 7.1947	5,000 Lire, blue. Type I, head of Italia at left and right, "Titoli Provvisori" in background, E4. Paper watermarked with head of Italia
		12.50
41.	8. 9.1947–22.11.1949	5,000 Lire, blue. As #40 but E5 on obverse (two signature varieties)
		10.00
42.	17. 1.1947	5,000 Lire, green and brown. Type II, two seated women (Venice and Genoa) E4. Paper watermarked with head of Dante at left, head of Italia at right
		25.00
43.	1948– 7. 1.1963	5,000 Lire, green and brown. As #42 but E5 on obverse
		20.00

10,000 Lire Notes

44.	4. 8.1945–12. 7.1947	10,000 Lire, red brown. Type I, head of Italia at left and right "Titoli Provvisori" in background, E4. Paper watermarked with head of Italia
		16.50
45.	8. 9.1947–12. 6.1950	10,000 Lire, red brown. As #44 but E5 on obverse (two signature varieties)
		15.00

245
×
125

| 46. | 1948–24. 3.1962 | 10,000 Lire, brown and orange. Type II, two seated women (Venice and Genoa), E5. Paper watermarked with head of Verdi at left, head of Galileo at right | 45.00 |

Biglietti di Stato (State Notes)

47.	17.12.1882	5 Lire, blue. King Umberto I at left (three signature varieties)	8.50
48.	11. 3.1883	10 Lire, blue. King Umberto I at left on obverse and reverse	35.00
49.	5–17.2.1888	10 Lire, blue and light brown. King Umberto I. Numerals only on the reverse (eight signature varieties)	6.50
50.	9–17.5.1895	25 Lire, blue and green. Bust of Italia at left	70.00
51.	23.3–9.4.1902	25 Lire, blue. King Victor Emmanuel III at left	65.00
52.	7–19.10.1904	5 Lire, blue and light brown. King Victor Emmanuel III at right (six signature varieties)	2.50

150 × 98

| 53. | 20. 8.1923 | 25 Lire, brown. Head of Italia at right with eagle above (as #1) | 30.00 |

54.	18. 6.1935	10 Lire, blue. King Victor Emmanuel III at left. On bottom edge:	
		a. 1935	.40
		b. 1938	.40
		c. 1939	.40
		d. 1944	.40
55.	27.10.1939	5 Lire, lilac brown. King Victor Emmanuel III at left. On bottom edge:	
		a. 1940	.40
		b. 1944	.40
56.	14.11.1939	1 Lira, brown. Statue of Caesar Augustus on reverse	.40
57.		2 Lire, blue violet. Statue of Julius Caesar on reverse	.40
58.	23.11.1944	1 Lira, lilac brown. Head of Italia at left (three signature varieties)	.60
59.		2 Lire, green and yellow. Head of Italia at left (three signature varieties)	.60
60.		5 Lire, lilac brown. Helmeted female head at left (three signature varieties)	.70
61.		10 Lire, blue. Head of Jupiter at left (three signature varieties)	.70
62.	31.12.1951	50 Lire, green. Bust of Italia at left (two signature varieties)	.75
63.		100 Lire, lilac brown. Bust of Italia at left (two signature varieties)	.75
64.	31. 3.1966–20. 6.1966	500 Lire, blue and brown. Eagle with serpent at left, head of Arethusa at right	—

Buoni di Cassa (State Notes)

65.	4. 8.1893 (15 or 16.9.1893 on reverse)	1 Lira, brown and green. Head of King Umberto I at left	2.50
66.	21. 2.1894 (22 or 23.2.1894 on reverse)	2 Lire, blue and brown. Head of King Umberto I at left	3.50
67.	22. 7.1894 (15 or 16.9.1893 on reverse)	1 Lira, brown and green. Head of King Umberto I at left	4.50
68.	18. 8.1914 (19 or 20.8.1914 on reverse)	1 Lira, brown on blue. Head of King Victor Emmanuel at left (three signature varieties)	2.25

69
82 × 46

69.		2 Lire, brown on light brown. Head of King Victor Emmanuel at left (three signature varieties)	2.25

Allied Military Currency

70.	1943	1 Lira, blue and brown	.75
71.		2 Lire, lilac and brown	.75
72.		5 Lire, green and brown	1.00
73.		10 Lire, black and brown	1.75
74.		50 Lire, blue	3.50
75.		100 Lire, lilac and blue	6.50
76.		500 Lire, green and blue	45.00
77.		1,000 Lire, black and blue	85.00

Notes # 70—77 exist both with and without "F" for the Forbes printing firm.

78.	1943A	5 Lire, green and brown	1.25
79.		10 Lire, black and brown	1.75
80.		50 Lire, blue	3.00
81.		100 Lire, lilac and blue	5.00

155 × 66

82.		500 Lire, green and blue	12.50
83.		1,000 Lire, black and blue	35.00

Banca d'Italia (Bank of Italy new types)

84.	3. 7.1962–12. 4.1962	10,000 Lire, brown, violet and lilac. Head of Michaelangelo at right	—
85.	14. 7.1962–28. 6.1962	1,000 Lire, blue, red and brown. Head of Giuseppe Verdi at right	—
86.	3. 9.1964–20. 8.1964	5,000 Lire, green and red. Head of Christopher Columbus at right	—
87.	3. 7.1967–27. 6.1967	50,000 Lire, brown and green. Head of Leonardo da Vinci at right	—
88.		100,000 Lire, brown. Head of Alessandro Manzoni at right	—
89.	25. 3.1969–26. 2.1969	1,000 Lire, blue and lilac. Head of Giuseppe Verdi at right. Paper with metallic fibres	—
90.	10. 5.1971–15. 5.1971	5,000 Lire, olive green. Christopher Columbus at right, mythical animal at left	—

Austrian occupation of Venice, 1918

Cassa Veneta dei Prestiti, Buoni di Cassa (Treasury Bills)

M1.	2. 1.1918	5 Centesimi, blue	.40
M2.		10 Centesimi, light brown	.40
M3.		50 Centesimi, red	.40
M4.		1 Lira, lilac (two control number varieties)	.75
M5.		2 Lire, green (three control number varieties)	1.25
M6.		10 Lire, blue (two control number varieties)	3.00
M7.		20 Lire, carmine (two control number varieties)	4.50

151 × 104

M8.	100 Lire, brown and green	10.00
M9.	1,000 Lire, brown	60.00

Banco di Napoli (Bank of Naples)

All notes read "Legge 10. Agosto 1893"

173 × 95

R1.	15. 7.1896	50 Lire, green. Woman with Mercury staff and book (Industry) at right (also with date 22.10.1903)	125.00
R2.	30. 6.1896	100 Lire, red brown. Woman with sickle and produce (Agriculture) at right (also with date 20.10.1903)	150.00

R3.	15. 6.1896	500 Lire, grey green and violet. Head of Leonardo da Vinci at left (also with dates 22.10.1903 and 20.7.1906)	250.00
R4.	1–2.3.1896	1,000 Lire, brown and blue. Head of Galileo Galilei at left (also with date 22.10.1903)	RRR
R5.	17. 8.1918	25 Lire, grey. Arms at left (also with date 4.6.1919)	125.00
R6.	30.12.1909	50 Lire, black and brown. Head of Salvator Rosa at left (also with dates 23.2.1911; 13.12.1914; 31.5.1915; 24.12.1917 and 16.8.1921)	35.00
R7.	10.11.1908	100 Lire, dark blue. Head of Torquato Tasso at left (also with dates 23.2.1911; 13.12.1914; 31.5.1915; 24.12.1917; 7.9.1918; 15.1.1921 and 16.8.1921)	35.00
R8.	7.12.1909	500 Lire, black on olive. Head of Gaetano Filangeri at left (also with dates 23.2.1911; 13.12.1914; 31.5.1915; 14.8.1917; 24.12.1917; 7.9.1918; 1.5.1919; 30.1.1920; 15.1.1921 and 16.8.1921)	75.00
R9.	7.12.1909	1,000 Lire. Head of Giambattista Vico at left (also with dates 23.2.1911; 13.12.1914; 31.5.1915; 14.8.1917; 24.12.1917; 24.12.1917; 7.9.1918; 1.5.1919; 30.1.1920; 15.1.1921 and 16.8.1921)	150.00

The bank's right to print paper money expired in 1926.

Banco di Sicilia (Bank of Sicily)

All notes read "Legge 10. Agosto 1893"

R10.	21. 2.1918	25 Lire, grey green. Statue of "Palermo" at left (also with date 6.8.1918)	85.00

R12
204 × 115

R11. 27. 4.1897   50 Lire, violet and brown. Statue of "Palermo" at
                          left (also with dates 8.12.1898; 18.12.1901;
                          27.12.1909; 16.12.1911; 24.12.1913; 18.5.1915;
                          22.6.1915;   24.12.1917;   30.5.1919   and
                          19.4.1920)   45.00
R12. 30.12.1896   100 Lire, blue. Statue of "Palermo" at left (also
                          with dates 18.12.1901; 27.12.1909; 24.12.1913;
                          18.5.1915; 22.6.1915; 24.12.1917; 30.5.1919
                          and 19.4.1920)   65.00
R13. 24.12.1897   500 Lire, red and blue. Statue of "Palermo" at
                          left (also with dates 18.12.1901; 27.12.1909;
                          24.12.1913; 18.5.1915; 22.6.1915; 24.12.1917;
                          22.3.1918; 30.5.1919; 19.4.1920; 23.5.1921)   150.00
R14. 15. 9.1897   1,000 Lire, brown and red. Statue of "Palermo" at
                          left (also with dates 18.12.1901; 27.12.1909;
                          24.12.1913; 18.5.1915; 22.6.1915; 24.12.1917;
                          30.5.1919; 12.4.1920; 19.4.1920 and 23.5.1921)   RR

The bank's right to print paper money expired in 1926.

During the period 1943–45, many notes were issued by partisan groups such as the
Garibaldi Brigade, Osoppo Brigade, Comitato Liberazione Ligure, etc. All of these
notes are RRR and seldom seen.

LATVIA (Latvija)

Latvia was under Russian control from 1772 until 1918 when it became an independent republic. In 1940 Latvia became part of the Union of Soviet Socialist Republics. During World War II, the country was first occupied by Russian troops, then by the Germans and finally retaken by the Russians.

1 Ruble = 100 Kapeikas
1 Lats = 100 Santimu

Notes of the western Volunteer Army of Col. Avalov-Bermondt circulated in Latvia during 1919 (see Russia R97 through R101).

Latwijas Walstskases Sihmes (State Bank Notes)

Notes in ruble values, many control number varieties

1.	1919	1 Ruble, blue and brown. Paper watermarked with waves	$5.00
2.		1 Ruble, light and dark green	
		a. Paper watermarked with waves	2.50
		b. Paper watermarked with light lines	1.75
3.		5 Rubles, light and dark blue. Woman's head in middle	
		a. Paper watermarked with waves	7.50
		b. Paper watermarked with light lines (three signature varieties)	5.00

129 × 82

4.	1919	10 Rubles, red brown and green. Sailing ship in middle	
		a. Paper watermarked with waves	6.50
		b. Paper watermarked with light lines (three signature varieties)	4.50
5.		25 Rubles, brown. Three stylized sheafs of produce on reverse	
		a. Paper watermarked with multiple waves	45.00
		b. Paper watermarked with stars	12.50
		c. Paper watermarked with light lines (two signature varieties)	10.00

6.		50 Rubles, green on grey	25.00
		Excellent Russian counterfeits exist.	
7.		100 Rubles, brown and dark brown. Oak tree on reverse (three signature varieties)	20.00
8.	1920	500 Rubles, light and dark green. Symbols of Agriculture, Industry and Shipping on reverse	
		a. Paper watermarked with light lines (two signature varieties)	85.00
		b. Paper watermarked with multiple waves	50.00
		Excellent Russian counterfeits exist.	

Latwijas Mainas Sihmes (Exchange Notes)

9.	(1920)	5 Kapeikas, red	.75
10.		10 Kapeikas, blue	.75
11.		25 Kapeikas, brown	.75
12.		50 Kapeikas, violet	.75
		Reverse inverted	8.50

Latvijas Bankas (Bank of Latvia)

13.	1920	10 Latu on 500 rubles. Red overprint on #8b	45.00
14.	1923	100 Latu, blue. Two seated women in national costumes on reverse (two signature varieties)	85.00
15.	1924	20 Latu, yellow, orange and grey. Peasant sowing seeds	RRR
		In circulation for very short time.	
16.		50 Latu, green and brown. Daugava river and city of Riga	175.00
17.	1925	20 Latu, black on yellow and green. President J. Cakste	18.50
18.	1928	25 Latu, black on yellow. K. Valdemars in middle	15.00

188 × 104

19.	1929	500 Latu, blue and brown. Girl in national costume at right	35.00
20.	1934	50 Latu, blue. Prime Minister K. Ulmanis	7.50
21.	1938	25 Lati, green. Folk hero Lacplesis the Bear-killer at right	10.00

155 × 80

22.   1939   100 Latu, red. Peasant family   10.00

Latvijas Valsts Kases Zimes (State Treasury Notes)

Notes in Lat values

23.	1925	10 Latu, red brown. Oaks and grain field (five signature varieties)	25.00
24.	1926	5 Lati, brown. Symbols of Commerce and Shipping on reverse	85.00
25.	1933	10 Latu, blue green. Seated woman in national costume on reverse	15.00
26.	1934	10 Latu, blue green. Type of #25 (three signature varieties)	16.50
27.	1935	20 Latu, brown. Riga castle	6.50
28.	1936	20 Latu, brown. Type of #27	6.50
29.	1937	10 Latu, dark brown and multicolored. Fisherman with net	4.50
30.	1938	10 Latu, dark brown and multicolored. Type of #29	4.50
31.	1939	10 Latu, dark brown and multicolored. Type of #29	4.50
32.	1940	10 Latu, dark brown and multicolored. Type of #29	6.50
33.		20 Latu, blue. Academy of Agriculture in Jelgava	200.00

140 × 75

Latvijas Valsts Kases Mainas Zimes (State Treasury Exchange Notes)

34.   1940   5 Lati, blue, grey and brown. Bridge over the Gauja River (two signature varieties)   12.50

The following notes exist with the apparently unofficial overprint "Latvija 1941, 1. Julijs:"

5 Lati, 1940 (#34)
10 Latu, 1937 (#29)
20 Latu, 1940 (#33)
100 Latu, 1939 (#22)
500 Latu, 1929 (#19)

Latgales Partizanu Pulks (Latgalian Partisan Regiments)

Russian notes stamped:

a. "Latgales Partizanu Pulks 2 Rotas Komandeers"
b. "Latgales Partizanu Pulks 3 Rotas Komandcers"

M1.   20 Rubles (1917 issue), stamp b
M2.   250 Rubles (1917 issue), stamp a
M3.   10 Rubles (1918 issue), stamp b
M4.   25 Rubles (1918 issue), stamp b
M5.   50 Rubles (1918 issue), stamp b
M6.   100 Rubles (1918 issue), stamp a
M7.   100 Rubles (1918 issue), stamp b
M8.   500 Rubles (1918 issue), stamp b
M9.   15 Rubles (undated issue, 1919), stamp a
M10.   15 Rubles (undated issue, 1919), stamp b
M11.   60 Rubles (undated issuc, 1919), stamp a
M12.   60 Rubles (undated issuc, 1919), stamp b
M13. 250 Rubles (1919 issue), stamp a
M14. 250 Rubles (1919 issue), stamp b

In the past few years many counterfeit overprints have been noted. Genuine notes are R to RRR.

LIECHTENSTEIN

A Principality since 1719, Liechtenstein left the German Confederation and associated itself with Austria through a customs union and defense treaty (1852–1919). In 1924, a customs union was established with Switzerland which is still in effect.

1 Krone = 100 Heller (to 1924)

1. (1920)   10 Heller, red and blue $1.00

71 × 45

2.   20 Heller, red and blue   1.00
3.   50 Heller, red and blue   1.00

LITHUANIA (Lietuva)

Along with Poland, Lithuania came under Russian control in 1795. In 1918 it was declared an independent republic but in 1940 the country was occupied by Russian troops, later by the Germans. At the end of World War II, Lithuania became a part of the Union of Soviet Socialist Republics.

1 Litas = 100 Centu

From 1919 to 1922 the notes of the Eastern German State Loan Office circulated in Lithuania. They were known as "Auksinas" and "Skatikas" after their inscriptions (see Germany R120–R134, also Memel).

Lietuvos Bankas (Bank of Lithuania)

80 × 53

1.	10. 9.1922	1 Centas, blue	$5.00
2.		5 Centai, green	5.00
3.		20 Centu, brown	8.50
4.		50 Centu, violet	15.00
5.		1 Litas, dark green	
		a. Paper watermarked with braids	25.00
		b. Paper watermarked with knots	30.00
6.		5 Litai, dark brown	50.00
7.	16.11.1922	1 Centas, blue and wine red	6.50
8.		2 Centu, dark green on grey violet	6.50
9.		5 Centai, blue on green	6.50
10.		10 Centu, brown on grey violet	6.50
11.		20 Centu, dark blue on grey	10.00
12.		50 Centu, violet and green	15.00
13.		1 Litas, brown on grey	20.00
14.		2 Litu, blue on grey	25.00
15.		5 Litai, blue, violet, brown and dark green. Peasant sowing seed in middle. Control number in black	35.00
16.		5 Litai, olive green, blue and black. Type of #15 but slight variations in the ornamentation. Control number in red	30.00
17.		5 Litai, brown and dark grey. Type of #16	45.00

18.		10 Litu, blue, yellow brown and dark green. Raftsman at right	65.00
19.		50 Litu, dark green and brown. Bust of Grand Duke Gediminas of Lithuania at right	125.00
20.		100 Litu, blue and violet. Bust of Grand Duke Vytautas the Great	250.00

198 × 92

21.	11.12.1924	500 Litu, brown	RR
22.		1,000 Litu, grey and dark blue. Girl in Lithuanian national costume at left, seated youth at right	RR
23.	24.11.1927	10 Litu, green. Peasant working in field at right	25.00
24.	31. 3.1928	50 Litu, dark blue. Head of Dr. J. Basanavicins at left	25.00
25.		100 Litu, dark violet, Seated woman at left, boy with Mercury staff at right	45.00
26.	24. 6.1929	5 Litai, brown. Head of Grand Duke Vytautas the Great	18.50
27.	5. 7.1930	20 Litu, brown. Grand Duke Vytautas the Great at left, Vytautas Church in middle	25.00
28.	1938	10 Litu, green and orange. Portrait of President A. Smetona at left	RR

LUXEMBOURG (Letzeburg)

The 1815 Congress of Vienna joined the Grand Duchy of Luxembourg in personal union with the Netherlands. The Grand Duchy remained a member of the German Confederation until 1866. After dissolution of the union with the Netherlands, Luxembourg was ruled by the House of Nassau: Adolf 1890–1905; Wilhelm 1905–12; Marie Adelaide 1912–19; Charlotte 1919–64; Jean 1964– . Luxembourg joined in a customs union with Belgium in 1922.

1 Taler = 30 Groschen
1 Mark = 100 Pfennig
1 Franc = 100 Centimes

Banque Internationale à Luxembourg (International Bank in Luxembourg)

1.	1. 9.1856	10 Taler, yellow. Seated woman with three cupids on reverse	RRR
2.		25 Francs = 20 Mark, yellow. Type of #1	RRR
3.		100 Francs = 80 Mark, yellow. Type of #1	RRR

An issue in Dutch gulden was authorized but no notes were issued.

4.	1. 7.1900	20 Mark, blue, brown and multicolored. Mill and foundry worker at left	RR
5.		50 Mark, green and red brown. Miner at left, peasant at right	RR
6.	5. 8.1914	1 Mark, blue	$65.00
7.		2 Mark, brown	125.00
8.		5 Mark, blue	250.00
9.	10. 2.1923	100 Francs, yellow and blue. City of Luxembourg. Vianden Castle on reverse	150.00
10.	18.12.1930	100 Francs. Type of #9	100.00

#11
183 × 109

11.	1. 8.1936	100 Francs. Type of #9	85.00
12.	15. 5.1947	100 Francs, brown and blue. Grand Duchess Charlotte. Peasant woman at left, man at right	25.00
13.	21. 4.1956	100 Francs, dark green. Grand Duchess Charlotte. Peasant woman at left, man at right	16.50
14.	1. 5.1968	100 Francs, green blue and blue on multicolor. Grand Duke Jean at right	—

Die Grossherzoglich Luxemburgische Nationalbank (National Bank of the Grand Duchy of Luxembourg)

15.	1. 7.1873	5 Taler	RRR

139 × 94

16.		10 Taler	RRR
17.		20 Taler	RRR
18.	25. 3.1876	5 Mark	RRR
19.		10 Mark	RRR
20.		20 Mark	RRR

Bon de Caisse (State Treasury Notes)

21.	28.11.1914	1 Frank = 80 Pfennig, blue background	12.50
22.		2 Franken = 1 Mark 60 Pfennig, rose and green background	20.00
23.		5 Franken = 4 Mark, brown violet and green	30.00
24.		25 Franken = 20 Mark, violet and green	75.00
25.		125 Franken = 100 Mark	150.00
26.	28.11.1914– 11.12.1918 (issued 1919)	50 Centimes, lilac and violet background	6.50
27.		1 Franc, blue background	8.50
28.		2 Francs, rose and green background	12.50
29.		5 Francs, brown violet and green	20.00
30.		25 Francs, violet and green	65.00
31.		125 Francs	125.00
32.		500 Francs. Rose underprinting	RR
33.	(1919)	10 Francs. Woman with Mercury staff at left, woman with hammer and tongs at right (specimen note, not issued)	RR

| 34. | (1923) | 10 Francs, blue. Peasant woman at left, worker at right. Grand Duchess Charlotte at left on reverse | 50.00 |

150 × 78

35.	28.11.1914– 11.12.1918 (issued 1926)	20 Francs, violet and green. Grand Duchess Charlotte with buildings at left and right on reverse	65.00
36.	(1927)	100 Francs. Grand Duchess Charlotte at left. Twelve coats-of-arms on reverse	85.00
37.	1.10.1929	20 Francs, blue. Grapes. Peasant plowing on reverse	12.50
38.	1.10.1932	50 Francs, green blue. Grand Duchess Charlotte at right. Palace in Luxembourg on reverse	10.00
39.	(1934)	100 Francs, green reverse. Grand Duchess Charlotte at left. Seated woman with globe and anvil on reverse	16.50
40.	1. 9.1939 (issued 1940)	1,000 Francs, dark brown and green. Arms in middle	RR
41.	20. 4.1940	10 Frang. Man's head at left	RR
42.	1943	20 Frang. Grand Duchess Charlotte. Peasant with sickle and sheaf at left on reverse	6.50
43.	(1944)	5 Francs, olive green. Grand Duchess Charlotte in middle. Printed by American Bank Note Company	4.50
44.		10 Francs, violet. Type of #43	6.50
45.		50 Frang, dark green. Grand Duchess Charlotte. Vianden castle on reverse. Text overprinted with guilloche ornament	16.50

#47
184 × 108

46.		50 Frang, dark green. Type of #45 but no text at bottom of reverse and no guilloche	5.00
47.		100 Francs, blue. Reverse brown. Type of #39	12.50
48.	(1954)	10 Francs, green. Grand Duchess Charlotte at right. Vianden castle on reverse	3.50
49.	(1955)	20 Francs, blue. Grand Duchess Charlotte at right. View of Mosel river and village of Ehnen	4.50
50.	15. 6.1956	100 Francs, red brown. Grand Duchess Charlotte at right. Industrial plant on reverse	12.50
51.	6. 2.1961	50 Francs, dark brown. Grand Duchess Charlotte. Landscape on reverse	4.50
52.	18. 9.1963	100 Francs, red brown. Grand Duchess Charlotte. Foliage on reverse	8.50
53.	7. 3.1966	20 Francs, blue. Grand Duke Jean	—
54.	20. 3.1967	10 Francs, green. Grand Duke Jean	—
55.	15. 7.1970	100 Francs, red. Grand Duke Jean	—
56.	25. 8.1972	50 Francs, dark brown. Grand Duke Jean	—

MALTA

A group of three Mediterranean islands between Sicily and Africa. Under British control from 1800, Malta became an independent republic in 1964.

1 Pound = 20 Shillings
1 Shilling = 12 Pence

Banco Anglo-Maltese

1.	(circulated during the 1920's)	1 Pound	RRR
2.	(circulated during the 1920's)	5 Pounds	RRR

Notes of the Bank of Malta circulated until 1886.

Government of Malta

3.	12. 8.1914	10 Shillings	$100.00
4.	13. 8.1914	5 Shillings	77.00
5.	14. 8.1914	5 Pounds	175.00
6.		10 Pounds	RRR
7.	20. 8.1914	1 Pound	125.00
8.	4. 9.1914	5 Shillings	65.00
9.	14. 9.1914	1 Pound	100.00
10.	20.11.1918	2 Shillings, green on light blue. King George V at right (not issued, see #11)	175.00

Malta did not have notes of its own from 1919 until 1939. Regular British notes were used in circulation.

120 × 70

11.	20.11.1918 (issued 1939/40)	1 Shilling on 2 shillings, green on light blue. Note #10 with red overprint of new value	35.00
12.	13. 9.1939 (date stamped)	2 Shillings 6 pence (2/6), lilac and blue. King George VI at right	10.00
13.		5 Shillings, green and red. King George VI at right	12.50

14.		10 Shillings, blue, lilac and olive. King George VI at right	16.50
15.		1 Pound. King George VI at right	25.00
16.	(1940)	1 Shilling, violet and lilac. King George VI in middle	6.50
17.		2 Shillings, brown and green. King George VI at right	8.50
18.		2 Shillings 6 Pence (2/6), lilac and blue. King George VI at right	10.00
19.		10 Shillings, blue, lilac and olive. King George VI at right	12.50
20.		1 Pound. King George VI at right	30.00
21.	1949	10 Shillings, green. King George VI at right	8.50

140 × 75

22.		1 Pound, brown. King George VI at right, cross at left	18.50
23.		10 Shillings, green. Queen Elizabeth II at right, cross at left	12.50
24.		1 Pound, brown. Queen Elizabeth II at right, cross at left	16.50
25.		10 Shillings, green, blue and multicolored. Queen Elizabeth II at right, cross in middle	10.00
26.		1 Pound, brown, lilac and multicolored. Queen Elizabeth II at right, cross in middle	12.50
27.		5 Pounds, blue and multicolored. Queen Elizabeth II at right, cross in middle	35.00

Central Bank of Malta

28.	1967	10 Shillings, red and multicolored. Type of #25	—
29.		1 Pound, green and multicolored. Type of #26	—
30.		5 Pounds, brown violet and multicolored. Type of # 27	—

Bank Centrali ta Malta

31.	1967	1 Lira, green. Arms at right, "Fiducia Fortis 1968"	—
32.		5 Liri, blue	—
33.		10 Liri, brown	—

MEMEL

In 1920 Memel separated from Germany and became an autonomous district under the administration of the League of Nations. The district was seized by Lithuania in 1923.

Handelskammer des Memelgebiets (Chamber of Commerce of the District of Memel)

Notes approved by the Interallied Commission

1.	22.2.1922	½ Mark, lilac. Lake on reverse	$2.25
2.		1 Mark, brown. Narrow strip of land on reverse	3.00
3.		2 Mark, blue and olive brown. View of Memel in 1630 on reverse	
		a. Paper watermarked with single-line chain	3.75
		b. Paper watermarked with double-line chain	3.75
4.		5 Mark, blue and yellow. View of market place on reverse	
		a. Paper watermarked with single-line chain	4.50
		b. Paper watermarked with double-line chain	4.50
5.		10 Mark, yellow brown and blue. Lighthouse on reverse	
		a. Paper watermarked with single-line chain	5.00
		b. Paper watermarked with double-line chain	5.00
6.		20 Mark, lilac and violet. Peasant house on reverse	
		a. Paper watermarked with single-line chain	6.50
		b. Paper watermarked with double-line chain	6.50

165 × 111

7.		50 Mark, brown on green and violet. Buoy in harbor on reverse	
		a. Paper watermarked with single-line chain	8.50
		b. Paper watermarked with double-line chain	8.50
8.		75 Mark, brown on blue and rose. Old and new sawmills on reverse	10.00
9.		100 Mark, blue and light brown. View of Memel	12.50

MONACO

Annexed by the French in 1793, the ruling Grimaldi family was restored in 1814. Monaco entered into a customs union with France in 1869.

1 Franc = 100 Centimes

1.	16.3.(20.3.)1920	25 Centimes, brown	$10.00
2.		25 Centimes, blue violet	6.50
3.		50 Centimes, blue grey	12.50

109 × 70

4.	1 Franc, brown. Thin paper	20.00
5.	1 Franc, blue grey and brown. Thicker paper	16.50

MONTENEGRO

This Balkan country became an independent principality in 1878 under Nicholas (1860–1918) who took the title of king in 1910. During World War I, Montenegro was occupied by Austrian troops and in 1918 it was merged with Serbia in the Kingdom of the Serbs, Croats and Slovenes (Yugoslavia).

1 Perper = 100 Para

(Treasury Notes) ГЛАВНА ДРЖАВНА БЛАГАЈНА

First Issue, dated 1912

1.	1.10.1912	1 Perper, blue	$3.50
2.		2 Perpera, lilac	3.75
3.		5 Perpera, green	6.50
4.		10 Perpera, brown	10.00
5.		50 Perpera, blue on brown	175.00
6.		100 Perpera	RR
7.	25. 7.1914	1 Perper, blue. Note #1 with red overprint of new date	4.50
8.		2 Perpera, lilac. Note #2 with red overprint of new date	6.50

Specimens of notes #1–8 pierced with large holes to cancel them are worth only 20% of the above prices.

Second Issue, dated 1914

Arms in middle on both sides. All notes are 155 × 107 mm. Prices are for notes without stamps.

9.	25. 7.1914	5 Perpera, blue	3.50
10.		10 Perpera, red	4.50

155 × 107

11.		20 Perpera, brown	8.50

12.		50 Perpera, olive	12.50
13.		100 Perpera, light brown	20.00
14.	11. 8.1914	100 Perpera, light brown (probably a trial note only)	RR

Third Issue, dated 1914. Arms in middle of all reverses. Prices are for notes without stamps.

15.	25.7.1914	1 Perper, blue (format 135 × 97 mm)	2.25
16.		2 Perpera, brown (format 135 × 97 mm)	2.50
17.		5 Perpera, red (format 135 × 97 mm)	3.00
18.		10 Perpera, blue. Arms above left (format 160 × 105 mm)	3.75
19.		20 Perpera, brown. Type of #18 (format 160 × 105 mm)	7.50
20.		50 Perpera, red. Two women with cornucopias and man plowing (format 186 × 110 mm)	8.50

186 × 110

| 21. | | 100 Perpera, blue. Type of #20 (format 186 × 110 mm) | 12.50 |

Austrian Military Government 1916–18

Notes #9–13 and #15–21 overprinted "K.u.K. Militar-Generalgouvernement in Montenegro, Kreiskommando (and place name)." Stamped in black, red or violet.

M1.	Stamped "Cetinje"	5 Perpera, second issue	2.25
	(place name 11 mm)	10 Perpera, ,, ,,	2.50
M3.		20 Perpera, ,, ,,	3.50
M4.		50 Perpera, ,, ,,	2.50
M5.		100 Perpera, ,, ,,	5.00
M6.		1 Perper, third issue	1.25
M7.		2 Perpera, ,, ,,	1.25
M8.		5 Perpera, ,, ,,	1.25
M9.		10 Perpera, ,, ,,	1.75
M10.		20 Perpera, ,, ,,	2.25
M11.		50 Perpera, ,, ,,	2.50
M12.		100 Perpera, ,, ,,	3.50
M13.	Stamped "Cetinje"	5 Perpera, second issue	1.75
	(place name 16 mm)		

M14.		10 Perpera, " "		2.25
M15.		20 Perpera, " "		2.50
M16.		50 Perpera, " "		2.25
M17.		100 Perpera, " "		4.50
M18.		1 Perper, third issue		.75
M19.		2 Perpera, " "		.75
M20.		5 Perpera, " "		.75
M21.		10 Perpera, " "		1.25
M22.		20 Perpera, " "		1.75
M23.		50 Perpera, " "		2.25
M24.		100 Perpera, " "		3.00
M25.	Stamped "Ipek"	5 Perpera, second issue		2.50
M26.		10 Perpera, " "		3.50
M27.		20 Perpera, " "		4.50
M28.		50 Perpera, " "		5.00
M29.		100 Perpera, " "		10.00
M30.		1 Perper, third issue		1.75
M31.		2 Perpera, " "		1.75
M32.		5 Perpera, " "		1.75
M33.		10 Perpera, " "		2.25
M34.		20 Perpera, " "		3.00
M35.		50 Perpera, " "		3.50
M36.		100 Perpera, " "		4.50
M37.	Stamped "Kolasin"	5 Perpera, second issue		3.00
M38.		10 Perpera, " "		3.75
M39.		20 Perpera, " "		5.00
M40.		50 Perpera, " "		6.50
M41.		100 Perpera, " "		16.50
M42.		1 Perper, third issue		1.25
M43.		2 Perpera, " "		1.25
M44.		5 Perpera, " "		1.25
M45.		10 Perpera, " "		1.75
M46.		20 Perpera, " "		2.25
M47.		50 Perpera, " "		2.50
M48.		100 Perpera, " "		3.50
M49.	Stamped "Nicsic"	5 Perpera, second issue		3.00
M50.	(place name 11 mm)	10 Perpera, " "		3.75
M51.		20 Perpera, " "		5.00
M52.		50 Perpera, " "		6.50
M53.		100 Perpera, " "		16.50
M54.		1 Perper, third issue		1.75
M55.		2 Perpera, " "		2.25
M56.		5 Perpera, " "		2.25
M57.		10 Perpera, " "		2.50
M58.		20 Perpera, " "		3.00
M59.		50 Perpera, " "		4.50
M60.		100 Perpera, " "		4.50
M61.	Stamped "Nicsic"	5 Perpera, second issue		2.25
M62.	(place name 14 mm)	10 Perpera, " "		2.50
M63.		20 Perpera, " "		4.50

M64.		50 Perpera, ,, ,,	4.50
M65.		100 Perpera, ,, ,,	10.00
M66.		1 Perper, third issue	1.25
M67.		2 Perpera, ,, ,,	1.75
M68.		5 Perpera, ,, ,,	1.75
M69.		10 Perpera, ,, ,,	2.25
M70.		20 Perpera, ,, ,,	2.25
M71.		50 Perpera, ,, ,,	2.50
M72.		100 Perpera, ,, ,,	3.50
M73.	Stamped "Pljevlje"	5 Perpera, second issue	2.50
M74.		10 Perpera, ,, ,,	3.50
M75.		20 Perpera, ,, ,,	4.50
M76.		50 Perpera, ,, ,,	5.00
M77.		100 Perpera, ,, ,,	15.00
M78.		1 Perper, third issue	1.25
M79.		2 Perpera, ,, ,,	1.25
M80.		5 Perpera, ,, ,,	1.25
M81.		10 Perpera, ,, ,,	1.75
M82.		20 Perpera, ,, ,,	2.25
M83.		50 Perpera, ,, ,,	2.50
M84.		100 Perpera, ,, ,,	3.50
M85.	Stamped "Podgorica"	5 Perpera, second issue	3.00
M86.	(small letters, 13 mm)	10 Perpera, ,, ,,	3.75
M87.		20 Perpera, ,, ,,	5.00
M88.		50 Perpera, ,, ,,	6.50
M89.		100 Perpera, ,, ,,	16.50
M90.		1 Perper, third issue	1.75
M91.		2 Perpera, ,, ,,	2.25
M92.		5 Perpera, ,, ,,	2.50
M93.		10 Perpera, ,, ,,	2.50
M94.		20 Perpera, ,, ,,	3.50
M95.		50 Perpera, ,, ,,	4.50
M96.		100 Perpera, ,, ,,	6.50
M97.	Stamped "PODGORICA"	5 Perpera, second issue	3.50
M98.	(capital letters, 13 mm)	10 Perpera, ,, ,,	4.50
M99.		20 Perpera, ,, ,,	6.50
M100.		50 Perpera, ,, ,,	8.50
M101.		100 Perpera, ,, ,,	18.50
M102.		1 Perper, third issue	3.50
M103.		2 Perpera, ,, ,,	4.50
M104.		5 Perpera, ,, ,,	6.50
M105.		10 Perpera, ,, ,,	8.50
M106.		20 Perpera, ,, ,,	12.50
M107.		50 Perpera, ,, ,,	15.00
M108.		100 Perpera, ,, ,,	16.50
M109.	Stamped "PODGORICA"	5 Perpera, second issue	2.25
M110.	(capital letters, 17 mm)	10 Perpera, ,, ,,	2.50
M111.		20 Perpera, ,, ,,	3.50
M112.		50 Perpera, ,, ,,	2.50
M113.		100 Perpera, ,, ,,	5.00

M114.		1 Perper, third issue	1.25
M115.		2 Perpera, " "	1.25
M116.		5 Perpera, " "	1.25
M117.		10 Perpera, " "	1.75
M118.		20 Perpera, " "	2.25
M119.		50 Perpera, " "	2.50
M120.		100 Perpera, " "	3.50
M121.	Stamped "Stari Bar"	5 Perpera, second issue	3.00
M122.	(imprint 11 mm wide)	10 Perpera, " "	3.75
M123.		20 Perpera, " "	5.00
M124.		50 Perpera, " "	6.50
M125.		100 Perpera, " "	16.50
M126.		1 Perper, third issue	4.50
M127.		2 Perpera, " "	6.50
M128.		5 Perpera, " "	8.50
M129.		10 Perpera, " "	10.00
M130.		20 Perpera, " "	12.50
M131.		50 Perpera, " "	15.00
M132.		100 Perpera, " "	16.50
M133.	Stamped "STARI BAR"	5 Perpera, second issue	3.00
M134.	(imprint 16 mm wide)	10 Perpera, " "	3.50
M135.		20 Perpera, " "	3.50
M136.		50 Perpera, " "	6.50
M137.		100 Perpera, " "	16.50
M138.		1 Perper, third issue	1.25
M139.		2 Perpera, " "	1.25
M140.		5 Perpera, " "	1.25
M141.		10 Perpera, " "	1.75
M142.		20 Perpera, " "	2.25
M143.		50 Perpera, " "	2.50
M144.		100 Perpera, " "	3.50
M145.	Stamped "Belgrad"	1 Perper, third issue	35.00
M146.	Stamped "Steuer-u. Zollamt Kolasin"	10 Perpera, " "	35.00
M147.	Stamped "Cetinje"	1 Perper, first issue	35.00

Specimens of overprinted notes have been observed with a narrow stamp of the place name on one side, a wide stamp of the place name on the other side.

Austrian Military Government 1916–18

Newly printed notes

M148.	1. 6.1917	10 Perpera = 5 Munzperper = 5 Kronen, blue and brown	4.50
M149.	5. 7.1917	1 Perper = 50 Munzpara = 50 Heller, blue green on orange	2.50
M150.		2 Perpera = 1 Munzperper = 1 Krone, violet on green	3.50

136 × 98

M151.		5 Perpera = 2 Munzperper 50 Para = 2 Kronen 50 Heller, lilac on green	4.50
M152.	20. 1.1917	20 Perpera = 10 Munzperper = 10 Kronen, red brown on green	6.50
M153.		50 Perpera = 25 Munzperper = 25 Kronen, lilac on green	12.50
M154.		100 Perpera = 50 Munzperper = 50 Kronen, blue on olive	25.00

During World War II Italian overprinted notes of Yugoslavia with "Verificato" were circulated in Montenegro. (See Yugoslavia R10–R15.)

NETHERLANDS (Nederland)

The Kingdom of the Netherlands including Belgium, was established in 1815 under King William I. Belgium seceded in 1830. The Dutch monarchs have been William II, 1840–49; William III, 1849–90; Wilhelmina, 1890–1948 and Juliana, 1948– .

1 Gulden = 100 Cents

The dates shown in parenthesis are examples taken from notes actually observed.

Muntbiljets (State Notes)

1.	dates to 1914	10 Gulden (1.9.1888; 15.1.1902)	$175.00
2.		50 Gulden	RR
3.		100 Gulden	RRR

Zilverbons (Silver Certificates)

104 × 68

4.	7. 8.1914	1 Gulden, brown. Numeral "1" in middle	15.00
5.		2½ Gulden, blue on green. Numerals "2,50" in middle	25.00
6.		5 Gulden, green	35.00
7.	30. 3.1915	2½ Gulden, blue. Numerals "2,50" in middle and the four corners	25.00
8.	31. 3.1916	2½ Gulden, blue. Type of #7	25.00
9.	1. 5.1916	1 Gulden, brown. Numeral "1" in middle and the four corners	10.00
10.	1. 8.1917	2½ Gulden, blue. Type of #7	12.50
11.	1.11.1917	1 Gulden, brown. Type of #9	10.00
12.	1. 7.1918	2½ Gulden, blue on grey. Numerals at left middle and right top and bottom	20.00
13.	1.10.1918	1 Gulden, brown. Type of #9	8.50
14.		2½ Gulden, blue on grey. Type of #12	15.00
15.	1. 2.1920	1 Gulden, brown on light green. Woman's head in relief	8.50
16.	1.10.1920	2½ Gulden, blue on grey. Type of #12	12.50

17.   1. 5.1922   2½ Gulden, blue on grey. Type of #12   12.50
Note dated 1.10.1922 is a counterfeit.

130 × 73

18.   1.12.1922   2½ Gulden, blue on grey. Type of #12   10.00
19.   1.10.1923   2½ Gulden, blue on grey. Type of #12   10.00
20.   1.10.1927   2½ Gulden, blue on grey. Type of #12   10.00

Nederlandsche Bank (Netherlands Bank)

Notes to 1945

21.   Type of 1860–90   25 Gulden, orange. Arms and lion above.
Blank reverse (27.9.1904; 2.10.1911;
13.2.1918; 13.9.1918; 15.6.1919)   85.00
22.   40 Gulden, green. As #21 (6.6.1910;
11.7.1921; 13.9.1921)   125.00

213 × 104

23.   60 Gulden, lilac-brown. As #21 (11.8.1910;
1.3.1912;   11.6.1918;   29.11.1921;
1.9.1922)   175.00
24.   100 Gulden, black. Blue reverse, helmeted
woman's   head   above   (1.3.1911;
2.1.1920; 13.10.1921)   200.00
25.   200 Gulden, black. Light brown reverse,
helmeted   woman's   head   above
(18.10.1910; 2.7.1921)   250.00

26.		300 Gulden, black. Green reverse, helmeted woman's head above (5.2.1909; 3.1.1921)	RR
27.		1,000 Gulden, black on blue. Red reverse, helmeted woman's head above (3.10.1910; 22.5.1916)	RR
28.	Type of 1904	10 Gulden. Blue reverse (29.7.1921)	65.00
29.	Type of 1904, modified 1922	10 Gulden	65.00
30.	Type of 1914	10 Gulden "Hulpbiljet," blue grey. Work and Welfare (7.10.1911; 23.10.1915; 16.5.1923)	65.00
31.		25 Gulden "Hulpbiljet" (no specimen known)	
32.		40 Gulden "Hulpbiljet" (no specimen known)	
33.		60 Gulden "Hulpbijet" (no specimen known)	
34.		100 Gulden "Hulpbiljet" (no specimen known)	
35.		1,000 Gulden, black on blue. As #27 but reverse not printed (1.8.1914)	R
36.	Type of 1921	25 Gulden, red. William of Orange above, Mercury at left, sailor at right. Bank building on reverse. Handwritten signature	
		a. "Amsterdam" in date 17 mm wide, thick letters before control numbers (30.9.1921)	35.00
		b. "Amsterdam" in date 19 mm wide, double-lined letters before control numbers (15.8.1921)	40.00
37.	Type of 1921, dates from 15.7.1929	25 Gulden, red. As #36 but no picture on reverse and signature printed (19.7.1929; 18.2.1930)	20.00
38.	Type of 1921, dates from 5.7.1927	25 Gulden, blue. As #37, handwritten signature (19.1.1928)	25.00

173 × 99

39.		40 Gulden, green. Prince Maurits above	65.00
40.		60 Gulden. Prince Frederik-Hendrik above	85.00

41. Type of 1921,   100 Gulden, blue. Seated woman at left
    dates from 23.1.1922   a. Letters and control numbers 4 mm
                             wide. No serial letters in background
                             on reverse (4.2.1922)   35.00
                          b. Letters and control numbers 4 mm
                             wide. Serial letters in background on
                             reverse. Text reads "Hijdie biljetten
                             . . ." (15.9.1924)   30.00
                          c. As #41b but reverse text reads "Het
                             namaken . . ." (12.3.1926)   27.50
                          d. Letters and control numbers 3 mm
                             wide, otherwise as #41c (11.2.1927;
                             4.12.1928)   25.00
42. Type of 1921,   200 Gulden, red brown. Seated woman at
    dates from 1.12.1922   left (8.4.1926)   85.00
43. Type of 1921,   300 Gulden, green. Seated woman at left
    dates from 2.12.1922   (9.4.1926)   125.00
44. Type of 1921,   1,000 Gulden, sepia. Seated woman at left
    dates from 23.6.1919   (24.6.1919)   100.00
45. Type of 1921,   1,000 Gulden, dark green and lilac. Seated
    dates from 1.10.1926   woman at left (two control number
                            and signature varieties, 2.10.1926;
                            24.9.1938)   65.00
46. Type of 1924,   10 Gulden, dark blue. Peasant girl of
    dates from 1.3.1924   Zeeland in middle
                          a. Signature in black. Letters only in
                             front of control numbers on reverse
                             (29.3.1924; 12.9.1925; 11.4.1927;
                             16.1.1929; 17.1.1930)   8.50
                          b. Signature in blue. Letters in front of
                             control numbers and also on edges at
                             lower left and upper right of reverse
                             (11.9.1930)   12.50
47. Type of 1926,   20 Gulden, olive. Sailor at rudder bar
    dates from 2.1.1926   (7.4.1926)   10.00

143 × 101

48. Type of 1929,   50 Gulden, grey blue. Head with helmet
    dates from 18.4.1929   at right (Wisdom) (18.4.1929)   30.00

49. Type of 1930, dates from 1.10.1930 — 100 Gulden, brown and olive. Woman's head at left and right (mirror images)
   a. Date in lower middle of reverse (three signature varieties; 9.3.1931; 2.12.1940; 28.5.1941) — 4.50
   b. Date at upper left and lower right of reverse (2.10.1942; 13.1.1944) — 4.50

50. Type of 1939, dates from 1.12.1930 — 500 Gulden, grey blue and multicolored. Stadholder William III in middle, ship in background (2.12.1930) — 150.00

51. Type of 1931, dates from 1.6.1931 — 25 Gulden, red. Bank President W.C. Mees at right (two signature varieties 25.2.1938; 9.2.1939; 19.3.1941) — 2.50

52. Type of 1933, dates from 1.6.1933 — 10 Gulden, dark blue. Head of old man (after Rembrandt) at right (18.11.1933; 11.6.1935; 12.5.1936; 25.11.1938; 22.6.1939) — 2.25

153 × 81

53. Type of 1939, dates from 20.7.1939 — 20 Gulden, violet. Queen Emma at right, warships of 1700's at left (16.12.1940; 19.3.1941) — 2.00

54. Type of 1939, dates from 19.3.1941 — 20 Gulden, violet. As #53 but date over-printed with "Amsterdam" above and "19.3.1941" below — 85.00

55. Type of 1940, dates from 9.7.1940 — 10 Gulden, blue and green. Head of young girl (after P. Moreelsen) at right
   a. Paper watermarked with head of old man (28.10.1940; 18.2.1941) — 2.25
   b. Paper watermarked with bunch of grapes (16.7.1941; 4.8.1942) — 1.75

56. Dates from 1.6.1940 — 10 Gulden, brown and dark green. Queen Emma at right (20.6.1940; 2.1.1941) — 3.00

57. Dates from 20.5.1940 — 25 Gulden, olive brown. Young girl (after P. Moreelsen) at right. Edge unprinted at left (20.5.1940) — 3.50

58.	Dates from 4.10.1943	25 Gulden, red brown. As #57 but frame bordered with "DNB" (5.10.1943; 6.4.1944)	1.75
59.	Type of 1941, dates from 2.1.1941	50 Gulden, dark brown and multicolored. Head of woman (after J. Steen), at left and right	
		a. "Amsterdam" in date is 17 mm wide (6.2.1941)	4.50
		b. "Amsterdam" in date is 16 mm wide (17.3.1941)	4.50
60.	Type of 1943, dates from 4.1.1943	10 Gulden, blue and multicolored. Man's head with hat (after Rembrandt) at right (29.1.1943; 9.11.1943; 3.2.1944)	1.50

Zilverbons (Silver Certificates)

61.	1.10.1938	1 Gulden, brown. Type of #15	.60
62.		2½ Gulden, blue. Type of #12	1.00
63.	16.10.1944	5 Gulden, green (two control number varieties)	2.50

Muntbiljets (State Notes)

64.	4. 2.1943	1 Gulden, red. Left-facing portrait of Queen Wilhelmina in middle. Printed by American Bank Note Company	2.00
65.		2½ Gulden, green. Type of #64	2.50
66.		10 Gulden, blue. Type of #64	25.00
67.		25 Gulden, olive. Type of #64	85.00

151 × 73

68.		50 Gulden, brown. Type of #64	200.00
69.		100 Gulden, black. Type of #64	RRR
70.	18. 5.1945	1 Gulden, brown on light green. Right-facing portrait of Queen Wilhelmina in middle	4.50
71.		2½ Gulden, blue on lilac. Type of #70 (two control number varieties)	4.50
72.	8. 8.1949	1 Gulden, brown on light green. Queen Juliana at left	1.00
73.		2½ Gulden, blue. Queen Juliana at left	1.75

Nederlandsche Bank (Netherlands Bank)

Notes after 1945

74.	7. 5.1945	10 Gulden, blue and brown violet. Arms and lion in middle	30.00
75.		10 Gulden, blue. King William I at right. Coal mining scene on reverse	
		a. 1788 date at right of portrait (counterfeit)	75.00
		b. 1772 date at right of portrait	35.00
76.		20 Gulden, brown. King William III at right	65.00
77.		25 Gulden, brown. Young girl	100.00
78.		50 Gulden, brown. King William II as a youth	125.00
79.		100 Gulden, brown	250.00
80.		1,000 Gulden, blue. William the Silent at right	RRR

155 × 87

81.	19. 3.1947	25 Gulden, red and green. Young girl's head with flowers at right	45.00
82.	9. 7.1947	100 Gulden, brown. Woman's head at right	75.00
83.	4. 3.1949	10 Gulden, blue. Obverse as #75b. Landscape with windmill on reverse	15.00
84.	1. 7.1949	25 Gulden, orange. King Solomon at right	30.00
85.	2. 2.1953	100 Gulden, dark brown. Erasmus at right	50.00
86.	23. 3.1953	10 Gulden, blue, brown and green, Hugo de Groot at right	6.50
87.	10. 4.1955	25 Gulden, red and orange. Christian Huygens at right	15.00
88.	8.11.1955	20 Gulden, green and lilac. Farm house at right	25.00
89.	15. 7.1956	1,000 Gulden, brown and green. Rembrandt at right	RRR
90.	26. 4.1966	5 Gulden, green. Vondel at right	
		a. Control numbers at upper left and lower right	—
		b. Control numbers at upper left and lower middle (smaller type — trial issue used only in the Province of Utrecht)	20.00
91.	25. 4.1968	10 Gulden, blue and violet. Frans Hals at right	—

92.	14. 5.1970	100 Gulden, dark brown. Portrait of Admiral Michiél Adriaensy de Ruyter at right	—
93.	10. 2.1971	25 Gulden, red. Portrait of composer Jan Pietersz Sweelinck at right	—
94.	30. 3.1972	1,000 Gulden, dark green. Portrait of philosopher Baruch d'Espinoza at right	—

Ministerie van Oorlog (Military money, Ministry of War)

Notes issued for use of Dutch troops in Germany

M1.	1 Gulden, brown	65.00
M2.	5 Gulden, green	100.00
M3.	25 Gulden, violet	175.00

A 10 gulden note was probably produced as well.

NORWAY (Norge)

The kingdom was united with Denmark from 1380 until 1814, when it was joined to Sweden following the Napoleonic Wars. This union was dissolved in 1905 and Norway became independent.

1 Krone = 100 Ore

Norges Bank (Bank of Norway)

Type I: Bust of bearded man at left, dates of issue handwritten

1.	1877–99	5 Kroner, blue	$75.00
2.		10 Kroner, yellow	100.00
3.		50 Kroner, green	200.00
4.		100 Kroner, rose	RR
5.		500 Kroner, brown	RRR
6.		1,000 Kroner, orange brown	RRR

Type II: Bust of man without beard (President Christie) at left, dates printed, "Hovedkasserer" below signature

7.	1901–25	5 Kroner, dark green	16.50
8.		10 Kroner, violet	25.00
9.		50 Kroner, blue green	45.00
10.		100 Kroner, violet	85.00

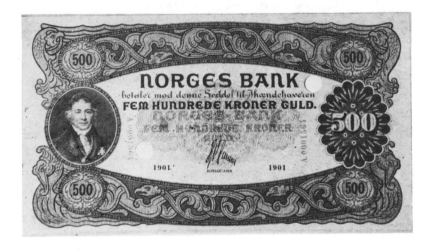

217 × 127

11.	500 Kroner, blue green	RR
12.	1,000 Kroner, violet	RR

1 and 2 Kroner notes

13.	1917	1 Krone, green	5.00
14.	1918	2 Kroner, rose	6.50
15.	1922	2 Kroner, rose	16.50
16.	1940–50	1 Krone, brown on green	1.75
17.		2 Kroner, rose	2.25

Also see #24 and 25.

Type II: As for notes #7–12 but "Hovedkasserer" printed wider

18.	1926–45	5 Kroner, dark green	1.25
19.		10 Kroner, violet	1.25
20.		50 Kroner, blue green	6.50

149 × 125

21.		100 Kroner, violet	10.00
22.		500 Kroner, blue green	45.00
23.		1,000 Kroner, violet	65.00

Type III: English printing, war issue

24.	1942	1 Krone, dark brown on green	15.00
25.		2 Kroner, rose	20.00
26.		5 Kroner, violet on green, red and brown	35.00
27.		10 Kroner, red on blue green and green	50.00

145 × 127

28.		50 Kroner, brown and multicolored	175.00
29.		100 Kroner, blue and multicolored	250.00
30.		500 Kroner, green and multicolored (not issued)	RRR
31.		1,000 Kroner, brown and multicolored (not issued)	RRR

Issues after 1945 (Also see #16 and #17)

125 × 70

32.	1945–54	5 Kroner, blue. Arms at left	5.00
33.	dates from 1955	5 Kroner, blue. Fridtjof Nansen at left	—
34.	1945–53	10 Kroner, yellow brown. Arms at left	18.50
35.	dates from 1954	10 Kroner, yellow brown. Statesman Christian Michelsen at left	—
36.	1945–50	50 Kroner, green. Arms at left	50.00
37.	1951–65	50 Kroner, green. Bjornstjerne Bjornson at left (format 142 × 128 mm)	16.50

38.	dates from 1966	50 Kroner, green. Type of #37 but different format (145 × 73 mm)	—
39.	1945–59	100 Kroner, red. Arms at left	85.00
40.	1950–62	100 Kroner, red. Henrik Wergeland at left (format 146 × 128 mm)	35.00
41.	dates from 1963	100 Kroner, red-violet. Type of #40 but different format (145 × 78 mm)	—
42.	1945–49	500 Kroner, dark green. Niels Henrik Abel at left	—
43.	1945–47	1,000 Kroner, light brown. Type of #23	RR
44.	dates from 1948	1,000 Kroner, brown. Henrik Ibsen at left	—

Military High Command, 1940

Notes issued by Major General Steffens with approval of the branch office of the Bank of Norway in Voss.

M1.	14.4.1940	5 Kroner	125.00
M2.		10 Kroner	RR
M3.		50 Kroner	RR
M4.		100 Kroner	RRR

Bear Island

Privately issued notes of the Bjornoen coal company in the values of 10 and 50 ore, 1, 10 and 20 kroner circulated on this island in the Barents Sea along with regular Norwegian money. All of these notes are RR.

POLAND (Polska)

After the various partitions of Poland during the 18th and 19th centuries, the remaining territory came under Russian rule. In 1918, Poland re-emerged as an independent republic. Following the Russo-German treaty of 1939, the country was again partitioned but was restored in 1945. A communist regime has governed since 1947.

1 Mark = 100 Fenigow
1 Zloty = 100 Groszy (since 1923)

Military Government of Warsaw (Zarzad General Gubernatorstwa Warszawkiego)

Notes issued during German occupation in World War I

Polska Krajowa Kasa Pozyczkowa (Polish National Land Loan Office)

Text reads "Zarzad jeneral-gubernatorstwa . . ."

1.	9.12.(Grudnia) 1916	½ Mark. Blue and olive reverse	$1.00
2.		1 Mark. Blue and red reverse	1.00
3.		2 Mark. Orange and green reverse	1.50
4.		20 Mark. Violet and light brown reverse	2.25

158 × 105

5.		50 Mark. Green and rose reverse	3.50
6.		100 Mark, blue and red	5.00

Text reads "Zarzad General-Gubernatorstwa"

7.	9.12.(Grudnia) 1916	½ Mark. Rev. Blue and olive. Type of #1	.40
8.		1 Mark. Rev. Blue and red. Type of #2	.40
9.		2 Mark. Rev. Orange and green. Type of #3	1.00

10.	5 Mark. Grey blue and yellow reverse. Text at left reads ". . . biletow Polskiej Krajowej . . ."	3.00
11.	5 Mark. Grey blue and yellow reverse. As #10 but text reads ". . . Biletow Kasy Pozyczkowej . . ."	2.00
12.	10 Mark. Lilac brown and green reverse. Text at left reads ". . . biletow Polskiej Krajowej . . ."	2.50
13.	10 Mark. Lilac brown and green reverse. As #12 but text reads ". . . Biletow Kasy Pozyczkowej . . ."	30.00
14.	20 Mark. Violet and light brown reverse. Type of #4	8.50
15.	100 Mark, blue and red	3.50
16.	1,000 Mark, brown and red	6.50

Republic of Poland

Polska Krajowa Kasa Pozyczkowa (Polish National Land Loan Office)

17.	15. 1.(Stycznia) 1919	500 Mark, green and red. Polish eagle at left	7.50

185 × 110

18.	15. 2.(Lutego) 1919	100 Mark, green and grey violet. Kosciuszko at left	
		a. Brownish paper watermarked with honeycomb. Engraver's name at lower left and right	1.50
		b. As #18a but without engraver's name	4.50
		c. Indistinct watermark of Polish eagle in white paper	6.50

19.	17. 5.(Maja) 1919	1 Mark, grey violet to violet (three control number varieties)	.40
20.		5 Mark, green. Rev. B. Glowacki at right	
		a. Engraver's name at lower left and right of reverse	.40
		b. As #20a but without engraver's name (two control number varieties)	.60
21.		20 Mark, brown. Kosciuszko in middle of reverse (two control number varieties)	1.75
22.		1,000 Mark, green and brown. Head of Kosciuszko at left	
		a. Brownish paper watermarked with honeycomb. Engraver's name at lower left and right on reverse (two control number varieties)	2.00
		b. As #22a but without engraver's name	2.50
		c. Indistinct watermark of Polish eagle in white paper. Engraver's name at lower left and right on reverse	2.00
		d. As #22c but without engraver's name (two control number varieties)	1.75
23.	23. 8.(Sierpna) 1919	1 Mark, red and brown. Woman's head at right (two control number varieties)	.40
		Error: Obverse without red plate	85.00
24.		5 Mark, green and brown. Man's head at right (two control number varieties)	.40
25.		10 Mark, blue and brown. Man's head at right (two control number varieties)	.40
26.		20 Mark, red and brown. Woman's head at right (two control number varieties)	.45
27.		100 Mark, blue and brown. Man's head at right (two control number varieties)	.40
28.		500 Mark, green and brown. Woman's head at right (two control number varieties)	.45

29.		1,000 Mark, violet and brown. Man's head at right (five control number varieties)	.40
30.	7. 2.(Lutego) 1920	½ Mark, green and brown. Man's head at right	.40
31.		5,000 Mark, blue and brown. Woman's head at left, man's head at right (two control number varieties)	.60
32.	11. 3.(Marca) 1922	10,000 Mark, grey green and yellow. Woman's head at left and right	.60
33.	10.10.(Pazdziernika) 1922	50,000 Mark, brown on olive	.60
34.	25. 4.(Kwietnia) 1923	250,000 Mark, grey brown (two control number varieties)	1.00
35.	30. 8.(Sierpnia) 1923	100,000 Mark, brown	1.50
36.	___	500,000 Mark, grey (five control number varieties)	1.75

189 × 94

37.		1,000,000 Mark, olive brown. City view at left (two control number varieties)	2.25
38.	20.11.(Listopada) 1923	5,000,000 Mark, brown and rose	4.50
39.		10,000,000 Mark, green and blue. City view at left (two towers)	8.50
40.		50,000,000 Mark. Blue background	100.00
41.		100,000,000 Mark. Red background	125.00

Ministerstwo Skarbu (Finance Ministry)

42.	28. 4.(Kwietnia) 1924	1 Groz. Red overprint on halved note #36	
		a. Left half	1.75
		b. Right half	1.75
43.		5 Groszy. Red overprint on halved note #39	
		a. Left half	2.50
		b. Right half	2.50

44.		10 Groszy, blue. Buildings with columns	1.75
45.		20 Groszy, brown. Copernicus Memorial	2.00
46.		50 Groszy, red. Equestrian statue (J. Poniatowski)	2.25
47.	1. 5.(Maja) 1925	2 Zloty, "Bilet Zdawkowy," grey violet on grey green	12.50
		Error: Reverse inverted	65.00

128 × 83

48.		5 Zloty, "Bilet Zdawkowy," green and brown	18.50
49.	25.10.(Pazdziernika) 1926	5 Zloty, "Bilet Panstwowy," dark olive. Woman's head in middle	16.50
50.	1.10.(Pazdziernika) 1938	1 Zloty, "Bilet Panstwowy," grey and yellow brown. Man's head with crown at right	4.50

Bank Polski (Bank of Poland)

51.	28. 2.(Lutego) 1919 (issued 1924)	1 Zloty, violet. Kosciuszko at left	3.50
52.		2 Zloty, light blue. Kosciuszko at left	16.50
53.		5 Zloty, brown. Prince Poniatowski at right	12.50
54.		10 Zloty, violet and brown. Kosciuszko at left	16.50
55.		20 Zloty, multicolored. Kosciuszko at left	20.00
56.		50 Zloty, brown lilac and violet. Kosciuszko at left	65.00
57.		100 Zloty, blue and brown. Kosciuzko at left	45.00
58.		500 Zloty, violet and green. Kosciuszko at left	35.00

182 × 110

59.		1,000 Zloty, brown. Kosciuszko at left (not officially issued)	85.00
		Pattern	150.00
60.		5,000 Zloty, green. Kosciuszko at left (pattern note)	175.00
61.	15. 7.(Lipka) 1924	5 Zloty, brown. Type of #53	6.50
62.		10 Zloty, violet. Type of #54	
		a. White paper	10.00
		b. Grey paper	10.00
63.		20 Zloty, multicolored. Type of #55	
		a. White paper	15.00
		b. Grey paper	15.00
64.	28. 8.(Sierpnia) 1925	50 Zloty, green, brown and blue. Peasant girl at left, Mercury at right	35.00
65.	1. 3.(Marca) 1926	20 Zloty, blue and olive. Type of #64	20.00
66.	20. 7.(Lipca) 1926	10 Zloty, olive brown and blue. Female allegorical figures at left and right	12.50
67.	2. 1.(Stycznia) 1928	10 Zloty. Youth's head at right (not issued)	RR
68.		20 Zloty (not issued)	RR
69.	20. 7.(Lipca) 1929	10 Zloty, olive brown and blue. Type of #66	2.50
70.	1. 9.(Wrzesnia) 1929	20 Zloty, blue and olive. Type of #65	85.00
71.		50 Zloty, green, brown and olive. Type of #64	2.50
72.	2. 1.(Stycznia) 1930	5 Zloty, grey blue. Woman's head at right	2.50
73.	20. 6.(Czerwca) 1931	20 Zloty, blue and brown. Emilie Plater at right	2.25
74.	2. 6.(Czerwca) 1932	100 Zloty, brown. Prince J. Poniatowski	1.75

75.	9. 9.(Listopada) 1934	100 Zloty, brown. Type of #74	1.50
76.	26. 2.(Lutego) 1936	2 Zloty, grey olive. Girl in Dabrowki costume	2.50
77.	11. 9.(Listopada) 1936	20 Zloty, blue. Emilie Plater at right	1.75
78.		50 Zloty. Man's head at right (not issued)	85.00
		Reverse only printed	35.00
79.	15. 8.(Sierpnia) 1939	1 Zloty, lilac (not issued)	125.00
80.		2 Zloty, green (not issued)	125.00
81.		5 Zloty, blue. Girl in costume cap at right (not issued)	125.00
82.		10 Zloty, red orange. Young woman with scarf (not issued)	125.00
83.		20 Zloty, blue. Old woman with scarf at right (not issued)	125.00

84.		50 Zloty, green. Man in costume at right (not issued)	125.00
85.		100 Zloty, brown. Man with moustache at right (not issued)	125.00
86.		500 Zloty, violet. Sailor at right (not issued)	125.00
87.	20. 8.(Sierpnia) 1939	20 Zloty, blue. Young woman in costume at right (not issued)	125.00
88.		50 Zloty, green. Young peasant woman at right (not issued)	125.00

Generalgouvernement (German Military Government)

Older notes overprinted during World War II "Generalgouvernement fur die besetzten polnischen Gebiete"

89.	2. 6.1932 (1939)	100 Zloty. Note #74 with red brown overprint	20.00
90.	9. 9.1934	100 Zloty. Note #75 with red brown overprint	18.50

Overprints have been frequently counterfeited.

Bank Emisyjny w Polsce (Emission Bank of Poland)

Notes issued during the German occupation

91.	1. 3.(Marca) 1940	1 Zloty, grey blue	1.25
92.		2 Zloty, brown. Woman's head with scarf	1.50
93.		5 Zloty, green blue. Girl's head at right	20.00

170 × 85

94.		10 Zloty, brown. Female allegorical figures at left and right	1.25
95.		20 Zloty, grey blue. Emilie Plater at right	1.50

179 × 100

96.	50 Zloty, green. Head of young man at right	10.00

97.		100 Zloty, brown. Aged Warsaw aristocrat at left	2.50
98.		500 Zloty, grey blue and olive. Man's head (Gorale) at right	3.00
99.	1. 8.(Sierpnia) 1941	1 Zloty, grey blue. Type of #91 (two control number varieties)	.60
100.		2 Zloty, brown. Type of #92	.75
101.		5 Zloty, green blue. Type of #93	1.00
102.		50 Zloty, dark green. Type of #96	1.50
103.		100 Zloty, brown and blue	1.50

Various notes of the series #91–103 are known stamped with the overprint of the Warsaw resistance fighters of 1944 "A. K. Regula, Pierwszy zold powstanczy, Sierpien, 1944," also "Okreg Warzawski-Dowodztwo zgrup IV" or "Braterstwo Broni Anglii Ameryki Polski Niech Zyje."

Narodowy Bank Polski (National Bank of Poland)

104.	1944	50 Groszy, red	2.25
105.		1 Zloty, dark green	1.25
106.		2 Zloty, brown. Text below reads "Obowiazkowym"	1.25
107.		2 Zloty, brown. Text below reads "Obowiazkowe"	2.25
108.		5 Zloty, lilac brown on green. Text as #106	2.00
109.		5 Zloty, lilac brown on green. Text as #107	2.25
110.		10 Zloty, blue on green. Text as #106	2.25
111.		10 Zloty, blue on green. Text as #107	2.00
112.		20 Zloty, green on lilac. Text as #106	2.50
113.		20 Zloty, green on lilac. Text as #107 (two control number varieties)	2.50
114.		50 Zloty, blue on lilac. Text as #106	4.50
115.		50 Zloty, blue on lilac. Text as #107	3.75
116.		100 Zloty, red on blue. Text as #106	6.50
117.		100 Zloty, red on blue. Text as #107	5.00

118.		500 Zloty, green black on light brown. Text as #106	12.50
119.		500 Zloty, green black on light brown. Text as #107	18.50
120.	1945	1,000 Zloty, brown	45.00

175 × 93

121.	15. 1.(Stycznia) 1946	500 Zloty, dark blue and green. Man with ship at left, fisherman at right	20.00
122.		1,000 Zloty, brown. Miner at left, worker at right (four control number varieties)	20.00
123.	15. 5.(Maja) 1946	1 Zloty, lilac	1.00
124.		2 Zloty, green	1.25
125.		5 Zloty, grey blue	1.50
126.		10 Zloty, brown on green	2.25
127.		20 Zloty, green on lilac	4.50
128.		50 Zloty, brown and violet. Ship at left and right	8.50
129.		100 Zloty, red. Peasant girl at left, peasant at right	15.00
130.	15. 7.(Lipca) 1947	20 Zloty, green	12.50
131.		100 Zloty, red. Peasant girl in middle	15.00
132.		500 Zloty, blue. Woman with rudder and anchor in middle	16.50
133.		1,000 Zloty, brown on olive. Worker in middle	20.00
134.	1. 7.(Lipca) 1948	2 Zloty, dark green	1.75
135.		5 Zloty, red brown	2.25
136.		10 Zloty, brown. Man's head at right	4.50
137.		20 Zloty, blue. Woman's head in scarf at right	—

138.		50 Zloty, green. Sailor's head	—
139.		100 Zloty, red. Man's head at right	—
140.		500 Zloty, dark brown. Miner at right	—
141.	29.10.(Pazdziernika) 1965	1,000 Zloty, multicolored. Copernicus at right	—

PORTUGAL

This small seafaring nation was an independent kingdom from 1140 until 1910. The last kings were Charles I (1889–1908) and Manuel II (1908–10). A revolution in 1910 led to the founding of a republic.

1 Milreis = 1,000 Reis
1 Escudo = 100 Centavos

Banco de Portugal (Bank of Portugal)

Notes in milreis values. The various types of notes are differentiated by their plate numbers ("Ch" for "Chapa" = plate) and various dates.

1.	dates to 1900	500 Reis Prata (silver). "Ch 1"	$16.50
2.	dates to 1905	500 Reis Prata. "Ch 2"	12.50
3.	dates to 1929	500 Reis Prata. "Ch 3." Woman's head on reverse	8.50

120 × 74

4.		500 Reis Prata. "Ch 3." Note #3 with overprint "Republica"	6.50
5.	dates to 1896	1 Milreis Prata. "Ch 1"	20.00
6.	dates to 1902	1 Milreis Prata. "Ch 2"	20.00
7.	dates to 1929	1 Milreis Prata. "Ch 3"	16.50
8.	dates to 1893	2½ Milreis Prata. "Ch 1"	35.00
9.	dates to 1904	2½ Milreis Prata. "Ch 2"	35.00
10.	dates to 1907	2½ Milreis Prata. "Ch 3"	30.00
11.	dates to 1928	2½ Milreis Prata. "Ch 4," Alf. de Albuquerque	20.00
12.	dates to 1890	5 Milreis Prata. "Ch 1"	45.00
13.	dates to 1891	5 Milreis Prata. "Ch 2"	45.00
14.	dates to 1895	5 Milreis Prata. "Ch 3"	45.00
15.	dates to 1901	5 Milreis Prata. "Ch 4"	35.00
16.	dates to 1903	5 Milreis Prata. "Ch 5"	35.00
17.	dates to 1911	5 Milreis Prata. "Ch 6"	30.00
18.	dates to 1916	5 Milreis Prata. "Ch 7"	30.00
19.		10 Milreis Ouro (gold). "Ch 1"	65.00
20.	dates to 1897	10 Milreis Ouro. "Ch 2"	65.00
21.	dates to 1917	10 Milreis Ouro. "Ch 3"	50.00

22.	dates to 1929	10 Milreis Ouro. "Ch 4"	50.00
22a.		10 Milreis Ouro. "Ch 4." Note #22 with over-print "Republica" on the reverse	50.00
23.	dates to 1900	20 Milreis Ouro. "Ch 7"	65.00
24.	dates to 1911	20 Milreis Ouro. "Ch 8"	57.50
25.	dates to 1913	20 Milreis Ouro. "Ch 8" (altered plate)	50.00
26.	dates to 1916	20 Milreis Ouro. "Ch 9"	50.00
27.	dates to 1901	50 Milreis Ouro. "Ch 2"	85.00
28.	dates to 1929	50 Milreis Ouro ."Ch 3," Bartholomew Diaz	75.00
29.	dates to 1929	50 Milreis Ouro. "Ch 4." Rev. Lusitania	65.00
30.	dates to 1916	100 Milreis Ouro. "Ch 1"	150.00
31.	dates to 1926	100 Milreis Ouro. "Ch 2" and "Arrival 8.3.1500"	85.00

Casa da Moeda (State Notes of the Mint)

32.	6. 8.1891	50 Reis, green on lilac	8.50
33.		50 Reis, blue	3.50
34.		100 Reis, grey brown. Type of #32	8.50
35.		100 Reis, brown. Type of #33	4.50
36.		100 Reis, brown. Drapery, man sitting on anvil at left, cupid at right	1.00
		Trial printings in various colors	8.50
37.	6. 8.1891 (crossed out)	5 Centavos Bronze, blue green (probably only a trial printing)	20.00
38.		5 Centavos Bronze, blue (probably only a trial printing)	20.00
39.	15. 8.1917	10 Centavos Bronze, dark brown. Type of #36	4.50
		Trial printings in various colors	6.50
40.		10 Centavos Bronze, dark blue half oval. Columns at left and right. Thin grey paper or thick yellow paper	3.50
		Trial printings in various colors	6.50
41.		10 Centavos Bronze, blue on green. Seated woman at left and right	
		a. Paper watermarked with oval	6.50
		b. Paper watermarked with "Casa da Moeda"	1.75
		c. Unwatermarked paper	1.75
42.		10 Centavos Bronze, brown. Seated figure at left, smokestacks, ships and bridge. Paper white, grey, yellow brown or brown	4.50
43.	5. 4.1918	5 Centavos Bronze, green on grey violet. Thin grey paper or thick yellow paper	2.00
44.		5 Centavos Bronze, red on yellow. Cupid at left, bust at right. Paper white or grey	2.00
45.		5 Centavos Bronze, red on light green	4.50

46.		5 Centavos Bronze, red without background color	4.50
47.		5 Centavos Bronze, dark brown on yellow brown. Paper white and yellow	2.25
48.		5 Centavos Bronze, dark brown without background color	3.50
49.	4. 8.1922	20 Centavos Copper Nickel, dark brown on blue	2.25
50.	15. 8.1917–11. 4.1925	10 Centavos, brown. Woman with torch. Printed by Waterlow	1.75

101 × 64

51.	4. 8.1922–11. 4.1925	20 Centavos, brown. Woman's head at left. Printed by Waterlow	2.50

Banco de Portugal (Bank of Portugal)

Notes in escudo values. The various types of notes are differentiated by their plate numbers ("Ch" for "Chapa" = plate). The notes carry various dates and signatures. The dates shown in parentheses are examples taken from notes actually observed.

52.	valid to 5. 2.1930	50 Centavos Prata, violet. "Ch 1," woman with ship in hand at left (5.7.1918; 25.6.1920)	4.50
53.	valid to 30. 1.1929	1 Escudo Prata, red and violet. "Ch 1," seated woman with book and lamp at left (7.9.1917; 29.11.1918; 25.6.1920)	6.50
54.	valid to 24. 6.1929	2 Escudos 50 Centavos Prata, green. "Ch 1," D. Nuno Alvarez Pereira (10.7.1920; 3.2.1922; 17.11.1922)	8.50
55.	valid to 31.12.1933	2 Escudos 50 Centavos Prata, blue. "Ch 2," M. da Silveira in middle (18.11.1925; 18.11.1926)	10.00
56.	valid to 7. 4.1931	5 Escudos Ouro. "Ch 1," Alexander Herculano	30.00
57.	valid to 7. 4.1931	5 Escudos Ouro, violet, brown and green. "Ch 2," Joao das Regras at left (10.7.1920; 14.6.1922; 13.1.1925)	16.50
58.		5 Escudos Ouro. "Ch 3"	30.00

138 × 80

| 59. | valid to 31.12.1933 | 5 Escudos Ouro, grey and yellow brown. "Ch 4," D. Alvaro Vaz d'Almada | 25.00 |
| 60. | valid to 24. 6.1929 | 10 Escudos Ouro. "Ch 1," Alf. de Albuquerque | 40.00 |

162 × 105

61.	valid to 31.12.1933	10 Escudos Ouro, brown and yellow green. "Ch 2," Marques de Sa da Bandeira (9.8.1920)	45.00
62.	valid to 31.12.1933	10 Escudos Ouro, black on red. "Ch 3," Eca de Queiros (13.1.1925)	25.00
63.	valid to 24. 6.1929	20 Escudos Ouro. "Ch 1"	65.00
64.	valid to 24. 6.1929	20 Escudos Ouro. "Ch 2," J. de Castro	50.00
65.	valid to 7. 4.1931	20 Escudos Ouro. "Ch 3," Jose Estevao Coeho de Magalhaes	50.00
66.	valid to 31. 8.1934	20 Escudos Ouro, red. "Ch 4," Marques de Pombal (13.1.1925)	45.00
67.		20 Escudos Ouro, red brown. "Ch 5," M. de Albuquerque at left (17.9.1929; 13.5.1938)	25.00
68.	still valid	20 Escudos Ouro, green and violet. "Ch 6," D. Antonio Luiz de Menezas at right (26.6.1951; 27.1.1959)	—

69.		20 Escudos Ouro, dark green. "Ch 6A," D. Antonio Luiz de Menezas, altered design (26.7.1960)	—
70.		20 Escudos Ouro, olive and violet. "Ch 7," St. Anthony at right (26.5.1964)	—
71.	valid to 7. 4.1931	50 Escudos Ouro. "Ch 1," Manuel Passos	75.00
72.		50 Escudos Ouro. "Ch 2," Angel of Peace	75.00
73.	valid to 31. 8.1934	50 Escudos Ouro, blue on red and green. "Ch 3," Chr. da Gama (13.1.1925)	65.00
74.		50 Escudos Ouro, violet. "Ch 4," B. Carneiro in middle (17.9.1929)	65.00
75.		50 Escudos Ouro, violet. "Ch 5," Duke of Saldanha at left (18.11.1932; 24.4.1936)	50.00
76.	valid to 31.12.1963	50 Escudos Ouro, brown lilac. "Ch 6." Dark green reverse, Ramalho Ortigao at right (3.3.1938)	45.00
77.	valid to 31.12.1963	50 Escudos Ouro, brown lilac. "Ch 6A." Brown lilac and green reverse, Ramalho Ortigao, altered design (25.11.1941; 28.6.1949)	20.00
78.	still valid	50 Escudos Ouro, blue. "Ch 7," Fontes Pereira de Mello at right (28.4.1953; 24.6.1955)	20.00
79.		50 Escudos Ouro, blue. "Ch 7A," Fontes Pereira de Mello at right, altered design (24.6.1910)	—
80.		50 Escudos Ouro, brown lilac and rose. "Ch 8," Queen Isabella (28.2.1964)	—
81.	valid to 7. 4.1931	100 Escudos Ouro. "Ch 1," Pedro Alvarez Cabral	100.00

208 × 134

82.	valid to 31.12.1930	100 Escudos Ouro, brown. "Ch 2," Diogo do Couto at left (31.8.1920)	100.00

83.		100 Escudos Ouro. "Ch 3"	100.00
84.		100 Escudos Ouro, blue on green and red. "Ch 4," Gomes Freire at left (4.4.1928)	75.00
85.	valid to 1. 1.1959	100 Escudos Ouro, blue green and brown. "Ch 5," Joao Pinto Ribeiro (21.2.1935)	57.50
86.	still valid	100 Escudos Ouro, dark green and lilac. "Ch 6," Pedro Nunes at right (28.10.1947; 24.10.1950; 25.6.1957)	—
87.		100 Escudos Ouro, lilac, green and brown. "Ch 6A," Pedro Nunes at right, altered design (19.12.1961)	—
88.		100 Escudos Ouro, blue. "Ch 7," Camilo Castelo Branco at right (30.11.1965)	—
89.	valid to 17. 9.1929	500 Escudos Ouro. "Ch 1," Joao de Deus	125.00
90.	valid to 7.12.1925	500 Escudos Ouro. "Ch 2," Vasco da Gama	125.00
91.		500 Escudos Ouro. "Ch 3," Vasco da Gama	125.00
92.		500 Escudos Ouro, red violet. "Ch 4," Duke de Palmela at right (4.4.1928)	100.00
93.		500 Escudos Ouro, brown violet. "Ch 5," Jose da Silva Carvalho at left (18.11.1932; 31.8.1934)	100.00
94.	valid to 1. 1.1959	500 Escudos Ouro, red violet. "Ch 6," Don Henrique at right	85.00
95.	still valid	500 Escudos Ouro, brown violet and green. "Ch 7," Damiao de Goes at right (29.9.1942)	—
96.		500 Escudos Ouro, red brown and grey. "Ch 8," D. Joao IV at right (28.11.1944; 11.3.1952)	—
97.	valid to 31. 8.1967	500 Escudos Ouro, olive brown. "Ch 9," D. Francisco d'Almeida at right (27.5.1958)	125.00
98.	still valid	500 Escudos Ouro, brown and multicolored. "Ch 10," D. Joao at right (25.1.1966)	—
99.	valid to 20. 2.1926	1,000 Escudos Ouro. "Ch A," Duke de Terceira	RR
100.	valid to 14.10.1927	1,000 Escudos Ouro. "Ch 1," Luiz de Camoes	RR
101.	valid to 14. 8.1931	1,000 Escudos Ouro. "Ch 2," A. F. Castilho	250.00
102.	valid to 14. 8.1931	1,000 Escudos Ouro, blue. "Ch 3," Oliveira Martins (25.11.1927)	250.00
103.		1,000 Escudos Ouro, green. "Ch 4," Marques de Sa da Bandeira at right (17.9.1929)	250.00
104.		1,000 Escudos Ouro, dark green. "Ch 5," Conde de Castelo-Melhor at left (18.11.1932)	200.00
105.	valid to 1. 1.1959	1,000 Escudos Ouro, green on red brown. "Ch 6," Mestre de Avis in middle (17.6.1938)	175.00

164 × 103

106. still valid	1,000 Escudos Ouro, dark green and blue. "Ch 7," D. Alfonso Henrique at right (29.9.1942)	—
107.	1,000 Escudos Ouro, violet. "Ch 8," D. Felipa de Lencastre at right (31.1.1956)	—
108.	1,000 Escudos Ouro, blue green and lilac. "Ch 8A," D. Felipa de Lencastre at right, altered design (30.5.1961)	—
109. valid to 31. 8.1967	1,000 Escudos Ouro, green, blue and red brown. "Ch 9," D. Diniz at right (2.4.1965)	125.00
110. still valid	1,000 Escudos Ouro, blue. "Ch 10," Maria II at right (19.5.1967)	—

RUMANIA

A communist-dominated republic since 1947, Rumania came into being in 1859 when the principalities of Wallachia and Moldavia were united. The country became a kingdom in 1881 under Carol I (1881–1914).

1 Leu = 100 Bani

Bilets Hypothecar (State Notes of the Principality)

1.	12. 6.1877	5 Lei, blue. Two women with children	$85.00
2.		10 Lei, blue. Two women with children	100.00
3.		20 Lei, blue. Two Roman men and women at left	150.00
4.		50 Lei, blue. Two Roman men and women at left	175.00
5.		100 Lei, blue. Woman with children in middle	250.00
6.		500 Lei, blue. Five women and two children	RR

Ministerul Finantelor (Finance Ministry)

7.	1917	10 Bani, green. King Ferdinand I in middle	1.75
8.		25 Bani, brown. Type of #7	2.50
9.		50 Bani, blue and light brown. Type of #7	2.25

Notes of the Austro-Hungarian Bank with overprint "Romania Timbru Special" stamped on the German or Hungarian side of the note

10.	(1919)	10 Kronen. Austria #9 with overprint	16.50
11.		10 Kronen. Austria #19 with overprint	2.00
12.		20 Kronen. Austria #10 with overprint	RR
13.		20 Kronen. Austria #13 with overprint	5.00
14.		20 Kronen. Austria #14 with overprint	2.50
15.		50 Kronen. Austria #6 with overprint	RR
16.		50 Kronen. Austria #15 with overprint	3.00
17.		100 Kronen. Austria #11 with overprint	RR
18.		100 Kronen. Austria #12 with overprint	2.50
19.		1,000 Kronen. Austria #8 with overprint	8.50
20.		10,000 Kronen. Austria #25 with overprint	25.00

These notes are also known with additional overprints in the Yugoslavian or Hungarian language.

Banca Nacionala a Romaniei (National Bank of Rumania)

The numerous date varieties of the various note types make chronological classification difficult. The notes are, therefore, arranged by denomination with the known dates of issue indicated. The valuations shown are for the commonest varieties.

1, 2 and 5 Lei notes

21.	1 Leu, violet blue on light rose (12.3.1915)	1.75
22.	1 Leu, blue on light rose. As #21 but larger date on reverse (17.7.1920)	2.00
23.	1 Leu, brown on rose. As #22 but date on obverse. Two signature varieties (28.10.1937; 21.12.1938)	2.50
24.	2 Lei, violet blue on light rose. Two signature varieties (12.3.1915)	1.75
25.	2 Lei, violet blue on light rose. As #24 but larger date on reverse (17.7.1920)	2.00
26.	2 Lei, brown on rose. As #25. Two signature varieties (21.12.1938)	3.00
27.	5 Lei, Type I, violet. Peasant woman with distaff at left. Numeral of value in violet on reverse. Paper watermarked with heads of Trajan and Minerva. Six signature varieties (31.7.1914; 4.8.1916; 26.1.1917; 21.8.1917; 25.3.1920; 22.11.1928; 19.9.1929)	1.50
28.	5 Lei, Type I, lilac brown. As #27 but numeral of value on reverse in yellow. Paper watermarked with light and dark hemisphere. Format 133 × 79 mm or 139 × 87 mm (16.2.1917)	2.50

20 Lei notes

| 29. | 20 Lei, Type I, blue. Two boys in middle, one with Mercury staff. Seven signature varieties (19.1.1881; 28.2.1881; 3.6.1881; 30.9.1881; 18.11.1881; 7.4.1882; 21.6.1882; 25.8.1882; 10.11.1882; 30.3.1883; 10.11.1883; 3.9.1884; 19.6.1885; 6.11.1885; 25.6.1886; 20.5.1887; 9.7.1888; 19.4.1889; 31.8.1889; 12.10.1889; 4.5.1890; 2.8.1890; 10.11.1890; 11.7.1891; 26.6.1892; 18.3.1893; 31.8.1895) | 65.00 |
| 30. | 20 Lei, Type II, blue. Woman with six children in middle. Three signature varieties (14.3.1896; 5.12.1896; 25.9.1897; 15.5.1898; 25.11.1898; 20.1.1900; 7.9.1900; 12.4.1901; 20.9.1901; 5.12.1901; 29.8.1902; 6.3.1903; 8.1.1904; 27.5.1904; 30.6.1905; 3.11.1905; 18.5.1906; 28.9.1906; 1.2.1907; 7.6.1907; 6.9.1907; 23.1.1908; 1.5.1908; 28.8.1908) | 20.00 |

#31
161 × 95

31.   20 Lei, Type III, blue violet. Girl with fruit at left, boy with
       rudder at right. Twelve signature varieties (26.2.1909;
       29.10.1909; 12.11.1909; 14.1.1911; 31.3.1911; 2.6.1911;
       13.10.1911; 15.3.1912; 14.7.1912; 15.11.1912; 1.2.1913;
       6.3.1914; 27.3.1914; 30.6.1914; 15.1.1915; 12.5.1916;
       26.1.1917; 6.7.1917; 7.3.1919; 31.7.1919; 25.3.1920;
       21.1.1921; 3.11.1921; 26.5.1922; 1.2.1923; 23.8.1923;
       5.2.1924; 12.6.1924; 2.10.1924; 14.5.1925; 10.6.1926;
       16.12.1927; 7.6.1928; 18.10.1928; 31.1.1929)   3.50
32.   20 Lei, Type III, blue violet. As #31 but only two signatures
       (19.9.1929)   6.50

100 Lei notes

33.   100 Lei, Type I, blue. Two cupids at upper left and right, eagle in
       middle. Nine signature varieties (28.2.1881; 3.6.1881;
       16.7.1881; 18.11.1881; 7.4.1882; 25.8.1882; 18.5.1883;
       7.9.1883; 5.9.1884; 19.6.1885; 12.11.1886; 14.4.1888;
       19.4.1889; 15.9.1889; 25.10.1889; 2.8.1890; 30.8.1890;
       11.4.1891; 22.8.1891; 5.11.1892; 13.5.1893; 17.2.1894;
       14.8.1896; 8.5.1897; 15.5.1898; 29.4.1899; 20.1.1900;
       3.1.1902; 29.8.1902; 6.3.1903; 30.9.1904; 18.8.1905;
       23.3.1906; 12.4.1907; 12.10.1907; 11.11.1907)   50.00
34.   100 Lei, Type II, violet blue. Seated woman in costume at left.
       Nine signature varieties. Paper watermarked with heads of
       Trajan and Minerva (14.10.1910; 20.5.1910; 2.6.1911;
       15.3.1912; 13.11.1912; 7.9.1913; 23.1.1914; 6.3.1914;
       27.3.1914; 1.10.1915; 12.5.1916; 22.12.1916; 22.6.1917;
       8.10.1919; 25.3.1920; 14.6.1920; 9.2.1921; 24.11.1921;
       26.5.1922; 1.2.1923; 23.8.1923; 1.11.1923; 8.5.1924;
       14.5.1925; 4.2.1926; 12.1.1927; 10.3.1927; 28.6.1928;
       17.1.1929; 31.1.1929)   20.00
35.   100 Lei, Type II, lilac. As #34 but paper watermarked with
       light and dark hemisphere (16.2.1917)   16.50
36.   100 Lei, Type II, violet. As #34 but only two signatures. Paper
       watermarked with heads of Trajan and Minerva (19.9.1929)   20.00
37.   100 Lei, Type II, olive brown. As #36. Three signature varieties
       (13.5.1930; 16.10.1930; 5.12.1931; 31.3.1931; 22.10.1931;
       3.12.1931; 13.5.1932)   20.00
38.   100 Lei, Type II, dark brown. As #36, paper watermarked with
       heads of Trajan and Minerva (19.2.1940)   12.50
39.   100 Lei, Type II, dark brown. As #38 but paper watermarked
       with "BNR" (19.2.1940; 1.11.1940)   16.50

500 Lei notes

40.   500 Lei, Type I, violet blue. Woman with boy at left, seated
       peasant woman at right. Six signature varieties (11.2.1916;
       7.4.1916; 18.8.1916; 26.1.1917; 29.3.1918; 30.8.1918;
       26.4.1919; 31.7.1919; 12.2.1920)   8.50

41.	500 Lei, Type II, multicolored. Peasant woman with distaff at left, woman with infant at right. Three signatures (12.6.1924)	16.50
42.	500 Lei, Type II, multicolored. As #41 but only two signatures. Six signature varieties (1.10.1925; 4.2.1926; 15.12.1927; 13.5.1930; 16.10.1930; 16.2.1931; 31.3.1931; 22.10.1931; 3.12.1931; 13.5.1932; 27.10.1932; 21.4.1933; 21.9.1933; 14.12.1933; 15.3.1934; 27.1.1938)	10.00
43.	500 Lei, Type III, green. King Carol II in half profile at left (31.7.1934)	12.50
44.	500 Lei, Type IV, grey. King Carol II in profile at left (30.4.1936; 26.5.1939; 1.11.1940)	8.50
44a.	500 Lei, Type IV, grey. Type of #44 but two peasant women printed on reverse (20.5.1939)	16.50
45.	500 Lei, Type V, brown. Two peasant women at left (1.11.1940; 2.4.1941; 22.7.1941; 20.4.1942; 26.1.1943)	2.25

1,000 Lei notes

| 46. | 1,000 Lei, Type I, lilac. Woman with sickle at left, woman with rudder at right. Ten signature varieties (28.2.1881; 2.11.1883; 30.5.1884; 15.5.1885; 9.2.1889; 23.8.1890; 24.6.1893; 31.3.1894; 1.6.1895; 19.9.1902; 23.3.1906; 20.5.1910; 2.6.1911; 27.8.1911; 15.12.1911; 15.3.1912; 14.6.1912; 23.7.1915; 24.9.1915; 24.3.1916; 12.5.1916; 15.10.1916; 10.7.1917; 15.11.1917; 10.7.1919; 22.4.1920; 19.5.1920; 26.5.1922; 23.8.1923; 6.3.1924; 20.11.1924; 3.9.1925; 4.2.1926; 7.6.1928; 18.10.1928; 31.1.1929; 19.9.1929; 16.10.1930; 31.3.1931; 22.10.1931) | 65.00 |
| 47. | 1,000 Lei, Type I, multicolored (15.6.1933) | 125.00 |

219 × 129

| 48. | 1,000 Lei, Type II, multicolored. Bust of King Carol II at left (15.3.1934) | 45.00 |
| 49. | 1,000 Lei, Type III, brown and green. Two peasant women and two children at left and right. Paper watermarked with head of King Carol II with wreath (25.6.1936) | 8.50 |

50.   1,000 Lei, Type III, brown and green. As #49 but obverse over-
       printed with two peasant women (25.6.1936)   6.50
51.   1,000 Lei, Type III, brown and green. As #49 but no wreath in
       watermark (21.12.1938; 28.4.1939; 1.11.1940)   6.50
52.   1,000 Lei, Type III, brown and green. As #51 but obverse over-
       printed with two peasant women (21.12.1938; 28.4.1939;
       1.11.1940)   6.50
53.   1,000 Lei, Type III, blue and rose. As #49 but paper watermarked
       with head of Trajan. Three signature varieties (10.9.1941;
       23.3.1943; 2.5.1944; 10.10.1944; 20.3.1945)   3.50

2,000 and 5,000 Lei notes

54.   2,000 Lei, brown, violet and yellow. Peasant woman with distaff
       at left, woman with infant at right. Two signature varieties.
       Paper watermarked head of Trajan (18.11.1941; 10.10.1944)   2.25
55.   2,000 Lei, brown, violet and yellow. As #54 but paper water-
       marked with "BNR" in shield. Two signature varieties
       (23.3.1943; 1.9.1943; 2.5.1944)   1.75
56.   5,000 Lei, Type I, dark blue. Danube landscape at left, King
       Carol II at right (31.3.1931 overprinted 6.9.1940 at right)   40.00
57.   5,000 Lei, Type II, light blue. Two men's heads (Trajan and
       Decebal). Two signature varieties. Paper watermarked with
       head of Trajan (28.9.1943; 2.5.1944; 22.8.1944)   2.25
58.   5,000 Lei, Type II, light blue. As #57 but paper watermarked
       with "BNR." Two signature varieties (10.10.1944;
       15.12.1944; 20.3.1945; 21.8.1945; 20.12.1945)   1.75

10,000 to 5,000,000 Lei notes

59.   10,000 Lei, brown and red. Two peasant women with two children
       at left and right. Two signature varieties (18.5.1945;
       20.12.1945; 28.5.1946)   2.75
60.   100,000 Lei, green and grey. Woman with boys at left, peasant
       woman at right (1.4.1945; 7.8.1945; 28.5.1946; 21.10.1946;
       20.12.1946; 8.5.1947)   1.75
61.   100,000 Lei, lilac and multicolored. Two men's heads (Trajan and
       Decebal) in middle (25.1.1947)   8.50
62.   1,000,000 Lei, green and grey brown. Type of #61 (16.4.1947)   16.50

#63
207 × 106

63. 5,000,000 Lei, olive green and brown. She-wolf with Romulus and
        Remus in middle (25.6.1947)
        a. White paper   50.00
        b. Lined paper   65.00

1947 Currency Reform: *20,000 old Lei = 1 new Leu*

Ministerul Finantelor (Finance Ministry)

64.	1945	20 Lei, brown. King Michael in middle	.75
65.		100 Lei, blue. King Michael in middle	1.25
66.	(1947)	20 Lei, brown and green. Two men's heads at left (Trajan and Decebal). Two signature varieties. Paper watermarked with "M.F."	2.50
67.	(1948)	20 Lei, brown and green. As #66 but watermarked with "N.N.R." Text reads "Directorul General . . ."	2.50
68.		20 Lei, brown and green. As #67 but "Directorul Bugetului"	2.50
69.	15. 6.1950	20 Lei, dark green. Girl's head at right	1.75
70.	1952	1 Leu, brown	.75
71.		3 Lei, lilac brown and green	1.25
72.		5 Lei, blue and brown. Girl's head at left	1.75

Banca Nacionala a Romaniei (National Bank of Rumania)

Notes issued after the currency reform of 1947

73.	25. 6.1947	100 Lei, brown. Three men with tools at right	2.50
74.		500 Lei, brown. Woman's head in middle	20.00
75.		1,000 Lei, blue. Tudor Vladimirescu	35.00
76.	27. 8.1947	100 Lei, brown. Type of #73	2.50
77.	30. 9.1947	1,000 Lei, blue. Type of #75	35.00
78.	5.12.1947	100 Lei, brown. Type of #73	2.50
79.		1,000 Lei, blue. Type of #75	35.00
80.	18. 6.1948	1,000 Lei, blue and multicolored. Tudor Vladimirescu in middle	6.50

Second currency reform 1952: *20 old Lei = 1 new Leu*

Banca Republicii Populare Romane, Banca de Stat (Bank of the Peoples Republic of
Rumania)

#81

156 × 73

81.	15.10.1949	500 Lei, brown. Three men's heads	12.50
82.	20. 9.1950	1,000 Lei, blue. N. Balcescu at left	15.00
83.	1952	10 Lei, brown. Worker's head at left	1.75
84.		25 Lei, blue violet. Tudor Vladimirescu at left	3.50
85.		100 Lei, blue. N. Balcescu at left	8.50

Banca Nacionala a Republicii Socialiste Romania (National Bank of the Socialist Republic of Romania)

86.	1966	1 Leu, brown	—
87.		3 Lei, blue grey	—
88.		5 Lei, lilac brown	—
89.		10 Lei, lilac	—
90.		25 Lci, multicolored. Tudor Vladimirescu at left	—
91.		50 Lei, dark green. Alexander Cuza at lcft	—
92.		100 Lei, dark blue. N. Balcescu at left	—

Banca Generala Romana (General Bank of Rumania)

Notes issued during the German occupation in World War II

M1.	(1917)	25 Bani, olive brown	.75
M2.		50 Bani, blue	1.00
M3.		1 Leu, green	1.75
M4.		2 Lei, lilac rose	2.25
M5.		5 Lei, violet	6.50
M6.		20 Lei, brown	10.00
M7.		100 Lei, olive green	17.50
M8.		1,000 Lei, lilac brown	65.00

> Notes M1–M8 also exist with many different overprints of military units and Rumanian administrative authorities.

Comandamentul Armatei Rossii

Notes issued during the Russian occupation at end of World War II

M9.	1944	1 Leu	175.00
M10.		5 Lei	100.00
M11.		10 Lei, brown	45.00
M12.		20 Lei, blue	85.00
M13.		100 Lei, brown olive	65.00
M14.		500 Lei	200.00
M15.		1,000 Lei	200.00

RUSSIA—U.S.S.R.

The last Russian Czar, Nicholas II (1894–1917), was forced to abdicate after the February 1917 revolution. The Provisional Government of Alexander Kerensky followed but it in turn was overthrown by the October Revolution in 1917. During the civil war that followed, many organizations and national states were formed but the complete victory of the Red Army led to the formation of the Russian Socialist Federated Soviet Republic (R.S.F.S.R.). The name was later changed to the Union of Soviet Socialist Republics (U.S.S.R.).

1 Ruble = 100 Kopecks
1 Tscherwonez = 10 Gold Rubles

Empire

ГОСУДАРСТВЕННЫЙ КРЕДИТНЫЙ БИЛЕТЪ   (State Paper Money)
1898–1917

These notes carry signatures of the various State Bank Directors as follows:

E. Pleske, 1898–1904   A. Konschin, 1910–12
S. Timaschew, 1905–10   I. Schipow, 1912–17

			Pleske	Timaschew	Konschin	Schipow
1.	1898	1 Ruble, blue on brown	$0.75	$1.25	$1.75	$0.40
2.		3 Rubles, blue on brown	6.50	4.50	—	—
3.		5 Rubles, blue on multicolor	12.50	12.50	—	—
4.		10 Rubles, red on multicolor	16.50	20.00	—	—
5.		100 Rubles, green background	20.00	18.50	20.00	—

272 × 126

6.	500 Rubles	20.00	20.00	16.50	—

No.	Year	Denomination				
7.	1899	25 Rubles, violet	20.50	16.50	—	—
8.		50 Rubles, green background	50.00	45.00	4.50	2.50
9.	1905	3 Rubles, green and multicolor	—	2.50	.75	.40
10.	1909	5 Rubles, blue and multicolor Note with serial number, see #35.	—	—	.45	.40
11.		10 Rubles, green and red	—	4.50	.45	.40
12.		25 Rubles, red and blue	—	—	1.75	.75
13.	1910	100 Rubles, light brown background	—	—	2.25	.75
14.	1912	500 Rubles, green and multicolor	—	—	2.50	.75
15.	1898 (issued 1915)	1 Ruble, blue on brown. As #1 but serial number instead of control number	—	—	—	.40

Some of the Schipow notes were re-printed by the Provisional Government and again by the Soviet government. The re-prints have brighter colors than those printed under the empire.

Postage Stamp Currency

Postage stamps of the Romanov Tercentenary issue were printed on thin cardboard for use as small change. The reverses are imprinted with text and an eagle.

No.	Date	Denomination	Price
16.	(1915–17)	1 Kopeck, brown. Stamp side overprinted "1"	1.00
17.		1 Kopeck, brown. As #16 without overprint	20.00
18.		2 Kopecks, green. Stamp side overprinted "2"	1.00
19.		2 Kopecks, green. As #18 without overprint	20.00
20.		3 Kopecks, red	1.25
21.		10 Kopecks, blue	.75
22.		15 Kopecks, brown	.75
23.		20 Kopecks, green	.75

For postage stamp money without eagle on reverse, see #32–34.

КАЗНАЧЕЙСКІЙ РАЗМѢННЫЙ ЗНАКЪ (Small Denomination Notes)

No.	Date	Denomination	Price
24.	(1915–17)	1 Kopeck, light brown	.75
25.		2 Kopecks, grey brown	.75
26.		3 Kopecks, green	.75
27.		5 Kopecks, blue	.75
28.		10 Kopecks, blue and rose	16.50

#29
80 × 44

29.		15 Kopecks, red brown and yellow	16.50
30.		20 Kopecks, green and lilac	16.50
31.		50 Kopecks, blue and yellow	.75

Provisional Government of Russia

Postage Stamp Currency

32.	(1917)	1 Kopeck, brown. As #16–17 but without eagle on reverse	1.00
33.		2 Kopecks, green. As #18–19 but without eagle on reverse	1.00
34.		3 Kopecks, red. As #20 but without eagle on reverse	1.00

ГОСУДАРСТВЕННЫЙ КРЕДИТНЫЙ БИЛЕТЪ (State Credit Notes)

35.	1909 (1917)	5 Rubles, blue and multicolor. As #10 but three digit serial numbers instead of control numbers	.40
		Error: Upper serial letters "AY" lower letters "YA"	45.00
36.	(1917)	250 Rubles, lilac. Swastika in background on reverse	.75
37.		1,000 Rubles, green. Swastika in background	1.75

Many signature varieties exist of notes #35–37.

КАЗНАЧЕЙСКІЙ ЗНАКЪ (So-called "Kerensky Rubles")

60 × 49

| 38. | (1917) | 20 Rubles, brown | .40 |
| 39. | | 40 Rubles, red on green | .40 |

ГОСУДАРСТВЕННЫЙ КРЕДИТНЫЙ БИЛЕТЪ

Notes printed in America for the Provisional Government (never issued)

40.	(1917)	50 Kopecks, orange (brownish with age)	.40
41.	1918	25 Rubles, dark blue on blue. Seated woman (varieties with and without signatures)	1.75
42.		100 Rubles, background brown and red brown. Seated woman (varieties with and without signatures)	2.25

Note #40 was released by Adm. Kolchak. Notes #41 and 42 were issued in the Far Eastern District with an overprint. Notes in denominations of 50, 250, 500 and 1,000 rubles dated 1919 were also ordered from the U.S. These are known only as trial printings or specimens (RR) and were never issued.

АКЦІОНЕРН КОММЕРЧ БАНКОВЪ   (Union of Russian Stock Commerce Banks)

43.	(1917)	25 Rubles, green	150.00
44.		50 Rubles, brown	200.00
45.		100 Rubles	200.00
46.	1917	100 Rubles	RR
47.		500 Rubles	RR

Russian Socialist Federated Soviet Republic

БИЛЕТЪ ГОСУДАРСТВЕННАГО КАЗНАЧЕЙСТВА (State Treasury Notes)

48.	1915	(issued 1918)	25 Rubles, green on lilac	1.75
49.	1908	,, ,,	50 Rubles, brown on green	6.50

155 × 138

50.	1912	,, ,,	50 Rubles, brown on green	5.00
51.	1913	,, ,,	50 Rubles, brown on green	4.50
52.	1914	,, ,,	50 Rubles, brown on green	1.75
53.	1915	,, ,,	50 Rubles, brown on green	1.75
54.	1908	,, ,,	100 Rubles, dark blue on rose	12.50
55.	1912	,, ,,	100 Rubles, dark blue on rose	8.50
56.	1913	,, ,,	100 Rubles, dark blue on rose	6.50
57.	1914	,, ,,	100 Rubles, dark blue on rose	2.25
58.	1915	,, ,,	100 Rubles, dark blue on rose	1.75
59.	1915	,, ,,	500 Rubles, dark blue on blue	2.50
60.	1916	,, ,,	500 Rubles, dark blue on blue	3.50

5 % КРАТКОСРОЧНОЕ ОБЯЗАТЕЛЬСТВО ГОСУДАР.
КАЗНАЧЕЙСТВА (5% Short-term State Treasury Notes)

61.	1916	(issued 1918)	1,000 Rubles (12 month), lilac brown	6.50
62.	1917	,, ,,	1,000 Rubles (9 month), lilac brown	6.50
63.	1917	,, ,,	1,000 Rubles (12 month), lilac brown	3.50

64.	1916–17	,,	,,	5,000 Rubles (12 month), orange	6.50
65.	1916	,,	,,	10,000 Rubles (12 month), red	12.50
66.	1916	,,	,,	10,000 Rubles (9 month), red	16.50
67.	1917	,,	,,	10,000 Rubles (12 month), red	12.50
68.	1916	,,	,,	25,000 Rubles (12 month)	25.00
69.	1917	,,	,,	25,000 Rubles (9 month)	30.00
70.	1917	,,	,,	25,000 Rubles (12 month)	20.00
71.	1916–17	,,	,,	50,000 Rubles (12 month)	30.00
72.	1917	,,	,,	50,000 Rubles (9 month)	35.00
73.	1916–17	,,	,,	100,000 Rubles (12 month)	53.00
74.	1916–17	,,	,,	500,000 Rubles (12 month)	85.00
75.	1917	,,	,,	500,000 Rubles (9 month)	100.00
76.	1916–17	,,	,,	1,000,000 Rubles (12 month)	125.00

5 % ОБЛИГАЦІЯ ЗАЙМЪ СВОБОДЫ (5% Obligations of Freedom Loan)

These notes are known with and without an overprint of their value.

				without	with
77.	1917 (issued 1918)	20 Rubles, yellow		1.75	1.25
78.		40 Rubles		1.75	1.25
79.		50 Rubles, green		1.50	1.25
80.		100 Rubles, brown		1.50	1.25

Many kinds of interest coupons from certificates of the various Russian loans also circulated as money.

РАСЧЕТНЫЙ ЗНАК (Accounting Notes)

81.	(1919)	1 Ruble, brown. Multicolor reverse	.40
82.		2 Rubles, dark brown. Multicolor reverse	.40
83.		3 Rubles, green. Multicolor reverse. Paper watermarked with lozenges	.40
84.	(1921)	3 Rubles, both sides green	
		a. Paper watermarked with spades	1.75
		b. Paper watermarked with stars	.75
85.		5 Rubles, both sides dark blue	
		a. Paper watermarked with lozenges	.40
		b. Paper watermarked with spades	4.50
		c. Paper watermarked with stars	5.00
		d. Unwatermarked paper	1.75

ГОСУДАРСТВЕННЫЙ КРЕДИТНЫЙ БИЛЕТЪ (State Credit Notes)

86.	1918	1 Ruble, brown	.60
87.		3 Rubles, green	.60
88.		5 Rubles, blue	.60
89.		10 Rubles, red	.60
90.		25 Rubles, red brown	.70
91.		50 Rubles, dark brown	.75
92.		100 Rubles, brown	.75

147 × 100

93.		250 Rubles, green	.75
94.		500 Rubles, dark green	1.25
95.		1,000 Rubles, brown	1.75
		Error: Inverted reverse	25.00
96.		5,000 Rubles, blue. Swastika in background	2.25
97.		10,000 Rubles, brown. Swastika in background	2.50

Many signature varieties exist of notes #86–97.

РАСЧЕТНЫЙ ЗНАК (Accounting Notes)

Because of the multi-language text, these notes are sometimes called "Babylonians."

98.	(1919)	15 Rubles, brown	.40
99.		30 Rubles, green	.40
		Error: inverted reverse	16.50
100.		60 Rubles, grey	.40
101.	1919 (issued 1920)	100 Rubles, brown on light brown	.40
102.		250 Rubles, violet	
		a. Paper watermarked with "250"	.60
		b. Paper watermarked with stars	1.25
103.		500 Rubles, olive	
		a. Paper watermarked with "500"	.60
		b. Paper watermarked with stars	2.00
104.		1,000 Rubles, green	
		a. Paper watermarked with "1000"	.60
		b. Paper watermarked with small stars	1.25
		c. Paper watermarked with large stars	1.25
		d. Paper watermarked with lozenges	1.25

165 × 115

105.		5,000 Rubles, blue	
		a. Paper watermarked with broad waves	1.00
		b. Paper watermarked with narrow waves	1.75
		c. Paper watermarked with stars	3.00
106.		10,000 Rubles, red	
		a. Paper watermarked with broad waves	1.50
		b. Paper watermarked with narrow waves	2.50
		c. Paper watermarked with stars	3.50

РАСЧЕТНЫЙ ЗНАК (Accounting Notes)

107.	(1921)	50 Rubles, brown	
		a. Paper watermarked with lozenges	1.25
		b. Paper watermarked with large stars	.60
		c. Paper watermarked with small stars	1.50
108.		100 Rubles, yellow	1.75
109.		100 Rubles, orange	1.25
110.		250 Rubles, green	
		a. Paper watermarked with "250"	1.25
		b. Paper watermarked with stars	2.25
111.		500 Rubles, blue	
		a. Paper watermarked with "500"	1.25
		b. Paper watermarked with stars	2.25
		c. Paper watermarked with lozenges	2.50
112.		1,000 Rubles, red	
		a. Paper watermarked with "1000"	1.00
		b. Paper watermarked with small stars	1.75
		c. Paper watermarked with large stars	2.50
		d. Paper watermarked with lozenges	1.75
113.		5,000 Rubles, blue	1.25
		Error: "PROLETAPIER"	2.50
114.		10,000 Rubles, red brown	1.75
115.		25,000 Rubles, lilac	
		a. Paper watermarked with large stars	1.75
		b. Paper watermarked with small stars	3.50

116.		50,000 Rubles, green	
		a. Paper watermarked with large stars	1.75
		b. Paper watermarked with small stars	4.50
		c. Paper watermarked with crosses	8.50
117.		100,000 Rubles, red	2.25
118.		50,000 Rubles, War loan type	16.50
119.		100,000 Rubles, War loan type	20.00

Currency Reform 1921: *10,000 old Rubles = 1 new Ruble*

КРАТКОСРОЧНОЕ ОБЯЗАТЕЛЬСТВО (Short-term Obligations)

120.	1921	1,000,000 Rubles, black on yellowish paper	12.50
121.		5,000,000 Rubles, black on bluish paper	15.00
122.		10,000,000 Rubles	16.50
123.	1922	5,000 Rubles	16.50
124.		10,000 Rubles, black on grey-blue paper	20.00
125.		25,000 Rubles (known only as a pattern)	45.00

ГОСУДАРСТВЕННЫЙ ДЕНЕЖНЫЙ ЗНАК (State Promissory Notes)

126.	1922	50 Kopecks (trial printing only)	RRR
127.		1 Ruble, light brown	1.00
128.		3 Rubles, green	1.00
129.		5 Rubles, blue	1.00

155 × 80

130.		10 Rubles, red brown	1.25
131.		25 Rubles, brown lilac	1.75
132.		50 Rubles, blue	1.75
133.		100 Rubles, red	2.50
134.		250 Rubles, dark green	3.50
135.		500 Rubles, dark blue	5.00
136.		1,000 Rubles, brown	10.00
137.		5,000 Rubles, violet	16.50
138.		10,000 Rubles, red	25.00

Many signature varieties exist of notes #127–138.

БАНКОВЫЙ БИЛЕТ (State Bank)

139.	1922	1 Tscherwonez. Multicolored guilloche (ornament) at left	25.00
140.		2 Tscherwonez (known only as a pattern)	175.00
141.		3 Tscherwonez	45.00

142:		5 Tscherwonez	65.00
143.		10 Tscherwonez	100.00
144.		25 Tscherwonez	125.00
145:		50 Tscherwonez (known only as a pattern)	175.00

ГОСУДАРСТВЕННЫЙ ДЕНЕЖНЫЙ ЗНАК (State Promissory Notes)

Notes #146–151 are the promissory note type; notes #152–156 are coin notes without the promissary designation.

146.	1922	1 Ruble, brown and yellow	1.75
147.		3 Rubles, green	1.75
148.		5 Rubles, blue	2.25
149.		10 Rubles, red	2.25
150.		25 Rubles, violet	2.50
151.		50 Rubles, green	2.50
152.	1923	10 Kopecks	RRR
153.		15 Kopecks	RRR
154.		20 Kopecks	RRR
155.		50 Kopecks, blue	2.50

Second Currency Reform 1923: *1,000,000 old Rubles = 1 new Ruble*

ГОСУДАРСТВЕННЫЙ ДЕНЕЖНЫЙ ЗНАК (State Promissory Notes)

Reverse text reads ОДИН РУБЛЬ . . . in seven lines

156.	1923	1 Ruble, brown	.75
157.		5 Rubles, green	.75
158.		10 Rubles, violet	.75
159.		25 Rubles, blue	.75
160.		50 Rubles, olive	1.25

161

141 × 95

| 161. | | 100 Rubles, violet and multicolored | 1.50 |
| 162. | | 250 Rubles, dark blue | 2.00 |

Many signature varieties exist of notes #156–162.

Reverse text reads ДЕНЕЖНЫЕ ЗНАКИ . . . in eight lines

163.	1923	1 Ruble, brown	.75
164.		5 Rubles, green	.75
165.		10 Rubles, violet	
		a. Paper watermarked with lozenges	.75
		b. Paper watermarked with stars	1.75
166.		25 Rubles, olive brown	
		a. Paper watermarked with lozenges	.75
		b. Paper watermarked with stars	1.75
167.		50 Rubles, brown	
		a. Paper watermarked with lozenges	1.25
		b. Paper watermarked with stars	2.50
168.		100 Rubles, violet and multicolored	
		a. Paper watermarked with lozenges	1.25
		b. Paper watermarked with stars	1.75
169.		500 Rubles, dark brown	6.50
170.		1,000 Rubles, red	10.00
171.		5,000 Rubles, green	15.00

Many signature varieties exist of notes #163–171.

Third Currency Reform 1924: *5,000 Rubles = 1 Gold Ruble*

ПЛАТЕЖНОЕ ОБЯЗАТЕЛЬСТВО НКФ РСФСР (Payment Commitments)

Known only as patterns

172.	1923 (1924)	100 Gold Rubles	RR
173.		250 Gold Rubles	RR
174.		500 Gold Rubles	RR
175.		1,000 Gold Rubles	RR

ТРАНСПОРТНЫЙ СЕРТИФИКАТ КПС (Transport Certificates)

176.	1923 1.3.1924	3 Gold Rubles	125.00
177.		5 Gold Rubles. Series 1–5	50.00
178.	1.5.1924	5 Gold Rubles. Series 6–10	45.00
179.		5 Gold Rubles. Series 11–15. As #178 but text differences	45.00
180.		5 Gold Rubles. Series 16–24. As #179 but further text differences	35.00

Union of Soviet Socialist Republics

ГОСУДАРСТВЕННЫЙ ДЕНЕЖНЫЙ ЗНАК (State Promissory Notes)

155 × 77

181.	1923 (issued 1924)	10,000 Rubles, lilac on green. View of Kremlin	6.50
182.		15,000 Rubles, brown. Man's head	8.50
183.		25,000 Rubles, dark blue and green on violet. Soldier	8.50

Many signature varieties exist of notes #181-183.

ПЛАТЕЖНОЕ ОБЯЗАТЕЛЬСТВО НКФ СССР (Payment Commitments)

184.	1924	100 Gold Rubles (known only as patterns)	85.00
185.		500 Gold Rubles (known only as patterns)	85.00

ГОСУДАРСТВЕННЫЙ КАЗНАЧЕЙСКИЙ БИЛЕТ (State Treasury Notes)

186.	1924	1 Gold Ruble, blue on light brown. Vertical format, with and without	8.50
187.		3 Gold Rubles, green. Two reclining men	10.00

182 × 88

188.		5 Gold Rubles, blue. Tractor plowing	15.00
189.	1925	3 Rubles, dark green	3.50
190.		5 Rubles, dark blue. Head of worker at left	3.50

Small Denomination Notes (vertical format)

191.	1924	1 Kopeck, light brown	1.50
192.		2 Kopecks, brown	1.50
193.		3 Kopecks, green	1.50

194.		5 Kopecks, blue	1.50
195.		20 Kopecks, brown on rose (known only as a pattern)	45.00
196.		50 Kopecks, blue on brown	4.50

БИЛЕТ ГОСУДАРСТВЕННОГО БАНКА СССР (State Bank Notes)

197.	1924	3 Tscherwonez, dark blue. Peasant sowing seeds at left	40.00
198.	1926	1 Tscherwonez, dark blue	20.00
199.	1928	2 Tscherwonez, green	
		a. Signature in green	20.00
		b. Signature in black	18.50
200.		5 Tscherwonez, dark blue	50.00

156 × 88

201.	1932	3 Tscherwonez, green	18.50
202.	1937	1 Tscherwonez, grey. Lenin at right	1.00
203.		3 Tscherwonez, red. Lenin at right	.75
204.		5 Tscherwonez, green. Lenin at right	1.00
205.		10 Tscherwonez, dark blue. Lenin at right	2.25

ГОСУДАРСТВЕННЫЙ КАЗНАЧЕЙСКИЙ БИЛЕТ (State Treasury Notes)

206.	1928	1 Gold Ruble, blue on light brown. With and without СЕРИЯ	4.50
207.	1934	1 Gold Ruble, blue. With signature	6.50
208.		1 Gold Ruble, blue. Without signature	1.00
209.		3 Gold Rubles, green. With signature	6.50
210.		3 Gold Rubles, green. Without signature	1.00
211.		5 Gold Rubles, grey blue on light blue. With signature	8.50
212.		5 Gold Rubles, grey blue on light blue. Without signature	1.25
213.	1938	1 Ruble, brown. Miner at right	.75
214.		3 Rubles, dark green. Soldiers	.75
215.		5 Rubles, dark blue. Aviator	1.25
216.	1947	1 Ruble, blue on brown. Arms surrounded by 16 inscribed ribbons	1.50
217.		1 Ruble, blue on brown. As #216 but 15 ribbons (later issue)	.75
218.		3 Rubles, green. Type of #216	1.75
219.		3 Rubles, green. Type of #217	1.00

220.		5 Rubles, blue. Type of #216	2.50
221.		5 Rubles, blue. Type of #217	1.50
222.	1961	1 Ruble, brown	—
223.		3 Rubles, green. View of Kremlin	—
224.		5 Rubles, blue	—

БИЛЕТ ГОСУДАРСТВЕННОГО БАНКА СССР (State Bank Notes)

225.	1947	10 Rubles, blue and multicolored. Arms surrounded by 16 inscribed ribbons. Lenin on reverse	8.50
226.		10 Rubles, blue and multicolored. As #225 but 15 ribbons	3.50
227.		25 Rubles, green. Type of #225. Lenin on reverse	10.00
228.		25 Rubles, green. Type of #226. Lenin on reverse	4.50
229.		50 Rubles, blue on green and multicolored. Type of #225. Lenin on reverse	12.50
230.		50 Rubles, blue on green and multicolored. Type of #226. Lenin on reverse	6.50

230
×
115

231.		100 Rubles, multicolored. Type of #216 with Lenin at left. View of Kremlin on reverse	18.50
232.		100 Rubles, multicolored. Type of #217 with Lenin at left. View of Kremlin on reverse	10.00
233.	1961	10 Rubles, red brown. Lenin	—
234.		25 Rubles, violet. Lenin	—
235.		50 Rubles, green. Lenin	—
236.		100 Rubles, olive. Lenin	—

Archangel Government
АРХАНГЕЛЕСКАЯ ГУБЕРН

R1.	(1918)	3 Rubles, green	3.50
		Error: Obverse without black plate	16.50
R2.		3 Rubles, green. As R1 but reverse with red overprint	5.00
R3.		5 Rubles, grey blue	3.50
R4.		10 Rubles, red brown	1.50
		Error: Obverse without black plate	16.50
R5.		10 Rubles, red brown. As R4 but reverse with black overprint	5.00

165 × 104

| R6. | | 25 Rubles, grey blue | 5.00 |
| R7. | | 25 Rubles, grey blue. As R6 but reverse with red overprint | 6.50 |

Armenian Republic
РЕСПУБЛИКИ АРМЕНИИ

Notes dated August (АВГУСТЬ) 1919 on obverse, 15 November (НОЯБРЯ) 1919 on reverse. Large format (175 × 104 mm)

R8.	1919	100 Rubles, green. Value numerals in black	12.50
R9.		250 Rubles, orange. Type of R8	12.50
R10.		500 Rubles, blue. Type of R8	10.00
R11.		1,000 Rubles, lilac. Type of R8	12.50
R12.		25 Rubles, dark grey. Value numerals in middle and four corners	25.00
		Error: Printed in brown	65.00
R13.		50 Rubles, green. Type of R12	45.00
R14.		50 Rubles, green. Value numerals ornamented	6.50
R15.		100 Rubles, light green. Type of R14	5.00
		Error: Printed in yellow	16.50
R16.		250 Rubles, light brown. Type of R14	8.50
R17.		500 Rubles, blue. Type of R14	8.50
R18.		1,000 Rubles, lilac. Type of R14	12.50

Notes dated 15 November (НОЯБРЯ) 1919 on reverse. Small format (110 × 65 mm)

R19.	1919	5 Rubles, blue, without Armenian text	2.25
R20.		10 Rubles, rose	2.50
		Error: Background inverted	8.50
R21.	1919	5 Rubles, grey blue. With Armenian text	2.25
	(issued 1920)	Error: Text reads ГОСКУДАРСТВЕ<u>Н</u>АГО	3.50
		Error: Reverse overprinted on obverse	6.50
R22.		10 Rubles, rose brown	2.25
		Error: Text reads ГОСКУДАРСТВЕ<u>Н</u>АГО	4.50
		Error: Background inverted	3.50
		Error: Text reads Д<u>ЕЕ</u>СЯТЬ	5.00
R23.		25 Rubles, brown	2.50
		Error: Text reads ГОСКУДАРСТВЕ<u>Н</u>АГО	5.00
		Error: Text reads ДВАД<u>ЧАШЬ</u>	8.50

109 × 68

R24.	50 Rubles, turquoise	2.50
	Error: Background inverted	4.50
	Error: Reverse text inverted	4.50
	Error: Text reads ГОСКУДАРСТВЕ<u>Н</u>АГО	3.75
R25.	100 Rubles, yellow green	3.50
	Error: Reverse text inverted	5.00
	Error: Text reads ГОСКУДАРСТВЕ<u>Н</u>АГО	8.50
	Error: Text reads МИ<u>НС</u> — ТЕРСТВОМЪ	10.00

Notes dated 15 January (ЯНВАРЯ) 1920 on reverse. Large format (175 × 104 mm)

R26.	250 Rubles, rose. Background of waves on reverse	12.50
R27.	500 Rubles, light blue	20.00
R28.	1,000 Rubles, lilac	16.50
R29.	50 Rubles, green. Background of groups of waves on reverse	12.50
R30.	500 Rubles, light blue	10.00
R31.	25 Rubles, grey brown. Signature stamped on reverse	8.50
	Error: Obverse background inverted	16.50
	Error: Reverse text inverted	16.50
R32.	50 Rubles, green blue	8.50
R33.	100 Rubles, light green	3.50
R34.	250 Rubles, rose	3.00
	Error: Text reads ПЯТЬДЕС<u>ТЯ</u>Ъ	8.50
	Error: Reverse text inverted	6.50

R35.		500 Rubles, light blue to grey blue	3.50
		Error: Background inverted	6.50
R36.		1,000 Rubles	
		a. Light violet	3.50
		b. Orange brown	3.25
		c. Rose	3.50
		Error: Reverse text inverted	7.50
		Error: Background inverted	6.50

176 × 106

R37.		5,000 Rubles	
		a. Grey	2.75
		b. Violet	3.75
		Error: Background inverted	6.50
R38.		10,000 Rubles, green. Signature stamped on reverse	2.25
		Error: Numerals of value inverted	7.50
		Error: Reverse text inverted	6.50
		Error: Edge text at left reads from top to bottom	5.00
		Also see R45.	
R39.		25 Rubles, brown. Reverse signature facsimile printed	2.25
		Error: Reverse text inverted	4.50
		Error: Background inverted	3.50
R40.		250 Rubles, yellow brown. Numerals of value in black	6.50
R41.		250 Rubles, yellow brown. Numerals of value in light blue	12.50

Printed by Waterlow and Sons Ltd., London

R42.	1919	50 Rubles, brown. Dragons at left and right	2.25
R43.		100 Rubles, green. Landscape with mountains	2.50
R44.		250 Rubles, violet on green. Rev. Woman spinning	3.00

Armenia, Soviet Socialist Republic
СОВЕТСКАЯ СОЦИАЛИСТИЧ РЕСПУБЛИКА АРМЕНИИ

| R45. | August (НОЯБРЯ) 1919 | 10,000 Rubles, light green. As R38 but reverse signature facsimile printed | 4.50 |

R46.	1921	5,000 Rubles, blue	2.25
R47.		10,000 Rubles	
		a. Rose, watermarked paper	2.50
		b. Rose to brown, unwater-marked paper	3.50
		c. Lilac, unwatermarked paper	4.50
		d. Trial printing in green	R
R48.	1922	25,000 Rubles, blue. Setting sun	
		a. Watermarked paper	4.50
		b. Unwatermarked paper	5.00
R49.		100,000 Rubles, grey green on yellow	6.50
R50.		500,000 Rubles	4.50
R51.		1,000,000 Rubles, red	10.00
R52.		5,000,000 Rubles, black on grey olive, ОБЯЗАТЕЛЬСТВО	
		a. Watermarked paper	5.00
		b. Unwatermarked paper	6.50
R53.		5,000,000 Rubles, blue-green on light green, ДЕНЕЖНЫЙ ЗНАКЪ	12.50

Azerbaijan, Independent Republic
АЗЕРБАЙДЖАНСКАЯ РЕСПУБЛИКА

Many variations of color, paper and serial numbers are known

R54.	1919	25 Rubles, lilac and brown	2.25
R55.		50 Rubles, blue green and brown	2.50
R56.		100 Rubles, brown. Text reads АЗЕРБАЙДЖАНСКОЕ ПРАВИТЕЛЬСТВО	4.50
R57.		100 Rubles, brown. Text reads АЗЕРБАЙДЖАНСКАЯ РЕСПУБЛИКА	3.50

151 × 95

R58.		250 Rubles, lilac and brown	3.50
		Trial printing in green, brown, rose	65.00
R59.	1920	500 Rubles, lilac and brown. Series I–LV (the later series fall, by rights, in the time of the Soviet Republic of Azerbaijan)	4.50
R60.		1 Ruble (unfinished trial printing)	15.00

Azerbaijan, Soviet Republic
АЗЕРБАЙДЖАНСКАЯ СОЦ. СОВ. РЕСПУБЛИКА

R61.	(1920)	5 Rubles. Worker and farmer. Factory on reverse	
		a. Yellow	2.50
		b. Orange	3.50
R62.		100 Rubles, olive and violet. Train engine	2.25
R63.	1920	1,000 Rubles, olive and multicolored (format 167 × 107 mm)	4.50
		Trial printing in grey and light blue	35.00
R64.		1,000 Rubles, green (format 107 × 66 mm)	2.50

147 × 93

R65.	1921	5,000 Rubles, multicolored. Worker at left, seated farmer at right	2.25
R66.		10,000 Rubles, rose and green. Worker and farmer standing	2.25
R67.		25,000 Rubles, brown and grey	
		a. Unwatermarked paper	2.50
		b. Watermarked paper	3.00
R68.		50,000 Rubles, grey green	3.50
R69.	1922	100,000 Rubles	
		a. Violet, unwatermarked paper	2.25
		b. Blue, unwatermarked paper	3.50
		c. Watermarked paper	3.50
R70.		250,000 Rubles, blue and brown	2.50
R71.		1,000,000 Rubles, red	2.75
R72.	1923	5,000,000 Rubles, green and light green	5.00

Don Cossack Government
ВСЕВЕЛИКОЕ ВОЙСКО ДОНСКОЕ

Values are for completely filled-out notes. Blank notes are worth very little. All notes are red brown and olive. Reverses indicate acceptance by the state bank branches as follows:

Nowotscherkassk (НОВОЧЕРКАССК)
Taganrog (ТАГАНРОГ)
Rostow (РОСТОВ)

R73.	1 January 1919	500 Rubles, Nowotscherkassk	12.50
R74.	(ЯНВАРЯ)	1,000 Rubles, Nowotscherkassk	15.00
R75.		5,000 Rubles, Nowotscherkassk	18.50
R76.		10,000 Rubles, Nowotscherkassk	45.00
R77.		25,000 Rubles, Nowotscherkassk	70.00
R78.		50,000 Rubles, Nowotscherkassk	95.00
R79.	1 April 1919	500 Rubles	
	(АПРѢЛЯ)	a. Nowotscherkassk	10.00
		b. Taganrog	30.00
R80.		1,000 Rubles	
		a. Nowotscherkassk	15.00
		b. Taganrog	45.00
		c. Rostow	RRR
R81.		5,000 Rubles	
		a. Nowotscherkassk	30.00
		b. Taganrog	100.00
		c. Rostow	RRR
R82.		10,000 Rubles	
		a. Nowotscherkassk	150.00
		b. Taganrog	150.00
R83.		25,000 Rubles	
		a. Nowotscherkassk	70.00
		b. Rostow	RRR
R84.		50,000 Rubles, Nowotscherkassk	175.00
R85.	1 July 1919	500 Rubles	
	(ІЮЛЯ)	a. Nowotscherkassk	8.50
		b. Taganrog	12.50
R86.		1,000 Rubles	
		a. Nowotscherkassk	12.50
		b. Taganrog	15.00
R87.		5,000 Rubles	
		a. Nowotscherkassk	18.50
		b. Taganrog	18.50

307 × 117

R88.		10,000 Rubles	
		a. Nowotscherkassk	30.00
		b. Taganrog	45.00

R89.		25,000 Rubles	
		a. Nowotscherkassk	65.00
		b. Taganrog	45.00
R90.		50,000 Rubles	
		a. Nowotscherkassk	125.00
		b. Taganrog	RR
R91.	1 October 1919	500 Rubles	
	(ОКТЯБРЯ)	a. Nowotscherkassk	10.00
		b. Taganrog	8.50
R92.		1,000 Rubles	
		a. Nowotscherkassk	16.50
		b. Taganrog	12.50
R93.		5,000 Rubles	
		a. Nowotscherkassk	25.00
		b. Taganrog	18.50
R94.		10,000 Rubles	
		a. Nowotscherkassk	40.00
		b. Taganrog	35.00
R95.		25.000 Rubles, Taganrog	85.00
R96.		50,000 Rubles, Taganrog	100.00

Volunteer Western Army, Mitau, Col. Avaloff-Bermondt
ЗАПАДНАЯ ДОБРОВОЛЬЧЕСКАЯ АРМIЯ,
ПОЛК АВАЛОВЪ—БЕРМОНДТЪ

Treasury Notes, obverses in Russian, reverses in German

R97.	10.10.1919	1 Mark, black on light brown	
		a. With stamped imprint	1.75
		b. Without stamped imprint	1.00
R98.		5 Mark, black on violet blue	
		a. With stamped imprint	1.75
		b. Without stamped imprint	1.00

131 × 94

R99.		10 Mark, black on greenish background	
		a. With stamped imprint	16.50
		b. Without stamped imprint	4.50

Unfinished sheets of this note (printed on one side only)
were used to print Latvian postage stamps in 1920.

R100.		10 Mark, black. Without background on obverse	
		a. With stamped imprint	1.75
		b. Without stamped imprint	1.75
R101.		50 Mark. Grey green on brown reverse	
		a. With stamped imprint	6.50
		b. Without stamped imprint	2.50

Georgia, Independent Republic
ГРУЗИНСКАЯ РЕСПУБЛИКА

ОБЯЗАТЕЛЬСТВО КАЗНАЧЕЙСТВА   (Obligation Notes)

R102.	15.1.1919	25 Rubles	12.50
R103.		100 Rubles	10.00
R104.		500 Rubles	15.00
R105.		1,000 Rubles	16.50
R106.		5,000 Rubles	25.00

State Notes

R107.	(1919)	50 Kopecks, blue and light brown	2.25
R108.	1919	1 Ruble, rose background. Knight with lance	1.25
R109.		3 Rubles, green background. Type of R108	1.75
R110.		5 Rubles, dark green and orange. Type of R108	2.50
R111.		10 Rubles, brown and red brown. Type of R108	3.00
R112.		50 Rubles, violet and green. Type of R108	3.50
R113.		100 Rubles, green and lilac. Type of R108	3.75

163 × 102

R114.		500 Rubles, dark green and red brown. Seated woman with shield and lance	
		a. Paper watermarked with braided design	5.00
		b. Unwatermarked paper, thick and thin varieties	3.50
R115.	1920	1,000 Rubles, brown and blue. Knight with lance	
		a. Paper watermarked with braided design	7.50
		b. Unwatermarked paper	3.50

R116.   1921   5,000 Rubles, lilac to brown. Building with flags.
                                 Single circles around corner figures of value
                                 on both sides
                                 a. Paper watermarked with monogram   4.50
                                 b. Unwatermarked paper   2.50
                                 c. Lined reverse   6.50

Georgia, Soviet Socialist Republic
ГРУЗИНСКАЯ СОЦ. СОВЕТСКАЯ РЕСПУБЛИКА

R117.   1921   5,000 Rubles, lilac to brown. As R116 but double
                                 circles around corner figures of value
                                 a. Thick paper   2.50
                                 b. Thin paper, black printing   5.00
                                 c. Thin paper, blue printing   2.50
                                 Error: Background inverted   6.50

174 × 105

R118.   1922   10,000 Rubles. Buildings with flags
                                 a. Green background   3.50
                                 b. Light blue background   4.50
                                 Error: Background inverted   7.00

Obligation Notes, ОБЯЗАТЕЛЬСТВО НАРОДН БАНКА

R119.   31.5.1922   100,000 Rubles   5.00
R120.   500,000 Rubles   7.75
R121.   1,000,000 Rubles   10.00
R122.   5,000,000 Rubles   16.50

Crimea District Government
КРЫМСКОЕ КРАЕВОЕ ПРАВИТЕЛЬСТВО

ОБЯЗАТЕЛЬСТВО КРАЕВОГО КАЗНАЧЕЙСТВА (Obligation Notes)

R123.   1.9.1918   500 Rubles   35.00
R124.   1,000 Rubles   50.00
R125.   5,000 Rubles   100.00
Stamp Notes
R126.   (1918)   50 Kopecks, brown. Double-headed eagle   40.00

ДЕНЕЖНЫЙ ЗНАКЪ (Promissory Notes)

R127.	1918	5 Rubles, blue and brown. Map of the Crimea on the reverse	
		a. Control numbers 3 mm wide	2.50
		b. Control numbers 3½–6 mm (Soviet issue, 1920)	2.25
R128.		10 Rubles, red and brown. Map of the Crimea on the reverse	
		a. Control numbers 3 mm wide	3.50
		b. Control numbers 3½–6 mm (Soviet issue, 1920)	2.50
R129.		25 Rubles, green and lilac. Map of the Crimea on the reverse	
		a. Control numbers 3 mm wide	4.50
		b. Control numbers 3½–6 mm (Soviet issue, 1920)	2.50

Kuban, District Government
КУБАНСКОЕ КРАЕВОЕ ПРАВИТЕЛЬСТВО

These notes were not in circulation.

R130.	15.3.1918	5 Rubles	RRR
R131.	25.3.1918	3 Rubles	RRR
R132.		5 Rubles	RRR
R133.		10 Rubles	RRR
R134.		20 Rubles	RRR
R135.		100 Rubles	RRR
R136.	1.3.1920	250 Rubles, green	
		a. Reverse reads АПРѢЛЯ"	3.50
		b. Reverse reads АПРѢЛЯ"	2.50

Kuban, (Soviet) Republic
КУБАНСКАЯ РЕСПУБЛИКА

Loan Notes

Russian notes #77–80 with a four-cornered counter stamp

R137.	(1918)	20 Rubles	10.00
R138.		40 Rubles	12.50
R139.		50 Rubles	18.50
R140.		100 Rubles	8.50

ЕКАТЕРИНОДАРСКОГО ОТДЕЛЕНИЯ ГОСУДАРТВЕННОГО БАНКА

R141.	1918	10 Rubles, blue on brown	
		a. Guaranteed amount 25,000 rubles	5.00
		b. Guaranteed amount 50,000 rubles	5.00
		c. Guaranteed amount 100,000 rubles	5.00

R142.	(1918)	50 Rubles. Colored guilloche (ornament) at left. Promissory note paper	
		a. With perforation	4.50
		b. Without perforation	6.50

235 × 129

R143.		100 Rubles. Type of R142	5.00

Northern Army, Special Corp under General Rodzianko
ОТДѢЛЬНЫЙ КОРПЧСЪ СѢВЕРНОЙ АРМІИ, ГЕН. РОДЗЯНКО

R144.	(1919)	50 Kopecks, light green. Both sides printed	125.00
R145.		50 Kopecks, light green	
		a. Obverse only of R144	4.50
		b. Reverse only of R144	4.50
R146.		50 Kopecks, dark green	
		a. Obverse only of R144	10.00
		b. Reverse only of R144	10.00
R147.	1919	1 Ruble, brown on yellow	2.50
R148.		3 Rubles, green	3.50

101 × 68

R149.		5 Rubles, blue	10.00
R150.		10 Rubles, red	2.50

Northern District (Tschaikowskij)
СѢВЕРНОЙ ОБЛАСТИ

5 % КРАТКОСРОЧНОЕ ОБЯЗАТЕЛЬСТВО ВЕРХОВНАГО
УПРАВЛЕНІЯ СѢВЕРНОЙ ОБЛАСТИ (5% Obligation Notes)

R151.	15.8.1918	100 Rubles, yellow	16.50

R152.	500 Rubles, blue	20.00
R153.	1,000 Rubles, red	35.00
R154.	5,000 Rubles	65.00
R155.	10,000 Rubles	100.00

5% КРАТКОСРОЧНОЕ ОБЯЗАТЕЛЬСТВО ВЕРХОВНАГО ПРАВИТЕЛЬСТВА СѢВЕРНОЙ ОБЛАСТИ (5% Obligation Notes)

Notes exist both with and without *и* after ФИНАНСОВЪ

R156. 15.8.1918	50 Rubles, green	5.00
R157.	100 Rubles	
	a. With *и*	6.50
	b. Without *и*	10.00
R158.	500 Rubles, blue	
	a. Control numbers green or black. With *и*	8.50
	b. Without *и*	10.00
R159.	1,000 Rubles, red	
	a. With *и*	10.00
	b. Without *и*	12.50

Small Denomination Notes

Similar to the Czarist notes #28, 30 and 31 but text reads СѢВЕРНАЯ РОССІЯ

R160. (1919)	10 Kopecks, green and rose	2.25

90 × 52

R161.	20 Kopecks, brown and green	2.25
R162.	50 Kopecks, blue and yellow. Eagle with crown	2.25
R163.	50 Kopecks. Eagle without crown	6.50

Notes similar to Czarist issues #10–13 but text reads СѢВЕРНАЯ РОССІЯ
Eagle with crown, stamp on reverse reads ЧЛЕНЪ ГОРОДСКОЙ ЗМИССІОННОЙ КАССЫ

R164. 1918	5 Rubles, blue green (also known without reverse stamp)	8.50
R165.	10 Rubles, red and green	8.50
R166.	25 Rubles, rose and green	25.00
R167.	100 Rubles, brown, red and green	45.00

Notes similar to R164–R167 but reverse stamp reads ЧЛЕНЪ ГОСУДАРСТВ ЗМИССІОННОЙ КАССЫ

R168. 1918	5 Rubles, blue green	12.50
R169.	10 Rubles, red and green	12.50

R170.	25 Rubles, rose and green	
	a. Eagle overprinted	25.00
	b. Eagle without overprint	30.00
R171.	100 Rubles, brown, red and green	85.00
R172.	500 Rubles	125.00

Notes similar to issues #1 and #9–14 but text reads СѢВЕРНАЯ РОССІЯ
Eagle without crown

R173.	1919	1 Ruble	8.50
R174.		3 Rubles	10.00
R175.		5 Rubles, green and brown	12.50
R176.		10 Rubles	18.50

178 × 106

R177.	25 Rubles, rose and green	25.00
R178.	100 Rubles	85.00
R179.	500 Rubles	125.00

Notes of the Czarist and the Provisional Government with perforation "CO"
Many counterfeits exist.

R180.	50 Kopecks. Note #31 with perforation	2.50
R181.	1 Ruble. Note #1 with perforation	4.50
R182.	1 Ruble. Note #15 with perforation	1.75
R183.	3 Rubles. Note #9 with perforation	2.25
R184.	5 Rubles. Note #3 with perforation	8.50
R185.	5 Rubles. Note #10 with perforation	4.50
R186.	5 Rubles. Note #35 with perforation	1.25
R187.	10 Rubles. Note #4 with perforation	16.50
R188.	10 Rubles. Note #11 with perforation	2.25
R189.	20 Rubles. Note #38 with perforation	3.50
R190.	20 Rubles. Note #77 with perforation	8.50
R191.	25 Rubles. Note #12 with perforation	4.50
R192.	25 Rubles. Note #48 with perforation	7.00
R193.	40 Rubles. Note #39 with perforation	3.50
R194.	40 Rubles. Note #78 with perforation	8.50
R195.	50 Rubles. Note #8 with perforation	9.00

R196.	50 Rubles. Note #49 (but dated 1909) with perforation	20.00
R197.	50 Rubles. Note #52 with perforation	6.50
R198.	50 Rubles. Note #53 with perforation	7.50
R199.	50 Rubles. Note #79 with perforation	7.50
R200.	100 Rubles. Note #5 with perforation	20.00
R201.	100 Rubles. Note #13 with perforation	8.50
R202.	100 Rubles. Note #56 with perforation	20.00
R203.	100 Rubles. Note #57 with perforation	8.50
R204.	100 Rubles. Note #58 with perforation	8.50
R205.	100 Rubles. Note #80 with perforation	7.50
R206.	250 Rubles. Note #36 with perforation	4.50
R207.	500 Rubles. Note #6 with perforation	30.00
R208.	500 Rubles. Note #14 with perforation	12.50
R209.	500 Rubles. Note #59 with perforation	10.00
R210.	500 Rubles. Note #60 with perforation	10.00
R211.	1,000 Rubles. Note #61–63 with perforation	12.50
R212.	1,000 Rubles. Note #37 with perforation	4.50
R213.	5,000 Rubles. Note #64 with perforation	16.50
R214.	10,000 Rubles. Note #65–67 with perforation	20.00
R215.	100,000 Rubles. Note #73 with perforation	35.00

North Caucasian Soviet Socialist Republic

СЕВЕРО—КАВКАЗСКАЯ СОВ. СОЦ. РЕСПУБЛИКА

ВРЕМЕН. ЦЕНТР. УПРАВЛ. ОТД. НАРОД. БАНКА

Notes printed on promissory note paper

R216.	1918	25 Rubles, blue green	3.50
R217.		50 Rubles, yellow brown	3.50
R218.		100 Rubles, green	3.50
R219.		10 Rubles, red and yellow brown. Sickle and grain	
		a. Obverse text reads ОБЩЕГО<u>СУ</u>ДАР . . . <u>О</u>ГО	3.50
		b. Obverse text reads ОБЩЕГОО<u>У</u>ДАР . . . <u>А</u>ГО	3.50

131 × 82

R220.	25 Rubles, violet, yellow and green. Sickle and grain	
	a. Obverse text reads ОБЩЕГО<u>СУ</u>ДАР . . . <u>О</u>ГО	3.50
	b. Obverse text reads ОБЩЕГОО<u>У</u>ДАР . . . <u>А</u>ГО	3.50

КРАЕВОГО ИСПОЛНИТ. КОМИТЕТА СОВЕТОВ СЕВ. КАВКАЗА
ДЕНЕЖНЫЙ ЗНАК

R221.	5 Rubles, blue and rose	4.50

R222.		50 Rubles, green	5.00
R223.		100 Rubles, brown	7.50
R224.		250 Rubles	8.50
R225.		500 Rubles, multicolored	10.00

North Caucasian Emirate

СЕВЕРО—КАВКАЗСКИЙ ЭМИРАТ

Notes of Terek and North Caucasia with the stamp of the Iman or Vizier Kjamil-Khan

R226.	(1919)	50 Rubles. Note R303b with round stamp of the Vizier	100.00
R227.		50 Rubles. Note R303a with round stamp of the Vizier	16.50
R228.		100 Rubles. Note R304 with oval imprint of the ring of the Iman	100.00
R229.		100 Rubles. Note R304 with oval imprint of the ring of the Iman and the round stamp of the Vizier. Signature and date	50.00
R230.		100 Rubles. Note R304 with only the round stamp of the Vizier. Signature and date handwritten	100.00
R231.		100 Rubles. Note R304 with only the round stamp of the Vizier but without signature and handwritten date	25.00
R232.		100 Rubles. Note R223 with round stamp of the Vizier, signature and handwritten date	150.00
R233.		100 Rubles. Note R223 with round stamp of the Vizier but without signature and handwritten date	150.00
R234.		500 Rubles. Note R225 with round stamp of the Vizier, signature and handwritten date	150.00

КРЕДТНЫЙ БИЛЕТЪ

Scale with rifle and sabre on all notes

62 × 65

R235.	1919	5 Rubles, blue green. Mountain with flags	
		a. Printed top to top	8.50
		b. Reverse inverted	12.50
R236.		25 Rubles	
		a. Printed top to top	12.50
		b. Reverse inverted	16.50
R237.		50 Rubles	
		a. Printed top to top	12.50
		b. Reverse inverted	16.50
		c. Obverse design repeated on reverse	45.00
R238.		100 Rubles, green and light brown. Mountain and flag	
		a. No text below the Arabic numeral of value in background on reverse	8.50
		b. As R238a but with Arabic text	10.00
		c. As R238b but reverse inverted	12.50

| R239. | | 250 Rubles, green. Large arms | 15.00 |
| R240. | | 250 Rubles, light blue. Small arms | 10.00 |

R241.		500 Rubles, light blue and light brown. Mountains and sea with setting sun	
		a. Printed top to top	12.50
		b. Reverse inverted	15.00
R242.		1,000 Rubles. Reverse blank (not issued)	RRR

Northwest Front (under General N. N. Judenitch) Field Notes
СЕВЕРО—ЗАПАДНЫЙ ФРОНТЪ

ДЕНЕЖНЫЙ ЗНАКЪ

The reverses of all notes show a double eagle without crown and the memorial to Peter the Great in the middle.

R243.	1919	25 Kopecks, yellow green	1.50
R244.		50 Kopecks, grey	1.50
R245.		1 Ruble, light and dark green	1.75
R246.		3 Rubles, rose and green	
		a. Control number without letters (1st issue)	2.00
		b. A in control number (2nd issue)	2.50
R247.		5 Rubles, blue	
		a. Type of R246a	1.75
		b. Type of R246b	2.25
R248.		10 Rubles, blue green and brown	
		a. Type of R246a (1st issue)	1.75
		b. Type of R246b (2nd issue)	2.25
		c. Control number (3rd issue)	2.50

160 × 73

R249.		25 Rubles, violet background	
		a. Type of R246a	3.00
		b. Type of R246b	3.50
		c. Type of R248c	4.50
R250		100 Rubles, brown and green	3.50
R251.		500 Rubles, green and brown	5.00
R252.		1,000 Rubles, red and violet	5.00

South Russia, Armed commandos of Generals Deniken and Wrangel
ГЛАВНОЕ КОМАНДОВАНІЕ ВООРУЖЕННЫМИ СИЛАМИ

Stamp Notes

| R253. | (1918) | 20 Kopecks, green. Ticket printed with text, eagle and St. George at right | 4.50 |

Small Denomination Notes

R254. (1918)   50 Kopecks, light brown   2.50

ДЕНЕЖНЫЙ ЗНАКЪ (Exchange Notes)

R255. 1918   1 Ruble, brown
                 a. White, thin paper   1.25
                 b. Yellow, thick paper   1.25
R256.   3 Rubles, green
                 a. White, thin paper without watermark   1.25
                 b. Grey, thin paper without watermark   1.25
                 c. Yellow, thick paper without watermark   1.25
                 d. Paper with watermark   3.50
R257.   5 Rubles, blue
                 a. Unwatermarked paper   1.75
                 b. Paper watermarked with monogram   1.75
R258.   10 Rubles, red brown and greenish
                 a. Unwatermarked paper   2.25
                 b. Paper watermarked with monogram   1.50
R259.   25 Rubles, lilac brown and green. Woman with sword
               at left
                 a. Unwatermarked paper   1.75
                 b. Paper watermarked with monogram   1.75
R260.   100 Rubles, dark brown and grey blue. Helmeted man's
               head and seated woman   2.25
R261.   250 Rubles, red brown and green. Seated women at left
               and right
                 a. White, unwatermarked paper   1.75
                 b. Yellowish, unwatermarked paper   1.75
                 c. Paper watermarked with monogram   1.50
R262.   500 Rubles, dark green and brown. Rev. Seated woman
               at left
                 a. White, unwatermarked paper   2.25
                 b. Yellowish, unwatermarked paper   2.25
                 c. Paper watermarked with monogram   2.25
R263. 1919   50 Rubles, brown, grey and blue. Rev. Woman with
               flag   1.75
R264.   100 Rubles, yellow green and multicolored. Warrior in
               armor with standard at right of reverse, memorial
               with two warriors
                 a. Unwatermarked paper   2.25
                 b. Paper watermarked with monogram   1.75
R265.   1,000 Rubles, grey green and red brown to blue violet.
               Woman seated with shield and sword in middle of
               reverse
                 a. Unwatermarked paper   2.25
                 b. Paper watermarked with monogram   1.75
                 c. Paper watermarked with mosaic design   1.75

R266.   5,000 Rubles, lilac and green. Warrior in armor with shield, flag and snake at left on reverse

      a. White, unwatermarked paper   2.25
      b. Grey, unwatermarked paper   2.50
      c. Paper watermarked with monogram   1.75
      d. Paper watermarked with mosaic design   2.00

БИЛЕТЪ ГОСУДАРСТВЕННАГО КАЗНАЧЕЙСТВА (State Treasury Notes)

R267. 1919   3 Rubles, green

      a. Unwatermarked paper   12.50
      b. Paper watermarked with mosaic design   2.25

R268.   10 Rubles, red brown. Memorial with two warriors on reverse

      a. Unwatermarked paper   2.25
      b. Paper watermarked with wavy lines   2.25

R269.   50 Rubles, background olive brown. Woman with two children

      a. Paper watermarked with lines   1.50
      b. Paper watermarked with spades   1.50

R270.   200 Rubles, lilac and grey violet. Equestrian statue and soldiers on reverse   2.50

R271.   1,000 Rubles, multicolored. Bell at left, St. George and dragon at right

      a. Unwatermarked paper (two control number varieties)   1.75
      b. Paper watermarked with mosaic design   1.75

R272.   10,000 Rubles, green and brown. Seated woman with lance at left, seated woman with sword at right   1.25

R273. 1920   5 Rubles, blue green

      a. Printed on both sides   RRR
      b. Printed on obverse only   6.50

R274.   25,000 Rubles, grey blue and brown (unfinished printing)   4.50

6 % КРАТК. ОБЯЗАТЕЛЬСТВО ГОСУД. КАЗНАЧЕЙСТВА
(6% Obligation Notes)

R275. 1.1.1920   100,000 Rubles, brown on red brown

      a. Maturity date (СРОК) 1. IV.   85.00
      b. Maturity date (СРОК) 15. VIII.   85.00
      c. Maturity date (СРОК) 15. XI.   20.00

БИЛЕТЪ ГОСУДАРСТВЕННАГО КАЗНАЧЕЙСТВА (State Treasury Notes)

Issued by General Wrangel. All reverses show memorial with cross.

R276. 1920   100 Rubles, red brown

      a. Paper watermarked with stars   2.00
      b. Paper watermarked with waves   2.50
      c. Paper watermarked with mosaic design   1.50

154 × 76

R277.	250 Rubles, lilac brown	
	a. Brown paper watermarked with spades	1.50
	b. White paper watermarked with mosaic design	1.25
R278.	500 Rubles, blue	1.25

ГОСУДАРСТВО РОССІЙСКОЕ КАЗНАЧЕЙСКІЙ ЗНАКЪ

English printing, not issued.

R279.	1 Ruble	RRR
R280.	3 Rubles	RRR
R281.	5 Rubles	RRR
R282.	50 Rubles, blue on yellow. Helmeted woman's head at left	2.25
R283. 1919	100 Rubles, brown on green. Helmeted woman's head at left on reverse. Serial letters in the plate or printed with control numbers	3.00
R284.	500 Rubles, green and orange. Type of R283	2.50

ХЕРСОНСКІИ ГУБ. УПОЛНОМОЧ. УПРАВЛ. ПРОДОВОЛЬСТВІЕМЪ
ОДЕССА (Food authorization notes for the Cherson district)

R285.	10.10.1919	25 Rubles	10.00
R286.		50 Rubles	10.00
R287.		100 Rubles	10.00
R288.		250 Rubles	10.00
R289.		500 Rubles	15.00

Terek-Daghestan District
ТЕРСКО=ДАГЕСТАНСКАЯ ОБЛАСТ

Pasted-on control stamps of savings banks. Reverses are printed with:
a. Narrow "Н" in date, no period after 1918 (issued by Iman Gozinskij)
b. Broad "Н" in date, period after 1918 (issued by Soviet Peoples Commissar)

			a.	b.
R290.	25.1(ЯНВАРЯ) .1918	25 Kopecks	20.00	10.00
R291.		50 Kopecks	25.00	10.00
R292.		1 Ruble	12.50	6.50
R293.		3 Rubles	15.00	10.00
		Error "БИЛЕТЕМИ"	—	20.00
R294.		5 Rubles	20.00	10.00

R295.		10 Rubles	8.50	6.50
R296.		25 Rubles	6.50	6.50
R297.		100 Rubles	10.00	6.50

Terek Republic
ТЕРСКАЯ РЕСПУБЛИКА

R298.	1918	1 Ruble, brown background		2.50
R299.		3 Rubles, green background		2.50
R300.		5 Rubles, blue on grey		2.50
		Error: Reverse inverted		4.50
R301.		10 Rubles, red background		2.50

152 × 96

R302.		25 Rubles, dark green	6.50
R303.		50 Rubles, yellow and orange background	
		a. Brown printing	2.25
		b. Black printing	2.40
R304.		100 Rubles	
		a. Brown on red brown printing	3.50
		b. Brown on light brown printing, at bottom left	4.50

Stamp Currency

Tickets with double-headed eagle in middle, text on reverse

R305.		10 Kopecks, blue	4.50
R306.		15 Kopecks, brown	4.50
R307.		20 Kopecks, green	4.50

Transcaucasian Commissariat
ЗАКАВКАЗСКІЙ КОМИССАРІАТЪ

All notes are known with and without a network of varnish as a background pattern.

R308.	1918	1 Ruble, blue on light blue	.75
R309.		3 Rubles, green background	1.50
R310.		5 Rubles, blue on grey	1.75

119 × 78

R311.		10	Rubles, red brown on olive	2.25
R312.		50	Rubles, blue grey background	2.40
R313.		100	Rubles, brown and blue green	2.50
R314.		250	Rubles, grey olive on pale lilac	3.00

Federation of Socialist Soviet Republics of Transcaucasia
ФЕДЕРАЦИЯ СОВ. СОЦ. РЕСПУБЛИК ЗАКАВКАЗЬЯ
ДЕНЕЖНЫЙ ЗНАК

All notes show a building with flags on their obverse. Ornamentation on the reverse runs in one direction.

R315.	1923	1,000	Rubles, yellow brown background	3.50
R316.		5,000	Rubles, lilac brown background	4.50
R317.		10,000	Rubles, grey on red background	2.50
R318.		25,000	Rubles, brown background	3.00
R319.		50,000	Rubles, green background	
			a. Paper watermarked with stars	16.50
			b. Unwatermarked paper	3.00
R320.		100,000	Rubles, red brown background	
			a. Paper watermarked with stars	16.50
			b. Unwatermarked paper	3.50

166 × 98

| R321. | | 250,000 | Rubles, green background | 3.50 |
| | | | Error: Reverse inverted | 12.50 |

R322.		500,000 Rubles, light blue blackground		
		a. Paper watermarked with stars		10.00
		b. Unwatermarked paper		3.50
R323.		1,000,000 Rubles, violet background		
		a. Paper watermarked with stars		8.50
		b. Unwatermarked paper		4.50
R324.		5,000,000 Rubles, green and lilac background		6.50
R325.		10,000,000 Rubles, blue, green, yellow and red background		6.50

ДЕНЕЖНЫЙ ЗНАК

Reverse ornamentation runs in various directions.

R326.	1923	5,000 Rubles, lilac brown background	3.50
R327.		10,000 Rubles, grey background	3.75
R328.		50,000 Rubles, green background	4.50
R329.		100,000 Rubles, red brown background	4.50
R330.		250,000 Rubles, green background	4.50
R331.		500,000 Rubles, light blue background	5.00
R332.		1,000,000 Rubles, violet background	5.00
R333.		5,000,000 Rubles, green and lilac background	5.00
R334.		10,000,000 Rubles, blue, green, yellow and red background	6.50

Transcaucasian Socialist Federation of Soviet Republics

R335.	1924	25,000,000 Rubles, grey background. Building with flag in middle	
		a. Watermarked paper	6.50
		b. Unwatermarked paper	6.50
		Error: Reverse inverted	18.50
R336.		50,000,000 Rubles, grey violet background. Type of R335 (format 167 × 100 mm)	10.00
R337.		50,000,000 Rubles, horizontal format. Printed on reverse side only (unfinished)	20.00
R338.		75,000,000 Rubles, brown background. Oil derrick on reverse	
		a. Watermarked paper	12.50
		b. Unwatermarked paper	10.00
R339.		100,000,000 Rubles, green background. Type of R335	10.00
R340.		250,000,000 Rubles, brown. Oil derrick on reverse	16.50
R341.		1,000,000,000 Rubles, lilac. Seated woman with fruit and grains on reverse	
		a. Text in green	18.50
		b. Text in black	20.00
R342.		10,000,000,000 Rubles	45.00

Ukrainian Peoples Republic
УКРАИНСЬКА НАРОДНЯ РЕСПУБЛИКА

1 Karbowanez (КАРБОВАНЕЦ) = *1 Ruble* = *2 Griwen* (ГРИВЕНЬ)
= *200 Schahiw* (ШАГІВ)

Central Control

R343. 1917	100 Karbowanez, brown, orange and yellow	
	a. Printed top to top	100.00
	b. Reverse inverted	8.50

ЗНАК ДЕРЖАВНОІ СКАРБНИЦІ (Treasury Notes)

R344. (1918)   25 Karbowanez, green. Man with spade at left, woman with sheafs at right. Without serial letters (issued in Kiev)
  a. Text reads КРЕДІТОВИМ   8.50
  b. Text reads КРЕДИТОВИМ   35.00

R345.   25 Karbowanez, green. As R344 but serial letters AO (issued in Odessa)   5.00

R346.   50 Karbowanez, green. Type of R344 (issued in Kiev)
  a. Text reads КРЕДИТОВИМ   12.50
  b. Text reads КРЕДИТОВИМИ   5.00

131 × 74

R347.   50 Karbowanez, green. As R346 but serial letters AKI or AKII (issued in Kiev)   1.75
  Error: Reverse printed only in red (AKII)   20.00

R348.   50 Karbowanez, green. As R346 but with serial letters AO (issued in Odessa)
  a. Serial numbers to 209   1.00
  b. Serial numbers from 210 (issued by General Deniken and labeled as false by the Ukrainian Government)   1.00

Postage Stamp Currency

Postage stamps (Michel catalogue #1–5 of Ukraine) printed on cardboard. Reverses have arms and text.

R349. (1918)   10 Schahiw, yellow brown. Arms   1.00

R350.		20 Schahiw, dark brown. Peasant	1.00
R351.		30 Schahiw. Ceres head	
		a. Ultramarine	1.00
		b. Grey violet	2.40
R352.		40 Schahiw, green. Arms	1.00
R353.		50 Schahiw, red	1.00

3.6 % БІЛЕТ ДЕРЖАВНОІ СКАРБНИЦІ   (3.6% Loan Notes and Interest Coupons)

R354.	1918	50 Griwen, green and brown	3.50
R355.		100 Griwen, brown on green and red	2.50
R356.		200 Griwen, blue	2.50
R357.		1,000 Griwen, brown on yellow brown	2.50
R358.		90 Schahiw, green	.60
R359.		1 Griwnja 80 Schahiw, red brown	.60
R360.		3 Griwnja 60 Schahiw, blue	.60
R361.		18 Griwen, yellow brown	.60

5 % КР. ОБЯЗАТ. ГОСУД. КАЗНАЧ (5% Obligation Notes)

With various stamps of the State Bank branches.

R362.	(1918)	1,000 Rubles, red brown on grey	12.50
R363.		5,000 Rubles	16.50
R364.		10,000 Rubles	35.00
R365.		25,000 Rubles	53.00
R366.		50,000 Rubles	69.00

ДЕРЖАВНИЙ КРЕДИТОВИЙ БІЛЕТ

R367.	1918	2 Griwen, green	
		a. Yellowish background, serial letter A	2.00
		b. Brown background, serial letter B	3.50
R368.		10 Griwen, red brown	2.00

R 369
174 × 114

R369.	100	Griwen, violet. Peasant woman at left, worker at right	
		a. Blue background, serial letter A	3.50
		b. Grey violet background, serial letter (not issued)	125.00
R370.	500	Griwen, green and orange. Woman's head in middle	3.50
R371.	1,000	Griwen, blue on orange and yellow	4.50
R372.	2,000	Griwen, red on blue	4.50

ЗНАК ДЕРЖАВНОІ СКАРБНИЦІ

Beginning with R374, the notes are issues of the Directorate under Sjemen Petljura.

R373.	1,000	Karbowanez, brown. Reverse brown, two allegorical female figures	
		a. Paper watermarked with wavy lines	3.50
		b. Zigzag lines of varnish printed on paper (appear as watermark)	5.00
R374.	1,000	Karbowanez, brown. As R373 but reverse violet brown	
		a. Paper watermarked with wavy lines	8.50
		b. Paper watermarked with stars	6.50
R375.	100	Karbowanez, brown and grey green	
		a. Paper watermarked with stars (two control number varieties)	3.50
		b. Paper watermarked with spades (two control number varieties)	57.50
R376.	250	Karbowanez, brown and olive (two control number varieties)	4.50
R377. (1919)	10	Karbowanez, brown on grey paper watermarked with spades (two control number varieties) Also see R383.	3.00
R378.	25	Karbowanez, violet brown. With and without control numbers	4.50

РОЗМІННИЙ ЗНАК ДЕРЖАВНОІ СКАРБНИЦІ

R379. (1920)	5	Griwen, grey	2.50
		Error: ГИВЕНЬ	85.00

ДЕРЖАВНИЙ КРЕДИТОВИЙ БІЛЕТ

Printing trials, Austrian printer

R380.	1920	50 Griwen, blue grey	RR
R381.		50 Griwen, brown	RR
R382.		1,000 Griwen, grey and orange	RRR

Ukrainian Soviet Republic

СОВЕТСКАЯ УКРАИНСКАЯ РЕСЛУБЛИКА

ЗНАК ДЕРЖАВНОІ СКАРБНИЦІ

R383.	(1920)	10 Karbowanez, red brown. As R377 but white paper and no control numbers	2.50
R384.		50 Karbowanez. Trial printings	
		a. Green	85.00
		b. Light blue	85.00
		c. Violet	85.00
		d. Brown	85.00

РАСЧЕТНАЯ БОНА ВУЦИК

All notes printed in green blue on obverses, lilac figures of value on reverses. Control numbers are handwritten. R385–R389 also have control numbers printed.

R385.	1923	5 Kopecks	6.50
R386.		10 Kopecks	6.50

75 × 55

R387.	25 Kopecks	7.50
R388.	50 Kopecks	8.50
R389.	1 Ruble	10.00
R390.	3 Rubles	12.50
R391.	5 Rubles	16.50
R392.	10 Rubles	16.50
R393.	25 Rubles	35.00
R394.	50 Rubles	50.00

German Occupation during World War II

Zentralnotenbank Ukraine (Central Ukrainian Bank)

R395.	10.3.1942	1 Karbowanez, olive	2.50
R396.		2 Karbowanez (not issued)	RRR
R397.		5 Karbowanez, brown violet. Head of child at right	3.00
R398.		10 Karbowanez, red brown. Head of peasant woman at right	3.00
R399.		20 Karbowanez, grey brown. Head of industrial worker at right	3.50

R400.   50 Karbowanez, green. Head of miner at right   6.50

176 × 92

R401.   100 Karbowanez, blue. Head of sailor at right   10.00
R402.   200 Karbowanez, olive. Peasant woman at right   16.50
R403.   500 Karbowanez, violet. Chemical worker at right   25.00

Notes also exist of the Bank of Kiev (1941 1 ruble, 1 and 5 tscherwonez) but they were not circulated.

Ukrainian Revolutionary Army–Ukrainski Powstanscha Armyia (У П А)

R404.   (1946)   5 Karbowanez, brown violet and multicolored. Soldier at machine gun and soldier with hand grenade   RRR

SAAR (Sarre)

The rich Saar district was occupied by France after World War I. Governed by the League of Nations, the area was returned to Germany after a plebiscite vote in 1935. Following World War II, the Saar was again declared an autonomous district to be returned to Germany in 1957.

Mines Domaniales de la Sarre, Etat Francaise (Mining interests of the **Saar**, French State)

1.	dates to 1.1.1930	50 Centimes, blue grey. Woman's head at left	$3.50
2.	1919 to 1.1.1930	1 Franc, red brown. Woman's head at right	5.00

Issue of 1947 (without any identification of issuing authority)

3.	1947	1 Mark, blue and brown. Bearded head of man	8.50
4.		2 Mark, lilac and brown. Type of #3	35.00
5.		5 Mark, rose and violet. Type of #3	12.50
6.		10 Mark, multicolored. Woman's head	35.00
		Error: Reverse without text	125.00

130 × 84

7.	50 Mark, multicolored. Type of #6	100.00
8.	100 Mark, multicolored. Type of #6	RR

SERBIA

At the beginning of the 19th century Serbia became an autonomous principality under the Turks, breaking away completely in 1878. In 1882 the country became a kingdom under Milan II who ruled until 1889. After the Balkan War of 1912–13 and World War I, Serbia became part of the Kingdom of Yugoslavia.

1 Dinar (ДИНАР) = *100 Para* (ПАРА)

Dinar in gold = ДИНАР У ЗЛАТУ
Dinar in silver = ДИНАР У СРЕВРУ

Government Notes

1.	1. 7.1876	1 Dinar	$150.00
2.		5 Dinar	250.00
3.		10 Dinar	RR
4.		50 Dinar	RR
5.		100 Dinar	RR
6.	1.11.1885	10 Dinar	RR

Privilegovana Narodna Banka Kraljevine Srbije (Privileged National Bank of the Kingdom of Serbia) ПРИВИЛЕГОВАНА НАРОДНА БАНКА КРАЉЕВИНЕ СРБИЈЕ

7.	2. 7.1884	100 Dinar Zlatu (gold), green on brown. Woman with tablet at left and at right	RR

157 × 95

8.	1. 5.1886	50 Dinar Zlatu, green on light brown. Woman in costume at left, woman with sword at right	RR

9.	14. 1.1887	10 Dinar Srebru, (silver), blue. Woman with sword at left, allegorical figures at right	150.00
10.	2. 1.1893	10 Dinar Srebru, blue on brown. Woman with musical instrument	16.50
11.	5. 1.1905	20 Dinar Zlatu, blue on brown. Woman at left, man with sword at right	175.00
12.		100 Dinar Srebru, blue on brown. Woman with sword at right	20.00
13.	1. 8.1914	50 Dinar Srebru	250.00
14.	(1916–17)	5 Dinar Srebru, blue. Man's helmeted head	6.50

Also see Yugoslavia #36–47.

Postage Stamp Currency, 1915

Due to the war, only two values, the 5 and 10 para, of an already prepared set of postage stamps were released for use on mail. The other five values, all showing King Peter II and his Military Staff on the battlefield, were circulated as emergency currency. The stamps were all perforated but some imperforate specimens from unfinished sheets are known.

15.	(1915)	5 Para, light green	2.25
16.		10 Para, vermilion	2.25
17.		15 Para, grey black	5.00
		Error: Dark blue	100.00
18.		20 Para, brown	2.50
19.		25 Para, dark blue	15.00
20.		30 Para, light olive	10.00
21.		50 Para, red brown	25.00

The 15 para stamps pasted onto cardboard with text and value overprinted were local issues of emergency currency (*Osijek, Prima Frankova tiskara*).

Austrian Military Government, 1917–18

Notes #10 and 12 with stamp "K.u.K. Militar-Gouvernement in Serbien, Kreis-kommando (area)" were issued during the Austrian occupation.

M1.	(1917–18)	10 Dinar (dated 2.1.1893), stamped "Belgrad"	35.00
M2.		100 Dinar (dated 5.1.1905), stamped "Belgrad"	65.00
M3.		10 Dinar, stamped "Belgrad-Land"	45.00
M4.		100 Dinar, stamped "Belgrad-Land"	75.00
M5.		10 Dinar, stamped "Čačak"	45.00
M6.		100 Dinar, stamped "Čačak"	75.00
M7.		10 Dinar, stamped "Gornji Milanovac"	150.00
M8.		100 Dinar, stamped "Gornji Milanovac"	150.00
M9.		10 Dinar, stamped "Kragujevac"	35.00
M10.		100 Dinar, stamped "Kragujevac"	75.00

M11.	10 Dinar, stamped "Kruševac"	45.00
M12.	100 Dinar, stamped "Kruševac"	75.00
M12a.	10 Dinar, stamped "Mitrovica"	150.00
M12b.	100 Dinar, stamped "Mitrovica"	150.00
M13.	10 Dinar, stamped "Šabac"	50.00
M14.	100 Dinar, stamped "Šabac"	85.00
M15.	10 Dinar, stamped "Semendria"	60.00
M16.	100 Dinar, stamped "Semendria"	90.00

138 × 84

M17.	10 Dinar, stamped "Smederevo"	45.00
M18.	100 Dinar, stamped "Smederevo"	65.00
M19.	10 Dinar, stamped "Užice"	60.00
M20.	100 Dinar, stamped "Užice"	100.00
M21.	10 Dinar, stamped "Valjevo"	75.00
M22.	100 Dinar, stamped "Valjevo"	100.00

Notes of 20 and 50 dinar (#11 and 13) were probably also overprinted.

SLOVAKIA

The eastern part of Czechoslovakia, Slovakia was declared an independent state led by Dr. Joseph Tiso under German protection. The area was returned to Czechoslovakia after World War II.

1 Krone = 100 Heller

As with the paper money of Czechoslovakia, Slovakian notes marked "Specimen" were supplied to collectors. The values indicated in the first column are for regular notes, those in the second column for specimens.

Government Notes

1.	(June 1939)	100 Kronen, green. Czech note #24 (dated 10.1.1931) with red overprint "Slovensky Stat"	$85.00	$8.50
2.	(April 1939)	500 Kronen, red. Czech note #22 (dated 2.5.1929) with blue overprint "Slovensky Stat"	150.00	16.50
3.	(April 1939)	1,000 Kronen, green and blue. Czech note #26 (dated 25.5.1934) with lilac overprint "Slovensky Stat"	RR	25.00
4.	15. 9.1939	10 Kronen, blue and brown. A. Hlinka at right	16.50	3.50
5.		20 Kronen, brown. A. Hlinka at right	25.00	4.50
6.	11. 9.1942	20 Kronen, brown and blue. Poet J. Holly at right	3.50	1.25
7.	20. 7.1943	10 Kronen, blue and violet. Poet L. Stur at right	6.00	1.25
8.	(1950)	5 Kronen, lilac and brown. Girl's head at right	3.50	1.25

Slovenska Narodna Banka (Slovakian National Bank)

9.	7.10.1940	100 Kronen, blue. Prince Pribina at right	7.50	2.25
10.		100 Kronen, blue. As #9 but "II Emisia" at left edge of reverse	10.00	2.25
11.	15.10.1940	50 Kronen, violet and lilac. Two girls in Slovakian costume at left	4.50	1.25

191 × 90

12.	25.11.1940	1,000	Kronen, brown. King Swatopluk and his three sons at right	16.50	3.50
13.	12. 7.1941	500	Kronen, green. Young man in costume at right	12.50	3.50
14.	18.12.1944	5,000	Kronen, brown and green. Prince Knieza Mojmir on reverse	35.00	5.00

For notes #9, #10, #12 and #13 with stamps affixed, see Czechoslovakia #51–54.

SPAIN (España)

As a result of the Carlist Wars, the weakened monarchy was deposed and a provisional government installed from 1868 to 1870. The monarchy was re-established under King Amadeo but he was forced to abdicate in 1873 and the First Republic came into being. It lasted only until 1875 when Alfonso XII was put on the throne. He was followed by Maria Christina who ruled as regent for her son Alfonso XIII from 1885 until 1902 when he came of age to rule in his own right. Alfonso ruled well but social unrest sent him into voluntary exile in 1931 and the Republic of Spain was created. Although Spain remained neutral during both world wars the country was devastated by a civil war that raged from 1936 to 1939.

1 Peseta = 100 Centimos

Issues of the First Republic and the Kingdom up to 1931

Banco de España (Bank of Spain)

1.	1. 7.1874	25	Pesetas	RR
2.		50	Pesetas	RR
3.		100	Pesetas	RR
4.		500	Pesetas	RRR
5.		1,000	Pesetas	RRR
6.	1. 7.1875	25	Pesetas	RR
7.		50	Pesetas	RR
8.		100	Pesetas	RR
9.		500	Pesetas	RRR
10.		1,000	Pesetas	RRR
11.	1. 7.1876	100	Pesetas	RR
12.		500	Pesetas	RR
13.		1,000	Pesetas	RRR
14.	1. 1.1878	50	Pesetas	RR
15.		100	Pesetas	RR
17.		250	Pesetas	RRR
18.		500	Pesetas	RRR
19.		1,000	Pesetas	RRR

The note previously listed as #16 has not been verified.

#20
174 × 90

20.	1. 4.1880	50	Pesetas	RR
21.		100	Pesetas	RR
22.		500	Pesetas	RR
23.		1,000	Pesetas	RR
24.	1. 1.1884	25	Pesetas	RR
25.		50	Pesetas	RR
26.		100	Pesetas	RR
27.		500	Pesetas	RR
28.		1,000	Pesetas	RR
29.	1. 7.1884	25	Pesetas	RR
30.		50	Pesetas	RR
31.		100	Pesetas	RR
32.		500	Pesetas	RR
33.		1,000	Pesetas	RR
34.	1.10.1886	25	Pesetas	$250.00
35.		50	Pesetas	250.00
36.		100	Pesetas	250.00
37.		500	Pesetas	RR
38.		1,000	Pesetas	RR
39.	1. 6.1889	25	Pesetas	175.00
40.		50	Pesetas	175.00
41.		100	Pesetas	150.00
42.	24. 7.1893	25	Pesetas	150.00
43.		50	Pesetas	175.00
44.		100	Pesetas	150.00
45.	1. 5.1895	1,000	Pesetas, black on light yellow	RR
46.	2. 1.1898	25	Pesetas	125.00
47.		50	Pesetas, dark blue on light yellow. Jovellanos at left	125.00
48.	24. 6.1898	100	Pesetas, blue on light yellow. Type of #47	100.00
49.	17. 5.1899	25	Pesetas, blue on green. Quevedo at left	85.00
50.	25.11.1899	50	Pesetas, black on green. Type of #49	100.00
51.	1. 5.1900	100	Pesetas, blue on green. Type of #49	125.00
52.	30.11.1902	50	Pesetas, black on yellow. Velasquez at left	115.00
53.	1. 7.1903	100	Pesetas, grey	RR
54.	1.10.1903	500	Pesetas	RR
55.	1. 1.1904	25	Pesetas	RR
56.	19. 3.1905	50	Pesetas, black on rose. Echegaray at left	100.00

#59
130 × 90

57.	30. 6.1906	100	Pesetas, multicolored. Seated woman at left and right	10.00
58.	24. 9.1906	25	Pesetas, multicolored. Seated woman at left	12.50
59.	24. 9.1906	50	Pesetas, multicolored. Woman with Mercury staff and globe in middle	12.50
60.	28. 1.1907	500	Pesetas, black on green and violet	150.00
61.	10. 5.1907	1,000	Pesetas, blue	RR
62.	15. 7.1907	25	Pesetas, background in green and red. Reclining woman in middle	12.50
63.		50	Pesetas, multicolored. Standing woman at left and right	15.00
64.		100	Pesetas, multicolored. Seated woman at left	10.00
65.		500	Pesetas, multicolored. Standing woman at left, three angels at right	85.00
66.		1,000	Pesetas, multicolored. Seated woman in middle	150.00
69.	1. 7.1925	100	Pesetas, blue and green. Philip II at left	1.25
70.		1,000	Pesetas, brown and violet. Charles I at right	7.50
71.	12.10.1926	25	Pesetas, blue and lilac. St. Xavier at left	7.50
72.	17. 5.1927	50	Pesetas, violet. Alfonso XIII at left, without stamp	16.50

For note with embossed stamp, see #80.

The notes previously listed as #67 and #68 have not been verified.

149 × 110

73.	24. 7.1927	500	Pesetas, blue and brown. Isabella the Catholic at right	16.50
74.	15. 8.1928	25	Pesetas, blue and brown. Calderon de la Barca at right	1.50
75.		50	Pesetas, lilac. Velasquez at right	1.50
76.		100	Pesetas, violet. Cervantes at left	1.50
77.		500	Pesetas, green and lilac. Cardinal Cisneros at left	6.50
78.		1,000	Pesetas, blue and yellow green. San Fernando at right	8.50

Banco de España (Bank of Spain)

Issues of the Second Republic, 1931–36

79.	(1931)	100 Pesetas. Note #69 (dated 1.7.1925) with embossed stamp "Gobierno Provisional de la Republica"	45.00
80.	(1931)	50 Pesetas. Note #72 (dated 17.5.1927) with colored stamp "Republica Espanol"	8.50
81.	25. 4.1931	25 Pesetas, green and multicolored. Vincente Lopez at right	2.25
82.		50 Pesetas, blue, lilac and multicolored. E. Rosales at left	1.50
83.		100 Pesetas, violet. G. F. de Cordoba at left	1.75
84.		500 Pesetas, brown and blue. Juan S. de Elcano at left	6.50
85.	1935	5 Pesetas, green. Woman's head at left	1.25
86.		10 Pesetas, red-brown. Woman's head at right	1.50
87.	7. 1.1935	500 Pesetas, blue and brown. Hernando Cortez at left	85.00
88.	22. 7.1935	50 Pesetas, lilac. Santiago Ramon Ygajal at right	1.25
89.	31. 8.1936	25 Pesetas, blue, brown and violet	RR

The notes previously listed as #90–92 have not been verified.

Ministerio de Hacienda (Ministry of Finance)

93.	1937	50 Centimos, blue. Woman's head in middle	1.00
94.		1 Peseta, brown and green. Nike of Samothrace at left	1.50
95.		2 Pesetas, blue, brown and green. Woman's head in middle	1.25

Postage Stamp Currency (1938)

Brown pasteboard printed on the obverse with the Spanish arms and "Plus Ultra." The reverse has a printed stamp or postage stamp attached. Initially issued only by the Finance Ministry but later also by banks as small denomination money.

96.	Printed stamps "Especial Movil" of 5, 10, 15, 30 centimos denominations	from	2.25
	Postage stamps of 5, 10, 15, 20, 25, 30, 40, 50, 60 centimos values	from	2.25

Banco de España (National Bank of Spain)

Issues since 1936

97.	21.11.1936	5 Pesetas, brown and blue green. Arms at right	85.00
98.		10 Pesetas, blue and orange. Arms at right	75.00
99.		25 Pesetas, blue and olive. Printed by Giesecke and Devrient	6.50

100.		50 Pesetas, brown. Type of #99	10.00
101.		100 Pesetas, green. Type of #99	15.00
102.		500 Pesetas, dark blue. Type of #99	50.00

181 × 105

103.		1,000 Pesetas, green. Type of #99	60.00
104.	18. 7.1937	5 Pesetas, brown. Woman with Mercury staff at right	25.50
105.	12.10.1937	1 Peseta, lilac and blue. Arms at left	5.00
106.		2 Pesetas, green. Buildings at left	16.50
107.	28. 2.1938	1 Peseta, brown and green. Arms at left	6.50
108.	30. 4.1938	1 Peseta, brown and green. Type of #107	4.50
109.		2 Pesetas, dark green Type of #106	5.00
110.	20. 5.1938	25 Pesetas, green and rose. Eagle in background	6.50
111.		50 Pesetas, red brown and green. Eagle in background	10.00
112.		100 Pesetas, lilac brown and orange. Eagle in background	15.00
113.		500 Pesetas, yellow green and lilac. Eagle in background	50.00
114.		1,000 Pesetas, blue and red. Eagle in background	65.00
115.	10. 8.1938	5 Pesetas, green and red brown. Printed by Giesecke and Devrient	5.00
116.	9. 1.1940	25 Pesetas, grey blue. Philip II at left	8.50
117.		50 Pesetas, green. Menendez Pelayo at left	10.00
118.		100 Pesetas, lilac brown. Columbus in middle	15.00
119.		500 Pesetas, dark green. John of Austria at right	40.00
120.		1,000 Pesetas, grey and brown. B. Murillo in middle	50.00
121.	1. 6.1940	1 Peseta, blue and orange. Cortez on horseback at right	6.50
122.	4. 9.1940	1 Peseta, multicolored. Sailing ship (Santa Maria) in middle	5.00
123.		5 Pesetas, orange and blue. Segovia castle at right	8.50
124.	21.10.1940	500 Pesetas, multicolored. Death scene of Count Orgaz at right	40.00
125.		1,000 Pesetas, lilac and violet. Charles I at left	50.00

126.	13. 2.1943	5 Pesetas, multicolored. Isabella the Catholic	5.00
127.	21. 5.1943	1 Peseta, dark brown and multicolored. Ferdinand the Catholic at left	1.75
128.	15. 6.1945	1 Peseta, brown. Isabella the Catholic at left	1.75
129.		5 Pesetas, green. Isabella and Columbus at left	3.50

122 × 78

130.	19. 2.1946	25 Pesetas, violet. Florez Estrada at left	4.50
131.		100 Pesetas, lilac brown. Goya at right	9.00
132.		500 Pesetas, blue. Francisco de Vitoria at right	35.00
133.		1,000 Pesetas, green and brown. J. L. Viveo at right	50.00
134.	12. 4.1947	5 Pesetas, brown lilac. Seneca on reverse	5.00
135.	5. 3.1948	5 Pesetas, green. Sebastian Elcano at right	2.25
136.	2. 5.1948	100 Pesetas, brown. Francisco Bayea at left	7.50
137.	19. 6.1948	1 Peseta, brown. Dame v. Elche at right	.75
138.	4.11.1949	1,000 Pesetas, black and green. Ramon Santillan at right	50.00
139.	16. 8.1951	5 Pesetas, green. J. Balmes at left	1.00
140.	15.11.1951	500 Pesetas, dark blue. Mariano Belliure at left	25.00
141.	19.11.1951	1 Peseta, brown. Don Quixote	.60
142.	31.12.1951	50 Pesetas, lilac. Santiago Rusinol at right	4.50
143.		1,000 Pesetas, green. J. Sorolla in middle	45.00
144.	7. 4.1953	100 Pesetas, brown. Julio Romero de Torres in middle	5.00
145.	22. 7.1953	1 Peseta, brown. Santa Cruz	.45
146.	22. 7.1954	5 Pesetas, green. Alfonso El Sabio at right	.75
147.		25 Pesetas, violet. Isaac Albeniz at left	2.25
148.		500 Pesetas, blue. Ignacio Zuloaga in middle	—
149.	29.11.1957	1,000 Pesetas, green. "Reyes Catolicos," the Catholic Monarchs in middle	45.00
150.	19.11.1965	100 Pesetas, brown. C. A. Becquer	—
151.		1,000 Pesetas, green. S. Isidoro at left	—

Bank of Spain, Bilbao

First issue, reverse not printed, name of issuing bank stamped at lower right. The following banks issued notes:

    a. Banco de Bilbao
    b. Banco Central de Bilbao
    c. Banco del Comercio de Bilbao
    d. Banco Guipuzcoano
    e. Banco Hispano Americano
    f. Banco Urquijo Vascongado
    g. Banco de Viscaya
    h. Caja de Ahorros Vizcaina
    i. Caja de Ahorros y Monte de Piedad Municipal de Bilbao

R1.	30.8.1936	5 Pesetas, red on olive. With stamps "a"–"i"	each	6.50
R2.	Various dates (stamped)	25 Pesetas, violet on olive. With stamps "a"–"i"	each	6.50
R3.		50 Pesetas, green on olive. With stamps "a"–"i"	each	6.50
R4.		100 Pesetas, blue on olive. With stamps "a"–"i"	each	8.50

Bank of Spain, Bilbao

Second issue, picture reverse, name of issuing bank imprinted at lower right. The following banks issued notes:

    a. Banco de Bilbao
    b. Banco del Comercio
    c. Banco Guipuzcoano
    d. Banco Hispano Americano
    e. Banco Urquijo Vascongado
    f. Banco de Vizcaya
    g. Caja de Ahorros Vizcaina
    h. Caja de Ahorros, y Monte de Piedad Municipal de Bilbao

Values indicated are for the commonest varieties. Seldom seen are:

    5 Pesetas: c, e
  10 Pesetas: g
  25 Pesetas: d, e
  50 Pesetas: g

R5.	1.1.1937	5 Pesetas, green. Shepherd with flock and tree on reverse. With bank names a, c, e, f, g, h	each	2.00
R6.		10 Pesetas, brown. Building entrance on reverse. With bank names a, f, g, h	each	2.40

R7.		25 Pesetas, brown. Blacksmith on reverse. With bank names b, d, e, g	each	2.50
R8.		50 Pesetas, blue. Worker on reverse. With bank names a, f, g, h	each	3.00
R9.		100 Pesetas, green. Peasant plowing with two oxen on reverse. With bank names a, f, h	each	6.50

158 × 103

R10.		500 Pesetas. With bank name b (not issued)	65.00
R11.		1,000 Pesetas, lilac. Stamped a. Factory on reverse. With bank name a (not issued)	65.00

Bank of Spain, Gijon

R12.	5.11.1936	5 Pesetas, rose with brown diagonal lines	3.00
R13.		10 Pesetas, rose with green diagonal lines	3.50
R14.		25 Pesetas, rose with blue diagonal lines	4.50
R15.		50 Pesetas, rose with light green diagonal lines	5.00
R16.		100 Pesetas, rose with red brown diagonal lines	7.50
R17.	Sept. 1937	100 Pesetas, blue on light brown. Two peasants at work on reverse	8.50

Bank of Spain, Santander

Name of issuing bank stamped at lower right. The following banks issued notes:

a. Banco de Bilbao-Santander
b. Banco Espanol de Credito
c. Banco Hispano Americano
d. Banco Mercantil
e. Banco de Santander
f. Monte de Piedad

R18.	1.11.1936	5 Pesetas, grey. With stamps "a"–"f"	each	8.50
R19.		10 Pesetas, grey. With stamps "a"–"f"	each	12.50
R20.		25 Pesetas, grey. With stamps "a"–"f"	each	16.50
R21.		50 Pesetas, grey. With stamps "a"–"f"	each	20.00
R22.		100 Pesetas, grey. With stamps "a"–"f"	each	35.00

Generalitat de Catalunya (Catalonia)

R23.	25. 9.1936	2.50 Pesetas, grey green. Worker and factory on reverse (two control number varieties)	2.50
R24.		5 Pesetas, brown. Weapons in middle, worker at left and peasant at right on reverse	4.50
R25.		10 Pesetas, green. Fishing boat on reverse	5.00

Notes R23–R25 are seldom seen in good condition.

Primitive-looking notes with a printed heading "Generalitat de Catalunya" in denominations of 10, 25, 50, 100, 500 and 1,000 pesetas, dated by machine are known. They are counterfeits presumably made for collectors.

Consejo de Asturias y León (Asturias and Leon)

R26.	(1936)	25 Centimos, grey violet and blue. Harbor work on reverse	1.25
R27.		40 Centimos, brown violet and green. Reverse as R26	1.75
R28.		50 Centimos, blue and violet. Blacksmith on reverse	3.00

103 × 56

R29.		1 Peseta, red brown and yellow. Seated woman with lion at left	1.75
R30.		2 Pesetas, grey violet and red. Type of R29	4.50

SWEDEN (Sverige)

The last separation of the Scandinavian states took place under King Oscar II when the personal union of Norway and Sweden was set aside. Under King Gustav V (1907–50) Sweden remained neutral during both world wars. Gustav VI Adolf became king in 1950.

1 Krona = 100 Ore

Sveriges Riksbank (Swedish Riksbank)

"Seated Svea" type, various dates of issue. All printing is black or dark brown on multicolored guilloche. Many signature varieties.

1.	1890–97	5 Kronor	$85.00
2.	1898–1905	5 Kronor. As #1 but with a letter at lower left and right on reverse	75.00

120 × 70

3.	1906–17	5 Kronor. As #2 but different background color	45.00
4.	1918–52	5 Kronor. As #3 but numerals of value in red	10.00
5.	1892–97	10 Kronor	100.00
6.	1898–1905	10 Kronor. As #5 but with a letter at lower left and right on reverse	85.00
7.	1906–17	10 Kronor. As #6 but different background color	50.00
8.	1918–40	10 Kronor. As #7 but numerals of value in red	16.50
9.	1896–97	50 Kronor	150.00
10.	1898–1903	50 Kronor. As #9 but with a letter at lower left and right on reverse	125.00
11.	1903–06	50 Kronor. As #10 but both signatures printed	115.00
12.	1907–17	50 Kronor. As #11 but different background color	105.00
13.	1918–54	50 Kronor. As #12 but numerals of value in red	95.00
14.	1955–57	50 Kronor. As #13 but with two letters at lower left and right on reverse	75.00
15.	1958–62	50 Kronor. As #14 but second signature at left	50.00
16.	1898–1903	100 Kronor	RR

#8

120 × 70

17.	1903–06	100 Kronor. As #16 but both signatures printed	250.00
18.	1907–17	100 Kronor. As #17 but different background color	175.00
19.	1918–54	100 Kronor. As #18 but numerals of value in red	150.00
20.	1955–58	100 Kronor. As #19 but with two letters at lower left and right on reverse	100.00
21.	1959–63	100 Kronor. As #20 but second signature at left	90.00
22.	1894–97	1,000 Kronor, bluish paper with red threads	RRR
23.	1898–1906	1,000 Kronor. As #22 but with a letter at lower left and right on reverse	RRR
24.	1907–08	1,000 Kronor. As #23 but different background color	RRR
25.	1909–17	1,000 Kronor. As #24 but different color paper (reddish with blue threads)	RR
26.	1918–31	1,000 Kronor. As #25 but numerals of value in red	RR
27	1932–50	1,000 Kronor. As #26 but both signatures printed	R R

134 × 76

28.	1874–75	1 Krona, green (format 134 × 76 mm)	27.50
29.	1914–21	1 Krona, green (format 120 × 70 mm)	
		a. 1914–16	15.00
		b. 1917–19	12.50
		c. 1920–21	8.50
		Error: 1 Krona 1920 wrong text "lagen om rikets mynt av den"	RR

"Seated Svea" type, additional issues

| 30. | 1948 | 5 Kronor, dark green. Jubilee issue for 90th birthday of King Gustav V (originally sold for double face value) | 18.50 |

#30   120 × 70

31.	1954–61	5 Kronor, dark brown. Portrait of King Gustav VI Adolf. Paper watermarked with king's portrait	6.50
32.	1962–63	5 Kronor, dark brown. As #31 but paper watermarked with portrait of Esaias Tegnér. Paper with metallic threads	8.50
33.	dates from 1965	5 Kronor, violet and multicolored. Gustav Vasa at right	—

119 × 69

34.	1940–52	10 Kronor, grey blue. Gustav Vasa at left. Date and control numbers in red	18.50
35.	1953–62	10 Kronor, grey blue. As #34 but date and control numbers in blue	10.00
36.	dates from 1962	10 Kronor, dark green. King Gustav VI Adolf	—
37.	(1968)	10 Kronor, blue and multicolored. "Sveriges Riksbank 1668–1968"	—
38.	dates from 1965	50 Kronor, blue. King Gustav III at right	—
39.	dates from 1962	100 Kronor, brown and blue. King Gustav II Adolf at right	—
40.	dates from 1952	1,000 Kronor, brown. Standing Svea	—
41.	1939	10,000 Kronor, black and blue. Arms	RRR
42.	dates from 1958	10,000 Kronor, green and multicolored. Svea with shield	—

Enskilda Banken (Private Banks)

After 1903, all private bank notes were recalled from circulation and the Swedish Riksbank given the exclusive right to issue paper money. The private bank notes still in circulation in 1900 were in denominations of 5, 10, 50, 100 and 500 kronor and are from the following banks (date in parenthesis is expiration of bank's authority to issue notes):

Bohus Lans Enskilda Bank (1901)
Boras Enskilda Bank (1902)
Christianstads Enskilda Bank (1901)
Enskilda Banken i Christinehamn (1902)
Enskilda Banken i Wenersborg (1902)
Gefleborgs Lans Enskilda Bank (1903)
Gotlands Enskilda Bank (1902)
Gotheborgs Privat Bank (1901)
Hallands Enskilda Bank (1902)
Helsinglands Enskilda Bank (1903)
Hernosands Enskilda Bank (1903)
Kalmar Enskilda Bank (1902)
Malare–Provinsernas Enskilda Bank (1902)
Norrbottens Enskilda Bank (1903)
Norrkopings Enskilda Bank (1902)
Ost-Gota Bank (1902)
Privat Banken i Orebro (1902)
Skaraborgs Lans Enskilda Bank (1902)
Skanska Priwat-Banken (1901)
Smalands Privat Bank (1902)
Stockholms Enskilda Bank (1902)
Stora Kopparbergs Lans och Berglags Enskilda Bank (1902)
Sundvalls Enskilda Bank (1903)
Sodermanlands Enskilda Bank (1902)
Uplands Enskilda Bank (1903)
Wermlands Provincial Bank (1901)

Nearly all of the above notes are rare and seldom available.

SWITZERLAND (Schweiz)

After the French occupation and the founding of the Helvetian Republic in 1803, renewed in 1815, the everlasting neutrality policy was established. In 1848 changes were made in the Constitution to strengthen the union of the States.

1 Franken = 100 Rappen

Concordat Notes

Uniform bank notes of the various Concordat banks with their individual names and authorized signatures imprinted. The notes issued from 1883 show the figure of Helvetia at left. The following banks issued Concordat notes (all R–RRR):

1.	Aargauische Bank, Aarau	50 Franken
2.		100 Franken
3.		500 Franken
4.		1,000 Franken
5.	Appenzell-Ausserhodische Kantonalbank, Herisau	50 Franken
6.		100 Franken
7.		500 Franken
8.	Appenzell-Innenhodische Kantonalbank, Appenzell	50 Franken
9.		100 Franken
10.	Banca Cantonale Ticinese, Bellinzona	50 Franken
11.		100 Franken
12.		500 Franken
13.		1,000 Franken
14.	Banca della Svizzera Italiana, Lugano	50 Franken
15.		100 Franken
16.		500 Franken
17.	Banca Popolare di Lugano	50 Franken
18.		100 Franken
19.		500 Franken
20.	Bank in Basel	50 Franken
21.		100 Franken
22.		500 Franken
23.		1,000 Franken
24.	Bank in Luzern	50 Franken
25.		100 Franken
26.		500 Franken
27.	Bank in St. Gallen	50 Franken
28.		100 Franken
29.		500 Franken
30.		1,000 Franken

31.	Bank in Schaffhausen	50	Franken
32.		100	Franken
33.		500	Franken
34.	Bank in Zurich	50	Franken
35.		100	Franken
36.		500	Franken
37.		1,000	Franken
38.	Banque Cantonale Fribourgeoise	50	Franken
39.		100	Franken
40.		500	Franken
41.		1,000	Franken
42.	Banque Cantonale Neuchateloise	50	Franken
43.		100	Franken
44.		500	Franken
45.	Banque Cantonale Vaudoise, Lausanne	50	Franken
46.		100	Franken
47.		500	Franken
48.		1,000	Franken
49.	Banque Commerciale Neuchateloise	50	Franken
50.		100	Franken
51.		500	Franken
52.	Banque du Commerce de Geneva	50	Franken
53.		100	Franken
54.		500	Franken
55.		1,000	Franken
56.	Banque de l'Etat de Fribourg	50	Franken
57.		100	Franken
58.		500	Franken
59.	Banque de Geneve	50	Franken
60.		100	Franken
61.		500	Franken
62.		1,000	Franken
63.	Banque Populaire de la Gruyere, Bulle	50	Franken
64.		100	Franken
65.		500	Franken
66.	Basellandschaftliche Kantonalbank, Liestal	50	Franken
67.		100	Franken
68.		500	Franken
69.		1,000	Franken
70.	Baseler Kantonalbank, Basel	50	Franken
71.		100	Franken
72.		500	Franken
73.		1,000	Franken
74.	Caisse d'Amortissement de la Dette publique a Fribourg	50	Franken
75.		100	Franken
76.		500	Franken
77.	Credit Agricole et Industriel de la Broye, Estavayer	50	Franken
78.		100	Franken
79.	Credit Gruyerien, Bulle	50	Franken
80.		100	Franken

81.	Credito Ticinese, Locarno	50	Franken
82.		100	Franken
83.		500	Franken
84.	Ersparnis-Cassa des Kantons Uri, Altdorf	50	Franken
85.		100	Franken
86.	Glarner Kantonalbank, Glarus	50	Franken
87.		100	Franken
88.		500	Franken
89.	Graubundner Kantonalbank, Chur	50	Franken
90.		100	Franken
91.		500	Franken
92.	Kantonalbank von Bern	50	Franken
93.		100	Franken
94.		500	Franken
95.	Kantonalbank Schwyz	50	Franken
96.		100	Franken
97.		500	Franken
98.		1,000	Franken
99.	Kantonale Spar-und Leihkasse von Nidwalden, with "Unterwalden nid dem Walde"	50	Franken
100.		100	Franken
101.	As #99 with "Nidwalden"	50	Franken
102.		100	Franken
103.	Luzerner Kantonalbank	50	Franken
104.		100	Franken
105.		500	Franken
106.		1,000	Franken
107.	Obwaldener Kantonalbank, Sarnen	50	Franken
108.		100	Franken
109.	St. Gallische Kantonalbank	50	Franken
110.		100	Franken
111.		500	Franken
112.		1,000	Franken
113.	Schaffhauser Kantonalbank	50	Franken
114.		100	Franken
115.		500	Franken
116.	Solothurnische Bank	50	Franken
117.		100	Franken
118.		500	Franken
119.		1,000	Franken
120.	Solothurner Kantonalbank	50	Franken
121.		100	Franken
122.		500	Franken
123.		1,000	Franken
124.	Spar-und Leihcasse des Kantons Luzern	500	Franken
125.		1,000	Franken
126.	Thurgauische Hypothekenbank, Frauenfeld	50	Franken
127.		100	Franken
128.		500	Franken

129.	Thurgauische Kantonalbank, Weinfelden	50 Franken
130.		100 Franken
131.		500 Franken
132.	Toggenburger Bank, Lichtensteig	50 Franken
133.		100 Franken
134.		500 Franken
135.	Zurcher Kantonalbank	50 Franken
136.		100 Franken
137.		500 Franken
138.		1,000 Franken
139.	Zuger Kantonalbank	50 Franken
140.		100 Franken
141.		500 Franken

All of the above notes are RR-RRR above their face value

Schweizerische Nationalbank (Swiss National Bank)

Founded in 1905, the Bank issued types similar to the Concordat issues but with a white cross in a red rosette at the upper right and changed text.

142.	1.2.1907	50 Franken, green	RR

180 × 115

143.	100 Franken, blue	RR
144.	500 Franken, green	RRR
145.	1,000 Franken, violet	RRR

New type notes

Notes #146–150 read "Gesetz vom 6. Okt. 1905," many date and signature varieties

146.	dates from 1. 1.1910	50 Franken, green. Woman's head. Wood-cutter on reverse	$125.00
147.		100 Franken, blue. Woman's head. Mower on reverse	RR
148.		500 Franken, red. Woman of Appenzell. Appenzell knitter on reverse	RRR
149.		1,000 Franken, violet. Woman's head. Foundry on reverse	RRR

150.	dates from 1.12.1911	20 Franken, blue, green and brown. Woman's head, "Vreneli"	65.00
151.	dates from 1. 8.1913	5 Franken. William Tell with background of Rutli Alp	
		a. Light brown (first issue)	45.00
		b. Dark brown (later issue)	6.50
152.	1.1.1918	100 Franken, blue and brown. Tell and Tellskapelle. Head of Tell in medallion at left. Letters "T.W." at lower left, "R.K." at lower right	200.00
153.		100 Franken, blue and brown. As #152 but altered portrait of Tell in medallion. Letters "Ekn. R.K." at lower right	RR

Die Eidgenossische Staatskasse (Confederation State Treasury)

154.	10.8.1914	5 Franken, blue. Liberty at left, Arnold v. Winkelried at right. German text	75.00
155.		5 Franken, blue. As #154 but French text	75.00
156.		5 Franken, blue. As # 154 but Italian text	RR
157.		10 Franken, blue. Liberty at left, Tell at right. German text	100.00

127 × 83

158.	10 Franken, blue. As #157 but French text	100.00
159.	10 Franken, blue. As #157 but Italian text	RR
160.	20 Franken, blue. Liberty at left, Arnold v. Winkelried right. German text	150.00
161.	20 Franken, blue. As #160 but French text	150.00
162.	20 Franken, blue. As #160 but Italian text	RRR

Darlehnkasse der schweizerischen Eidgenossenschaft (State loan office of the Swiss Confederation)

| 163. | 9.9.1914 | 25 Franken, dark green and yellow brown | 175.00 |

Treasury notes of 1 and 2 franken (dated 27.4.1915) and 100 franken (dated 9.9.1914) were printed but not issued.

Swiss National Bank

Notes as previous issues but text reads "Gesetz vom 7.4.1921."

| 164. | | 20 Franken, blue, green and brown. Type of #150 | RR |

165.	1.1.1923	100 Franken, blue. Type of #147	RR
166.		500 Franken, red. Type of #148	RRR
167.		1,000 Franken, violet. Type of #149	RRR

Notes as previous issue but text reads "Gesetzgebung uber die Schweizerische National Bank." Many date and signature variations.

168.	dates to 18. 4.1929	20 Franken, blue, green and brown. Type of #150	37.50
169.	dates to 20. 1.1949 and 29.10.1955	50 Franken, green. Type of #146	45.00
170.	dates to 20. 1.1949	100 Franken, blue. Type of #147	60.00

200 × 127

171.	dates to 20. 1.1949	500 Franken, red. Type of #148	RR
172.	dates to 16.10.1947 and 29. 4. 1955	1,000 Franken, violet. Type of #149	RRR

New Note Types

Many date and signature varieties

173.	21. 6.1929–28. 3.1952	20 Franken, blue. Pestalozzi	25.00
174.	dates from 25. 8.1955	10 Franken, red brown. Gottfried Keller	—
175.	dates from 1. 7.1954	20 Franken, blue. H. Dufour	—
176.	dates from 1. 7.1955	50 Franken, green. Girl's head	
		a. Printed by Waterlow & Sons	35.00
		b. Printed by Thomas de La Rue	—
177.	dates from 25.10.1956	100 Franken, blue. Boy's head	—
178.	dates from 31. 1.1957	500 Franken, red brown. Woman's head	—
		a. Printed by Waterlow & Sons	RR
		b. Printed by Thomas de La Rue	—
179.	dates from 30. 9.1954	1,000 Franken, violet. Woman's head	—

TURKEY (Turkiye)

During the 19th century, Turkey was forced out of the Balkan area. In the Balkan War of 1913 Turkey lost nearly all of her remaining European territories. Sultan Mohammed VI (1918–22) was deposed in 1922 and a new republic established. The first president of the republic was Kemal Ataturk.

1 Ghurush (piastre, later kurus) = *40 Para*
1 Pound (lira) = *100 Kurus*

Imperial Ottoman Bank, so-called "Kaime" Notes

Dates of Issue: ۱۲۹۳ = 1293 (1876), ۱۲۹۴ = 1294 (1877), ۱۲۹۵ = 1295 (1878), ۱۳۳۱ = 1331 (1913), ۱۳۳۲ = 1332 (1914), ۱۳۳۳ = 1333 (1915).

Numerals of value: ۱ = 1, ۲ = 2, ۳ = 3, ۴ = 4, ۵ — 5, ۶ — 6, ۷ = 7 , ۸ = 8, ۹ = 9, ۱۰ = 10, ۲۰ = 20, ۵۰ = 50, ۱۰۰ = 100.

The early dates on the following notes follow the Moslem calendar (A.H.) beginning with the year 1 equal to A.D. 622, the date of Mohammed's flight from Mecca.

1.	1876/77	1 Ghurush, grey to grey blue	
		a. Round stamp (15 mm) with 1294 on reverse. Line stamp with 1877	$2.50
		b. Round stamp (18 mm) with 1295 on reverse. Line stamp with 1877	4.50
2.		5 Ghurush, red brown	
		a. Round stamp with 1293 on reverse. Box stamp with 1876	6.50
		b. As # 2a but 1877, unwatermarked paper	5.00
		c. As #2b but paper watermarked with letters	6.50
		d. As #2b but 1294	4.50
		e. As #2d but 1795	6.50
3.		10 Ghurush, lilac on light green	
		a. Round stamp with 1293 on reverse. Box stamp with 1876	8.50
		b. Round stamp with 1293 on reverse. Box stamp with 1877	12.50
4.		20 Ghurush, brown lilac on yellow	
		a. Round stamp with 1293 on reverse. Box stamp with 1876	15.00
		b. Round stamp with 1293 on reverse. Box stamp with 1877	12.50
		c. Round stamp with 1294 on reverse. Box stamp with 1877	10.00

5. 1876/77   50 Ghurush, brown lilac on yellow. Vertical format
                a. Round stamp with 1293 on reverse. Box stamp
                   with 1876   15.00
                b. As #5a but 1877   12.50
                c. As #5a but 1294/1877   12.50
                d. As #5c but 1295   12.50
6.   100 Ghurush, brown lilac on grey. Vertical format
                a. Round stamp with 1293 on reverse. Oval stamp
                   with 1876   15.00
                b. As #6a but 1877   12.50
                c. As #6a but 1294/1877   12.50

178 × 112

7.   50 Ghurush, light blue. Round stamp with 1295 on
                   reverse. Box stamp with 1877. Horizontal format   18.50
8.   100 Ghurush, red brown. Horizontal format
                a. Round stamp with 1294 on reverse. Box stamp
                   with 1877   20.00
                b. Round stamp with 1295 on reverse. Box stamp
                   with 1877   27.50

During World War I and continuing until 1933, the Imperial Ottoman Bank issued notes that had no legal tender status as their face value exceeded their exchange value. The 1, 2, 5, 50 and 100 pound values are RR–RRR.

Notes of the Finance Ministry

Text and figures in Arabic script

9.   30 March 1331 (1915)   1 Pound, blue frame. Background rose,
                               green and brown   30.00
10.   5 Pounds   65.00
11. 18 Oct. 1331 (1915)   ¼ Pound, green background   10.00
12.   ½ Pound, rose background   16.50
13.   1 Pound, brown and multicolored back-
                               ground   20.00

14.	18 Oct. 1331 (1915)	5 Pounds, blue frame, rose, blue and brown background	50.00
15.	16 Dec. 1331 (1915)	½ Pound on left or right half of 1 pound note #9	100.00
16.		½ Pound on left or right half of 1 pound note #13	85.00
17.		2½ Pounds on left or right half of 5 pounds note #10	125.00
18.		2½ Pounds on left or right half of 5 pounds note #14	85.00
19.	22 Jan. 1331 (1916)	5 Piastres, brown background	5.00
20.		20 Piastres, violet background	8.50
21.		¼ Pound, green background	10.00
22.		½ Pound, rose background	15.00
23.		1 Pound, brown frame, blue, green and rose background	15.00
24.	2 March 1332 (1916)	⅛ Pound on left or right half of ¼ pound note #11	RR
25.	23 May 1332 (1916)	1 Piastre, green. River with palms and caravan	2.00
26.		2½ Piastres, rose. The Dardanelles	2.50

Notes previously listed as #27–31 have not been verified.

32.	6 August 1332 (1916)	5 Piastres, olive-green background. White paper	4.50
33.		20 Piastres, orange background	8.50
34.		½ Pound, rose background. Brownish paper, light blue and yellow	20.00

175 × 96

35.		1 Pound, green border, blue, green and rose background	
		a. Paper watermarked with hook design	20.00
		b. Paper watermarked with small quatrefoils	20.00

36.	6 August 1332 (1916)	5 Pounds, blue border, multicolored background	35.00
37.		10 Pounds, brown border, light blue background	50.00
38.		50 Pounds, light blue and yellow brown	
		a. Paper watermarked with hook design	150.00
		b. Paper watermarked with honeycomb and letters	150.00
39.		50 Pounds. As #38b but four stamps on reverse and "2eme Emission"	RR
40.		50 Pounds. As #38b but two stamps on reverse and "3eme Emission"	RR
41.		500 Pounds	RR
42.		50,000 Pounds	RRR
43.	4 February 1332 (1917)	5 Piastres, green background. Bluish paper	6.50
44.		20 Piastres, brown background. Bluish paper	10.00
45.		½ Pound, red background. Violet paper	16.50
46.		1 Pound, brown border, violet, rose and green background	
		a. Paper watermarked with hook design	16.50
		b. Paper watermarked with small quatrefoils	18.50
47.		2½ Pounds, orange and green	35.00
48.		10 Pounds, brown border, light blue background	70.00
49.		25 Pounds	150.00
50.		100 Pounds	RR
51.	28 March 1333 (1918)	1 Pound	35.00
52.		2½ Pounds, brown border, multicolored background	50.00
53.		5 Pounds, blue border, green and multicolored background	65.00
54.		25 Pounds, brown border, light blue background	150.00
55.		100 Pounds	RR
56.		1,000 Pounds	RRR
56a.	28 March 1334	2½ Pounds, orange and blue green	
		a. Stamped "Troisième Émission"	50.00
		b. Stamped "Cinquième Émission"	50.00
56b.		5 Pounds, cream brown	
		a. Stamped "Deuxième Émission"	65.00
		b. Stamped "Sixième Émission"	65.00
56c.		10 Pounds, cream brown. Light blue underprinting	
		a. Stamped "Deuxième Émission"	75.00
		b. Stamped "Quatrième Émission"	75.00

56d.	25 Pounds	175.00
56e.	100 Pounds	RR
56f.	500 Pounds	RR
56g.	1,000 Pounds	RRR

Postage Stamp Currency

Unissued postage stamps (#57 and #58) or tax stamps (#59) pasted on colored cardboard

57.	(1917)	5 Para, carmine on yellow or rose cardboard. Gun emplacement	2.50
58.		10 Para, green on bluish, greenish, yellowish or rose cardboard. Hagia-Sofia Mosque	2.50
59.		10 Para on 1 piastre, green and rose on bluish, yellowish or rose cardboard. Camel	7.50

Notes of the Finance Ministry

All notes with text in arabic and "Law no. 701 of 30. Dec. 1341 (1925)"

| 60. | 1 Pound, green. Peasant with two oxen | 8.50 |

170 × 91

61.	5 Pounds, blue. Springing wolf in middle	18.50
62.	10 Pounds, violet. Springing wolf at right	35.00
63.	50 Pounds, brown. Kemal Ataturk at right. View of Afyonkarahisar and mountain on reverse	75.00
64.	100 Pounds, green. Kemal Ataturk at right. View of new city of Ankara on reverse	125.00
65.	500 Pounds, red brown. Gok-Medres Mosque at left. Kemal Ataturk at right	RR
66.	1,000 Pounds, dark blue. Kemal Ataturk at right. Railroad canyon on reverse	RR

Turkiye Cumhuriyet Merkez Bankasi (Central Bank of Turkey)

All notes with Latin letters and date "11 Haziran (June) 1930." Pre World War II issue, obverse portrait of Kemal Ataturk without moustache.

67.	2½ Pounds, green. Memorial at the National Plaza on reverse	6.50
68.	5 Pounds, dark blue. Memorial in Ankara on reverse	12.50
69.	10 Pounds, red brown. Citadel of Ankara on reverse	20.00
70.	50 Pounds, violet. Farm house and Angora sheep on reverse	50.00
71.	100 Pounds, dark brown. The Dardanelles on reverse	85.00
72.	500 Pounds, olive green. Rumeli Hisar castle on reverse	250.00
73.	1,000 Pounds, blue. Memorial in Ankara on reverse	RR

Turkiye Cumhuriyet Merkez Bankasi (Central Bank of Turkey)

All notes have Latin letters and the date "11 Haziran (June) 1930." Obverse portrait of Ismet Inonu (with moustache) facing half left.

74.	50 Kurus, dark brown and lilac. Bank building on reverse. Printed by Bradbury (not issued)	2.25
75.	50 Kurus, brown and green. Bank building on reverse. Printed by Reichs Printing Office	8.50
76.	1 Pound, lilac. The Bosphorus on reverse	8.50
77.	2½ Pounds, dark brown. Family home on reverse	15.00
78.	5 Pounds. Three girls on reverse	20.00

155 × 65

79.	10 Pounds, brown and red brown. Three peasant girls on reverse	25.00
80.	10 Pounds, light brown. Sultan Ahmed fountain in Istanbul on reverse	30.00
81.	10 Pounds, red. As #80 but later issue	25.00
82.	50 Pounds, violet. Sheep on reverse	65.00
83.	50 Pounds, blue. As #82 but later issue	45.00
84.	100 Pounds, dark brown. Girl with grapes on reverse Also known half printed	65.00
85.	100 Pounds, violet. Rumeli Hisar castle on reverse	50.00
85a.	100 Pounds, green. Rumeli Hisar castle on reverse	65.00
86.	500 Pounds, olive green. Rumeli Hisar castle on reverse	200.00
87.	500 Pounds, olive green. Student	200.00
88.	1,000 Pounds, blue. Memorial in Ankara	RR
89.	1,000 Pounds, blue. Boy Scout	RR

Zentralbank Turkiye Cumhuriyet Merkez Bankasi

All notes with Latin letters and date "11 Haziran (June) 1930." Obverse portrait of Kemal Ataturk without moustache facing front. Post-war issue.

90.	2½ Pounds, lilac. Reverse lilac, bank building	3.50
91.	2½ Pounds, lilac. As #90 but brown reverse	2.50
92.	2½ Pounds, lilac. As #90 but red reverse	2.50
93.	2½ Pounds, lilac. As #90 but green reverse	2.25
94.	5 Pounds, blue. Reverse blue, three peasant girls. Without name of printer	3.50
94a.	5 Pounds, blue green. Type of #94 but different guilloche on obverse	3.50
95.	5 Pounds, blue. As #94 but different guilloche (ornament) on obverse. Reverse blue. Printed by Bradbury	2.50
96.	5 Pounds, blue. As #95 but green reverse	2.50
97.	10 Pounds, green. Reverse green, river and Maritza Bridge. Without name of printer	6.50
98.	10 Pounds, green. As #97 but red-brown reverse. Without name of printer	6.50
99.	10 Pounds, green. As #97 but different guilloche on obverse. Reverse brown. Printed by Thomas De La Rue	6.50
100.	10 Pounds, green. As #99 but green reverse	5.00
101.	10 Pounds, green. As #99 but red-brown reverse	5.00
102.	50 Pounds, brown. Reverse brown, soldier with arms. Printed by Bradbury Wilkinson	10.00
103.	50 Pounds, brown. As #102 but orange reverse	10.00
104.	50 Pounds, brown. As #102 but dark rose reverse	8.50
105.	50 Pounds, brown. As #102 but grey-green reverse	8.50

159 × 74

106.	50 Pounds, brown. As #102 but brown reverse without name of printer	8.50
107.	50 Pounds, brown. As #106 but different guilloche on obverse	8.50
108.	100 Pounds, olive green. Reverse olive green, park with bridge in Ankara. Printed by Bradbury	20.00
109.	100 Pounds, olive green. As #108 but light blue reverse	16.50
110.	100 Pounds, brown. As #108 but different guilloche on obverse. Without name of printer	16.50
111.	500 Pounds, brown. Plaza and mosque in Istanbul on reverse	85.00
112.	500 Pounds, grey brown. As #111	85.00
113.	1,000 Pounds, violet. The Bosphorus on reverse	—

Zentralbank Turkiye Cumhuriyet Merkez Bankasi

All notes with Latin letters and date "11 Haziran (June) 1930." Obverse shows portrait of Kemal Ataturk facing half left.

114.	5 Pounds, violet and multicolored. Waterfall on reverse	—
115.	10 Pounds, green	—
116.	20 Pounds, brown. Memorial on reverse	—
117.	100 Pounds, green. Park with bridge in Ankara on reverse	—
118.	100 Pounds, olive green. As #117 but different guilloche	—
119.	500 Pounds, brown. Plaza and Mosque of Sultan Ahmed in Istanbul on reverse	—
120.	500 Pounds, grey violet. As #119	—

Zentralbank Turkiye Cumhuriyet Merkez Bankasi

With date "14 Ocak 1970," Kemal Ataturk at right

121.	100 Pounds, dark green and multicolored. Mountain on reverse	—
122.	500 Pounds, blue, green and multicolored. Tower of Istanbul University on reverse	—

English notes with overprint

Issued during the World War I campaign of Gallipoli in Palestine and Iraq

R1.	60 Piastres on 10 shillings, red. British note #85 with overprint in Arabic letters	100.00
R2.	120 Piastres on 1 pound, black. British note #86 with overprint in Arabic letters	RR

YUGOSLAVIA

The Kingdom of Yugoslavia was formed after the break-up of the Austro-Hungarian Empire in 1918 from Serbia, Croatia, and Slovenia. King Alexander I ruled from 1921 until 1934, followed by his son, King Peter II, who was under the guardianship of a regent until 1941. Yugoslavia was occupied by German troops during World War II who supported the independent states of Serbia and Croatia. Since 1945 Yugoslavia has been a Federated People's Republic.

1 Dinar = 100 Para

Finance Ministry Notes

Notes of the Austro-Hungarian Bank with machine overprint МИНИСТАРСТВО ФИНАНСИЈА КРАЉЕВСТВА СРБА ХРВАТА И СЛОВЕНАЦА (Ministarstvo Finansija Kraljevstva Srba, Hrvata i Slovenaca)

1.	(1919)	10 Kronen (dated 2.1.1915). Austria #19	$12.50
2.		20 Kronen (dated 2.1.1913). Austria #13	R

162 × 99

3.		50 Kronen (dated 2.1.1914). Austria #15	20.00
4.		100 Kronen (dated 2.1.1912). Austria #12	16.50
5.		1,000 Kronen (dated 2.1.1902). Austria #8	50.00

Numerous local and state hand overprints exist on Austro-Hungarian bank notes, also Serbian overprints on Bulgarian notes. At the time of the second Yugoslavian overprint on the Austrian notes, a stamp was attached to each. The text on the stamp reads "Kraljevstvo Srba Hrvata i Slovenaca." On the stamps affixed to the 10, 20 and 50 kronen notes the text was in three languages—Serbian, Croatian and Slovenian—and only one type of stamp was used. The stamp fastened to the 100 and 1,000 kronen notes had text in only one language, Serbian, Croatian or Slovenian, thus there were three different types of stamps.

6.	10	Kronen. Orange stamp, three languages. Woman's head to left	2.50
7.	20	Kronen. Lilac stamp, three languages. Woman's head to left	3.50
8.	50	Kronen. Green stamp, three languages. Woman's head to left	5.00
9.	100	Kronen. Brown stamp	
		a. Serbian (Cyrillic alphabet)	4.50
		b. Croatian	4.50
		c. Slovenian	4.50
10.	1,000	Kronen. Blue, brown and orange stamp	
		a. Serbian (Cyrillic alphabet)	3.50
		b. Croatian	3.50
		c. Slovenian	3.50

Ministarstvo Finansija Kraljevstva Srba, Hrvata i Slovenaca (Finance Ministry Notes)

Newly printed notes without overprint

11.	1. 2.1919	½ Dinar, brown, rose and green	.60
12.	(1919)	1 Dinar, brown. Helmeted man's head at left	.60
13.	21. 3.1921	25 Para (¼ dinar), blue and olive. Buildings in middle	.60

Notes overprinted in kronen values "kypha-kruna-kron." Various colors were used for the overprint.

14.	1. 2.1919	½ Dinar = 2 Kronen. Note #11 with red overprint	.75
15.	(1919)	1 Dinar = 4 Kronen. Note #12 with red overprint	1.00
16.	(1919)	5 Dinar = 20 Kronen, lilac. Helmeted man's head at left	1.50
17.	1. 2.1919	10 Dinar = 40 Kronen, blue. Blacksmith at left	2.25
18.		20 Dinar = 80 Kronen, green. Farmer plowing with oxen at left	4.50

174 × 110

19.	(1919)	100 Dinar = 400 Kronen, lilac. Cupids at left and right	85.00
20.		1,000 Dinar = 4,000 Kronen, grey violet. Six allegorical figures	RRR

328 • Yugoslavia

Narodna Banka Kraljevine Srba Hrvata i Slovenaca (National Bank of the Kingdom of the Serbs, Croats and Slovenes)

21.	1.11.1920	10	Dinar, blue. Man with wagon wheel at left	5.00
22.	30.11.1920	100	Dinar, violet and yellow. Seated woman with sword at right	20.00
23.		1,000	Dinar, multicolored. St. George and the dragon at left	200.00
24.		1,000	Dinar, multicolored. As #23 but blue overprint on man's head (Karageorge), colored rosettes overprinted above and below	175.00
25.	26. 5.1926	10	Dinar, multicolored. Woman's head at right	4.50

Narodna Banka Kraljevine Jugoslavije (National Bank of the Kingdom of Yugoslavia)
НАРОДНА БАНКА КРАЉЕВИНЕ ЈУГОСЛАВИЈЕ

26.	1.12.1929	10	Dinar, multicolored. As #25	35.00
27.		100	Dinar, violet and yellow. As #22	
			a. Paper watermarked with head of Karageorge	15.00
			b. Paper watermarked with head of Alexander I	2.25
28.	1.12.1931	50	Dinar, brown and multicolored. Head of King Alexander I at left (first issued in 1941 as a Serbian note)	1.75
29.		1,000	Dinar, blue green and brown. Head of Queen Marie at left	2.25

171 × 104

30.	15. 7.1934	100	Dinar, blue and multicolored. Woman with boy at right (not issued)	35.00
31.	6. 9.1935	500	Dinar, green. King Peter II at left	2.00
32.		1,000	Dinar, multicolored. Group of six people with three horses and a lion (not issued)	65.00
33.	6. 9.1936	20	Dinar, brown and blue. King Peter II in middle	2.25
34.		10,000	Dinar, brown, yellow green and blue. King Peter II at left (not issued)	RR
35.	22. 9.1939	10	Dinar, green. Head of King Peter II at left	2.25

Srpska Narodna Banka (Serbian National Bank) СРПСКА НАРОДНА БАНКА

36.	1. 5.1941	10 Serbian Dinar, green. Arms at left. Reverse of #35 overprinted	2.50
37.		20 Serbian Dinar, brown. Man's head (Vuc Karadzic) at left	1.75
38.		100 Serbian Dinar, violet and yellow. Note #27 overprinted	2.25
39.		1,000 Serbian Dinar on 500 dinar, multicolored. Three seated women (the 500 dinar note was not issued without overprint)	2.50
40.	1. 8.1941	50 Serbian Dinar, brown and multicolored. Woman's head at left	1.25
41.	1.11.1941	500 Serbian Dinar, brown and multicolored. Woman in national costume in middle	
		a. Paper watermarked with head of King Alexander I	1.25
		b. Paper watermarked with woman's head	1.00
42.	1. 5.1942	20 Serbian Dinar, blue. As #37 (not issued)	35.00
43.		50 Serbian Dinar, brown. Man's head (Njegos) at left	1.50

163 × 84

44.		100 Serbian Dinar, brown and multicolored. Shepherd playing flute, sheep in background (not issued)	150.00
45.		500 Serbian Dinar, brown and multicolored. Seed sower at right	3.50
46.		1,000 Serbian Dinar, brown and multicolored. Black-smith at left, woman in costume at right	
		a. Paper watermarked with head of King Peter II	2.25
		b. Paper watermarked with woman's head	4.50
47.	1. 1.1943	100 Serbian Dinar, brown and blue. St. Sava at left	1.75

Demokratska Federativna Jugoslavija (Democratic Federation of Yugoslavia)

48.	1944	1 Dinar, olive brown. Soldier's head and rifle at right	.60
49.		5 Dinar, blue. Type of #48	.60

50.	1944	10 Dinar, black and orange. Type of #48	.75
51.		20 Dinar, orange. Type of #48 (three control number varieties)	2.25
52.		500 Dinar, brown and green. Type of #48 (two control number varieties)	8.50
53.		1,000 Dinar, dark green. Type of #48 (two control number varieties)	15.00
54.	(undated)	50 Dinar, violet. Type of #48 (two control number varieties)	2.25
55.		100 Dinar, dark green and violet (two control number varieties)	2.25

Gospodarska Banka za Istru Rijeku i Slovensko Primorje (State Bank for Istria, Fiume and the Slovenian Coast)

56.	1945	1 Jugolire, brown. Woman with soldier's cap at left	2.50
57.		5 Jugolire, green. Sail boat at right on reverse	1.25
58.		10 Jugolire, brown and green. Type of #57	1.75
59.		20 Jugolire, violet and green. Type of #57	2.25
60.		50 Jugolire, red brown. Type of #57 at right (two control number varieties)	3.50
61.		100 Jugolire, brown and blue. Type of #57 (two control number varieties)	10.00

134 × 75

| 62. | | 500 Jugolire, green. Type of #57 | 12.50 |
| 63. | | 1,000 Jugolire, lilac and light brown. Farmer plowing with oxen at right on reverse | 16.50 |

Narodna Banka Federativne Narodne Republike Jugoslavije (National Bank of the Federated People's Republic of Yugoslavia)

64.	1. 5.1946	50 Dinar, brown. Miner at left	.75
65.		100 Dinar, brown and multicolored. Blacksmith at left, farmer at right	1.00
66.		500 Dinar, brown. Soldier with rifle at right	8.50
67.		1,000 Dinar, brown. Woman with produce at right	7.50

149 × 77

68.	1. 5.1953	100 Dinar, multicolored. Four workers and two steam engine wheels	20.00
69.	1. 5.1955	100 Dinar, red. Woman in costume at left	1.25
70.		500 Dinar, green. Woman with sickle at left	3.50
71.		1,000 Dinar, brown. Worker at left	10.00
72.		5,000 Dinar, blue. Relief of Mestrovic at left	45.00

Narodna Banka Jugoslavije (National Bank of Yugoslavia)

73.	1. 5.1963	100 Dinar, red. As #69	2.50
74.		500 Dinar, green. As #70	8.50
75.		1,000 Dinar, brown. As #71	16.50
76.		5,000 Dinar, blue. As #72	65.00

Currency Reform, 1965: *100 old Dinar = 1 new Dinar*

77.	1. 8.1965	5 Dinar, green. Woman with sickle at left (format 134 × 64 mm)	1.25
78.		10 Dinar, brown. Worker at left (format 143 × 66 mm)	2.25
79.		50 Dinar, blue. Relief of Mestrovic at left (format 151 × 72 mm)	6.50
80.		100 Dinar, red. Equestrian statue "Peace"	—
81.	1. 5.1968	5 Dinar, green. Woman with sickle at left (format 123 × 59 mm)	—
82.		10 Dinar, brown. Worker at left (format 131 × 63 mm)	—
83.		50 Dinar, blue. Relief of Mestrovic at left (format 139 × 66 mm)	—

Savings Bank of Laibach Province

Issued during the German occupation, one side in Slovenian, the other in German

R1.	14. 9.1944	50 Lire, red. Peasant woman with produce	6.90
R2.		100 Lire, blue. Peasant with scythe	6.10
R3.		500 Lire, green. Man in costume	12.50
R4.		1,000 Lire, brown. Woman's head	20.00
R5.	28.11.1944	$\frac{1}{2}$ Lira, green. Child in costume	3.50
R6.		1 Lira, dark brown. Spire and dragon	2.50

R7.		2 Lire, brown. Woman and child	3.50
R8.		5 Lire, brown red. Man in costume	3.50
R9.		10 Lire, violet. Woman's head with costume cap	3.50

Many essays in various printing and overprint colors are known with text differences and such items as the 2 lire illustration appearing on the 1 lira note.

Montenegro, Italian Occupation

Yugoslavian notes stamped "Verificato."

R10.	(1941)	10 Dinar (dated 22.9.1939). Note #35 with stamp	12.50
R11.		20 Dinar (dated 6.9.1936). Note #33 with stamp	16.50
R12.		50 Dinar (dated 1.12.1931). Note #28 with stamp	10.00
R13.		100 Dinar (dated 1.12.1929). Note #27 with stamp	
		a. Paper watermarked with head of Karageorge	25.00
		b. Paper watermarked with head of King Alexander I	4.50
		Error: 100 Dinar of 30.11.1920 with stamp	R
R14.		500 Dinar (dated 6.9.1935). Note #31 with stamp	65.00
R15.		1,000 Dinar (dated 1.12.1931). Note #29 with stamp	30.00

Declining-value issue (Social dinar) with table of devaluations on reverse

R16.	1. 1.1945	10 Dinar, blue. Man with raised hands at left, burning house at right	25.00
R17.	1. 2.1945	100 Dinar, blue green on yellow. Lady giving a bearded man a drink	35.00
R18.		1,000 Dinar, ochre and brown. Rider with arm in sling	40.00

Partisan Notes

Gospodarsko Financni Odbor Osvobodilne Fronte

M1.		50 Lit, orange	3.50
M2.		100 Lit, lilac brown and blue (with and without control numbers)	4.50
		Also known with stamp "25RM," probably a forgery.	
M3.		500 Lit, red brown on grey olive	25.00
M4.		1,000 Lit, red brown on grey olive	45.00
M5.		5,000 Lit, red brown on grey olive	65.00
M6.		10,000 Lit, red brown on grey olive	85.00

Denarni Zavod Slovenije

M7.	20.2.1944–12.3.1944	1 Liro, blue green. Control number in black	6.50
		Error: No text on reverse	45.00
M8.		5 Lir, blue on light blue. Control number in black	8.50

M9.		10 Lir, red. Control number in black	16.50
		German propaganda note: Obverse as	
		M9, reverse "Ta denar je prav . . ."	45.00
M10.		1 Liro, blue on olive. Control number in	
		red	3.50
M11.		5 Lir, blue on grey. Control number in	
		red	4.50
M12.		10 Lir, brown on grey violet. Control	
		number in black	12.50
M12a.		50 Lir, green	25.00
M13.		100 Lir, brown on light brown. Control	
		number in black	16.50
M14.	Handwritten dates	1,000 Lir, green. Value handwritten	30.00
M14a.		1,500 Lir, green	35.00
M14b.		3,000 Lir, green	35.00

Izvršni Odbor Ocvobodilne Fronte Slovenskega Narodna

M15.	8.10.1943	20 RM, blue and red. Woman with bread, farmer	
		and blacksmith	25.00
M16.		50 RM, green and red. Type of M15	35.00
M17.		500 RM. Type of M15	53.00

153 × 91

M18.		100 Lir, blue and red. Type of M15	35.00
M19.		100 Lit, brown. Agricultural work at left and right	25.00
M20.		1,000 Lit, brown. Type of M19	45.00
M21.		10,000 Lit, brown. Type of M19	65.00

Potrdilo (Partisan Certificates)

Values and dates handwritten, crude printing or reproduction.

Glavno Poveljstvo Slovenskih Partizanskih cet Ljubljana

| M21a. | 2,000 Lit, blue. Peasant and partisan plowing | 45.00 |

Kanalski O.N.O.O. (O.F.)

| M22. | 100 Lir | 35.00 |
| M23. | 600 Lir, lilac. Tito at right | 35.00 |

Narodni Osvobodilni Svet za Primorsko Slovenijo

M24.	100 Lir	20.00
M25.	300 Lir	35.00
M26.	400 Lir	35.00
M27.	1,000 Lir, blue. Tito at right	25.00
M27a.	2,000 Lir, blue	45.00
M28.	5,500 Lir	45.00
M29.	10,000 Lir, green. Tito at right	45.00

200 × 103

M30.	12,000 Lir, green. Tito at right	50.00

Okrožni Odbor O.F. za Južno Primorsko

M30a.	250 Lir. Without underprinting	50.00

Okrožni Odbor O.F. za Zapadno Primorsko

M31.	128 Lir, blue. Tito at right	65.00

Okrožni Odbor O.F. za Slov. Istro

M32.	100 Lir, blue grey	35.00
M33.	400 Lir, blue grey	35.00
M34.	500 Lir, blue grey	35.00
M34a.	1,000 Lir, blue grey	35.00

OOOF (Okrožni Odbor O.F.) za Brkine

M35.	600 Lit, black	35.00

Okrožni N.O.O. za Brkine

M36.	1,000 Lir, green. Tito at right	25.00

Okrožni N.O.O. (Odbor O.F.) za Viparsko Okrožje

M36a.   500 Lir, black   65.00

Okrožni Narodno Osvobodilni Odbor za Brda

M37.   50 Lir, lilac. Tito at right   35.00
M37a.   600 Lir, brown   45.00
M38.   10,000 Lir, grey. Tito at right   45.00

Okrožni Narodno Osvobodilni Odbor za Kras

M39.   200 Lir, grey   16.50
M40.   500 Lir, grey   40.00

Okrožni Narodno Osvobodilni Odbor za Gorisko

M41.   250 Lir, green. Tito at right   35.00
M42. 1,000 Lir, green. Tito at right   35.00

Okrožni Narodna Osvobodilni Odbor za Idrijsko

M43.   100 Lir, grey   16.50

Okrožni Narodno Osvobodilni Odbor za Basko

M44.   50 Lir   16.50
M45.   100 Lir   25.00
M46.   400 Lir, grey. Red star at right   35.00
M47.   500 Lir, grey. Red star at right   35.00
M48. 5,000 Lir   45.00

Okrožni Narodna Osvobodilni Odbor za Tolminsko

M48a.   100 Lir, blue   45.00

Pokrajmski Odbor O.F. za Stajersko

M48b.   75 RM, blue   150.00